Critical Cι

Writing

ALSO PUBLISHED BY BLOOMSBURY:

The Bloomsbury Introduction to Creative Writing, Tara Mokhtari
Can Creative Writing Really Be Taught?, Stephanie Vanderslice
Creative Writing Innovations, edited by Michael Dean Clark,
Trent Hergenrader, and Joseph Rein
The Insider's Guide to Graduate Degrees in Creative Writing, Seth Abramson
Toward an Inclusive Creative Writing, Janelle Adsit

Critical Creative Writing

Essential Readings on the Writer's Craft

Edited by Janelle Adsit

BLOOMSBURY ACADEMIC
LONDON • NEW YORK • OXFORD • NEW DELHI • SYDNEY

BLOOMSBURY ACADEMIC
Bloomsbury Publishing Plc
50 Bedford Square, London, WC1B 3DP, UK
1385 Broadway, New York, NY 10018, USA

BLOOMSBURY, BLOOMSBURY ACADEMIC and the Diana logo are trademarks of Bloomsbury
Publishing Plc

First published in Great Britain 2019

Cover design: Eleanor Rose
Cover image © Christopher Squier

A catalogue record for this book is available from the British Library.

A catalog record for this book is available from the Library of Congress.

ISBN: HB: 978-1-3500-2333-8
PB: 978-1-3500-2332-1
ePDF: 978-1-3500-2335-2
eBook: 978-1-3500-2334-5

Typeset by Deanta Global Publishing Services, Chennai, India
Printed and bound in Great Britain

To find out more about our authors and books visit www.bloomsbury.com
and sign up for our newsletters.

Contents

Editorial Note and Introduction

For Students

Each piece of writing asks for something different from us, asks us to consider a certain set of things. There can be no universal set of rules for writing. There is no step-by-step recipe for your next story, script, essay, song, or poem. What you'll find in this book is a portrait of creative writing as a complex art form. It's an art form that has produced a range of questions that each writer is wise to consider.

Writers have been writing for centuries, and of course they've thought quite a bit about what it means to be doing what they do. Sometimes these writers take up the task of *writing about* the work they do: they write about the craft, techniques, and considerations involved in putting words to page. This type of writing has an element of the "meta," a prefix that denotes a self-referential quality, "aboutness": these authors are *writing about writing*.

"Writing about writing," when it focuses on literary craft, is sometimes called "craft-criticism." Included in this text are a series of critical essays about craft. These essays are written by writers, for writers, about writing.

While the essays included do not always mention the other authors you see in the Table of Contents, we can read these essays as participating in a conversation that involves all writers—questions such as,

1 Is writing always political? Or is there such a thing as "pure craft"? (Chapter 1)
2 What expectations are placed on writers of specific identity categories? (Chapter 2)
3 How are a writer's worldview, expectations, and beliefs about writing affected by the systems of inequity of which the writer is part? (Chapter 3)
4 What do writers need to consider in how they represent narrators and characters in their work? How can writers avoid stereotyping and other marginalizing practices? (Chapter 4)

5 What is at stake in our choice to write in one language or another? What is the relationship between language, identity, and culture? (Chapter 5)

6 What are the ethics of "borrowing" or "appropriating" from another text or culture in order to create something new? (Chapter 6)

7 Are there universal criteria for evaluating literary texts? What do creative writers mean by the terms "genre" and "literary" fiction? (Chapter 7)

All of the questions listed here are debatable, and the writers anthologized in this book take different stances on these questions and orient their work differently in relation to them.

You can see this book as an invitation to do your own "meta" writing about your craft. What from your experience as a writer, reader, and observer of the world could you share with other writers? What do you want to say in response to the essays you read in this book? After reading this text, you might decide to write a craft-criticism essay of your own, to consider publishing in a venue like *New Writing, Assay, Journal of Creative Writing Studies*, or the other publications mentioned in the pages that follow.

This book is meant to prompt your thinking, your reading, and your writing. It will offer you tools to consider both the texts you read and the writing you produce. The questions presented in the following pages are also good discussion-starters for workshop groups, writing circles, or classroom conversations.

The issues and debates you'll find in the essays collected here are issues that pertain to literature across the genres—poetry, fiction, creative nonfiction, playwriting, screenwriting, illustrated texts, and the many other genres creative writers work with and within. Use this opportunity to get to know the contributors' literary work, and read this work with their craft-criticism in mind. Based on what you read in *Critical Creative Writing*, what questions do you think the authors asked themselves as they were writing their novels, short stories, and poems? And would these questions be useful to you as well, in your composing process?

As you read across these authors' work, you may find that the difference between "literary" texts and "critical" texts begins to blur. Our categories for understanding texts are, at once, useful and insufficient. A text can arguably be read as part of, and escaping from, a genre category.

Craft-criticism is a genre category—a porous and shifting way of naming a group of texts. Together the authors in this collection represent a small sampling of this dynamic genre, as they reflect on the implications of a literary writer's choices.

As a sampling, this book does not offer a comprehensive survey. Instead, it is meant to prompt you to read more, and to read broadly. In addition to the bibliographies that some of the essays provide, there are suggested additional readings offered at the close of each chapter, many of which are easy to locate online. Direct links to some of the referenced titles are available on this book's companion website: criticalcreativewriting.org. Use the website to further your exploration. Bookmark the essays (whether in the print text or online) that are most relevant to your projects, that are most challenging to your thinking, or that most affirm your experience. Keep this text on your shelf as a reference point when you are writing. Return to these essays because they will have different meaning with each literary project you take up—remembering that each occasion of writing is uniquely in relation to the issues you'll find presented in the following chapters. Each text locates itself uniquely in the literary landscape.

This book is titled *Critical Creative Writing* because "critical" carries multiple meanings: the essays you're about to read are *critical* in that they are characterized by *incisive analysis* and they are *crucial* for the practicing writer to know. These essays are here for you as text-partners. Write in response to these essays and have discussions about them. Read this book with the expectation that you'll find more to say in conversation with your literary community.

A Note About the Book's Cover

The cover of this book presents an image by the artist Christopher Squier. The image is part of a series titled "Strange Fragments, Taken for the Whole" that depicts the adjustment brackets on the back of plastic chaise lounges found at many swimming pools. Perhaps you didn't recognize this object when you first saw it on the book's cover. The photograph defamiliarizes the object in such a way that we are able to look at it differently, perhaps more carefully and critically. The object when isolated in the close view of the photographic lens appears as a kind of blade, where it was before a taken-for-granted part of common poolside furniture. The artist looks closely at the object-within-object, at the idea within the idea. This is an excavating practice—one that perhaps has a parallel in the essays that follow.

For Instructors

Critical Creative Writing brings together into one volume some much-discussed texts in creative writing—texts that have prompted significant responses in social media and other forums. This is the first book of its kind to provide a guide to these conversations. The text anthologizes multiple perspectives on key issues in creative writing, including the politics of craft, language diversity in creative writing, and questions of identity, representation, and appropriation. The book provides students of creative writing the following:

- An invitation to join conversations taking place among contemporary creative writers about the politics of literary art-making.
- An examination of aesthetic considerations that transcend what can be covered in a typical craft handbook, including questions of linguistic diversity and the relationship between art and politics.
- A survey of the craft-criticism genre and its importance to the field of creative writing.
- A chance to engage with irresolvable debates in creative writing.

The goal is to help emerging writers discover their own nuanced perspectives on their craft and to write with a broader awareness of how their texts may be variously regarded by diverse members of literary communities.

"Craft-criticism," as a creative-analytical practice in which writers and artists challenge the inherited "lore" of creative writing, is an opportunity to interrogate cultural, historical, and institutional influences. The works included in the seven chapters that follow address a set of central questions:

1 What is the ideology of "pure craft"? What has the centering of craft pedagogy left to the margins of creative writing? What does it mean to intervene in politics through art-making, and what must writers consider as they write in an era fraught with strife, violence, and oppression? (Chapter 1)

2 What limiting expectations or demands are placed on writers of specific identity categories? How is the supposed divide between "aesthetic" texts and "cultural" texts born from, and sustaining of, a system of inequity and exclusion? How are writers implicitly or explicitly asked to benefit and affirm a white gaze? (Chapter 2)

3 How can creative writing, as a field, increase the diversity of the aesthetic traditions it represents and do more to interrogate the implications of

the values it maintains? How can we invite a deliberate examination of power and privilege in our work? (Chapter 3)

4   What disparities exist in creative writing? What forms of cultural humility and fluency does a writer need to present narrators and characters with complexity and dignity? How does a writer negotiate responsibility to what their cultural productions promote and affirm? (Chapter 4)

5   How can creative writing support linguistic diversity? What is at stake in an author's choice to write in one language or another? How is language grounded in community, and what does this relationship mean for our writing practice? How does a writer negotiate language's close tie to culture, history, and the politics of erasure? (Chapter 5)

6   How can we best think about the literary landscape as it is influenced by remix and sampling culture and the techniques of retelling, borrowing, and erasure? What ethical considerations are at stake in appropriative practices, and how can we respond adequately to instances of "art for art's sake" that do harm? (Chapter 6)

7   How does a writer negotiate the contingencies of literary value? What legacies of "high" art versus "low" art continue to influence creative writing today? (Chapter 7)

These questions operate across genres and serve to help writers think about how texts circulate and intervene in the world.

The book is meant to be read at multiple stages of one's career. Graduate students who are preparing for critical exams, beginning to write exegetical descriptions of their work, or teaching a creative writing class for the first time are likely to find the essays anthologized here to be important references. In order to ensure that *Critical Creative Writing* would also be accessible to intermediate-level students, I asked four writers from my 300-level workshop classes to help me edit this book. They reviewed the essays that I sought permissions for, and they wrote many of the discussion questions included at the end of each chapter.

This text can be mapped onto a semester course schedule in a variety of ways. The content is organized under simple headers—topics the craft-criticism responds to, critiques, or traces the contours of. Ultimately, my goal with the organization was to create clusters of texts that seemed to spark something together, but even a random clustering no doubt has the potential to create fire.

I have opted not to include a genre-based index because the essays cross, or even transcend, genre in useful ways; however, some essays may be more relevant to a poetry workshop (e.g., Nardone's chapter on conceptualism), and others more relevant to conversations about fiction (e.g., Row's essay on "American Fiction's Racial Landscape").

The essays provide language with which we can discuss several of the most challenging topics that arise in workshop conversations. A few of the essays (Salesses, Green, Mura, and others) comment directly on workshop conventions and what commonly (and, for some examples, unfortunately) gets said in those spaces. As such, these essays are useful to read as a class both before and during workshop. They occasion a conversation about anticipated concerns, and they can help a group think through community agreements that support a fruitful, inclusive, and open discussion.

A word about what is and isn't included in this collection: As teachers, we know the difficulty of selection; we face it every time we build a syllabus—what to include and what to leave out, however regretfully. In the case of this book, the vagaries and constraints of the permissions process—as we attempted to keep the book's purchase price affordable—had significant influence on what I was able to include in full here. The list of authors from whom reprint permissions were sought is significantly longer than the list you find in the table of contents. I hope that the suggestions for further reading included in each chapter can be a starting place for reading beyond these pages. Supplemental assignments might offer students the time and space to locate additional readings in craft-criticism, as they may also have the opportunity to produce their own craft-criticism for publication.

Critical Creative Writing also has a companion website: criticalcreativewriting.org. The site is updated regularly with supplemental materials. There is a live form on the website where requests can be made by students or teachers for additional resources, or to offer resources to be added to the site. The website provides links to craft-criticism and research in creative writing and announces new releases, tracking a growing conversation that will continue to grow as we engage students in it. It is with anticipation of this expansion that this book came into being.

1

Craft

"Pure Craft" Is a Lie

Matthew Salesses

> "'Pure Craft' Is a Lie" is a four-part essay that was originally posted in 2015 as a series of installments on the *Pleiades Magazine* blog. Part 1 explains the statement we find in the title. Part 2 asks: What's wrong with learning "pure craft" anyway? Why shouldn't people "know the rules before they can break them"? Part 3 returns to the issue of race and craft. Part 4 suggests ways forward, to combat the problems discussed in the opening sections. Matthew Salesses is the author of the novel *The Hundred-Year Flood*, an Amazon Bestseller, Best Book of September, and Kindle First pick. Salesses has written about adoption, race, and parenting in *NPR Code Switch*, *The New York Times Motherlode*, *Salon*, *The Toast*, *The Millions*, *The Rumpus*, The Center for Asian American Media, and elsewhere.

Part 1

Some alternate titles for this piece:
The MFA Story
Craft as Colonization
Craft vs POC
Why Writers of Color Don't Write Pure Craft Essays
A Lot of Craft, A Lot of Ideas

* * *

Just before the beginning of this semester, writer (and friend) Christine Hyung-Oak Lee was asking for craft essays by women and writers of color that she could teach in a graduate creative writing course. She was having trouble finding what she wanted. We started tweeting back and forth about why that might be. One of the things Christine wanted to know was why there weren't more "just craft" or "pure craft" essays by writers of color, why writers of color often wrote about race in their craft essays, instead.

I've written in a few places about race in craft, once about a kind of "moral craft" and once about inciting incidents in American novels and the difference between my adoption as a story and the way novel structure works in a (some) conventional American literary novel. Both of those essays, though, were really about how craft is cultural, how writers need to consider how (race and) culture shapes and is inseparable from craft.

I'm thinking about this a lot in terms of how we teach creative writing. Often what we are doing is teaching a kind of cultural norm. This is because we base "craft" off of what affects a literary, American reader. But that reader has already grown up with a world in which meaning is constructed in a certain way. This is already starting to get too abstract, so think of it this way: I teach my students that it can be to their advantage to write "say" and "ask" instead of other dialogue tags. This is something many creative writers teach. I give my class a reason why they should do this, and what I say is that it is because these dialogue tags are effectively "invisible" to readers, that it takes the focus off the tag and puts it on who is talking. That's the general purpose of dialogue tags, most of the time, to indicate to the reader who is talking. I tell my students that if the purpose becomes how the character is talking, instead, such as shouting or whispering, then those dialogue tags ("she shouted" or "they whispered") then become useful for the way they are not "invisible." We want the reader to register that the person is shouting or whispering. When we write "say" or "ask" we aren't trying to get the reader to register that the person is saying or asking.

I believe this is true and good advice. But I also know that it is cultural. The reason why we see "say" or "ask" as invisible isn't because they're actually invisible, of course, and isn't completely because of the nature of the words—"queried" or "commented" arguably don't add anything more than "asked" or "said" without a cultural context—but because we read other books where authors use "say" or "ask." Another way to say this is that we read the words "say" and "ask" A LOT. But if everyone started using "queried," then we would start to see "queried" as invisible. That's what I mean by culture. The culture is what makes using "say" or "ask" a good craft move. It's teaching the writer cultural rules, or how to use culture to her advantage.

This works if the writer is within the culture and writing to someone within the culture. Stay with me. An example would be someone writing "ask" in a culture where "queried" was the invisible term. Then "ask" would draw attention to itself. Or if the reader had never read a book before—she might question why the author always uses "ask," instead of "spicing it up" with other synonyms—something many of us heard as kids. I've had the experience of assigning Hemingway to ESL readers and having them ask exactly that—why the hell does Hemingway keep using the same dialogue tags over and over.

I've used this example because it's a simple one, but the same can be said about how we characterize someone, how a plot of causation is enjoyable to us, how a story where a character changes or fails to change affects us. Maybe not everything is cultural—though poststructuralists would probably argue that everything is—but certainly so damn much of it is.

Now imagine the writer who comes from the culture of "queried" enters our "ask" culture's creative writing workshop. See the dilemma? I sometimes feel like the "craft" I'm talking about is not so far from colonization. (I know that term is going to throw some people off, and I try to combat and acknowledge this norming in many ways, but still.)

Part 2

Some of you may be thinking, fine, what's wrong with teaching student writers to write using cultural norms? Why shouldn't we teach writers to reach a "wide" "mainstream" audience? And if people want to experiment, then they should know what they're experimenting "against." In other words, "you have to know the rules in order to break them."

I've heard those things plenty of times as well. But why should a writer have to know the rules first? Whose rules are they? Why are those the rules they have to learn?

Going back to our old example of the cultural value of "say" and "ask" versus other dialogue tags—culture makes these dialogue tags effective since we've learned to read them as "invisible"—why should we teach a hypothetical student who comes from a "query" and "comment" culture to use the terms "ask" and "said" instead?

Here's what we're doing if we do that (to make this simpler, let's call the writer from the hypothetical "query" culture q-writer from q-culture).

1   We're assuming that the q-writer is going to write to people from "our" culture. *Or* we are assuming that the q-writer needs to learn how to write to people from our culture in order to write to people from q-culture.

2 We're asking the q-writer to accept something that doesn't seem true to her. While other people in the class are probably much more receptive to the lesson of "say" and "ask."

3 We're asking the q-writer to learn a new culture on the fly without teaching the culture itself, only the terms the culture uses.

Of course, this is a simplified version of what happens in a creative writing workshop when some people are not as familiar with the dominant literary culture that the craft is taught from. I'll give you another example, one many creative writing teachers have probably experienced.

Say someone is teaching a workshop where most of the people in the class are interested in writing "literary" fiction but I and maybe a few other people are interested in writing "high fantasy" (I'm not totally familiar with fantasy, but I am familiar with this situation). The people who like literary fiction have also read a lot of literary fiction but not much fantasy. The people who like fantasy have read a lot of fantasy but not much literary fiction. (I'm using literary and fantasy as very sweeping terms here, terms I don't like, but I do so for the sake of the example.)

The instructor sets out to teach characterization and assigns a literary story with "complex, three-dimensional characters," and says something like, characters should not be "types." However, I the fantasy-writer am sitting there thinking that types are normal and pleasurable in fantasy and I'm even thinking "types" is a weird word, what about types as in wizards versus elves versus whatever. In those cases, doesn't the type dictate how someone acts and behaves? Plus, I hate this literary story the instructor assigned and I don't know why I should like it other than that is literary.

I find it hard then to accept the lesson based on the example.

Do I raise my hand and speak up? It's possible that I do and my objections lead to an interesting discussion of "types." But it's maybe more likely that, if I do speak up, we get into an argument. It's probably even likelier that I don't say anything at all. After all, I'm trying hard to keep up with what my instructor means by "types" and why I should like this literary story and what literary even is, while my classmates are well-versed in this stuff. I also feel like the "literary" is being valued and I feel kind of offended or I feel inadequate or shamed somehow, and so I stay quiet because of that feeling.

I'm also scared of this whole workshopping thing where these literary writers who know about what we're talking about and the terms we're using are going to critique me.

* * *

Many teachers might want the interesting discussion that could arise from the fantasy writer voicing her objections, but the (hypothetical) class is already set up to make an interesting discussion difficult.

Most of the class prefers literary fiction, and all of the class has read a literary story as the example text, and the teacher is talking more to the rest of the class than to the fantasy writer. How does that writer catch up to people who've had so much more experience reading the things the class is talking about? She starts at a disadvantage to the other students, and that disadvantage is *widened* when the class discussion builds on the culture she doesn't yet know instead of acknowledging (or even teaching) that culture.

I've been in this class, and I've taught a version of this class, though I do think the instructor can help take the class into an interesting discussion if the student does speak up. I know many creative writing teachers will think (and I do too) that if the fantasy writers can learn some of the literary techniques, it will probably help their fantasy writing. But in this scenario, at least, everything's already stacked against those students. Even if the creative writing teacher wants to convert the fantasy writers to "literary" writing (not my goal), this goal isn't being made available to them, either. It's not teaching them to incorporate "literary" strategies, it's teaching them that their knowledge of the world isn't useful in this discussion and needs to be discarded. The instructor is teaching to the rest of the class.

The "literary" writer enjoys a lot of privilege in this lesson. The rich get richer. She has a foundation of knowledge with which to immediately process the craft being taught (culturally). She is invested in the craft and the culture the craft is taken from, and she is invested in making more of that culture, for the people who are already reading it.

The fantasy writer has to learn a whole "culture" before she can start learning the craft the instructor is teaching. And she has to learn a whole "culture" and its craft before she can apply that craft or not to the context of high fantasy.

* * *

This isn't just a problem of genre, though. Of course it isn't. Imagine a workshop with twelve students all interested in "literary" writing, but three of those students are writers of color. Imagine that the readings are all by white writers, and the instructor is white and is teaching that a short story can't prioritize a political perspective.

I've been in that course, too. Many times.

Part 3

The writers of color in this workshop where the craft values are white, or the LGBT writers in a workshop where craft values are straight and cis, or women writers in a workshop where the craft values are male, end up in the position then where they are told that they need to "know the rules before they can break them," but the rules are never only "just craft," because the rules are cultural. This is where it starts to feel like colonizing.

Let's take the example of sensory details. Here are three things we might be taught:

1 Choose "striking" or "lasting" or "unusual" (or so forth) details.
2 Leave out unnecessary or "common" details.
3 Defamiliarize the familiar.

Now imagine a writer of color submits to a workshop of mostly white writers who have read mostly white texts and have a white instructor a story about people of color. Not hard to imagine, I would guess. Let's re-examine these three strategies through possible responses (responses I've seen and/or experienced) just to the writer of color's use of sensory details.

For the sake of my own experience, let's take a story about Korean Americans in Korea.

Let's take the first two strategies together and explore two possibilities, one of the writer taking the advice of cultural craft, and one of the writer resisting that craft.

In the first possibility, the writer does as instructed, including what he thinks are striking details of a fish a man is taking home on the subway, wearing an incorrectly buttoned coat, and the smell of unwashed bodies, the slickness of the bodies pressed close, all of which will cause some kind of plot that has to do with the man with the fish, perhaps. Meanwhile the writer leaves out details that seem unnecessary to that story.

In this example, it would not be surprising to me to see the workshop react by saying the writer has not done the things she did: that is, including unusual details and leaving out unnecessary details. Say the workshop starts asking the writer to include details like—an extreme example—passengers eating kimchi in their box lunches. The workshop might suggest this because the rules, again, are cultural and pertain to white culture. The idea is that the writer should be writing for white Americans who may have experienced the smell of unwashed bodies but would be "struck" by the "vivid" details of the smell of kimchi or so forth. There might even be a white American in the workshop who speaks up to say he's been to Korea and to give some examples.

In the second possibility, the writer resists the craft lessons and tries instead, perhaps following other writers of color she has read (and maybe resisting stories where white expats in Asia eat exotified food, maybe on the lunar new year, etc.) to include common details meant to let other Korean Americans recognize a similar experience, details like, I don't know, the way the man with the fish can tell by the protagonist's clothes that he's a kyopo, without explaining the term. Maybe the writer is reacting to the amount of fiction that doesn't seem to be about people like him, and he believes it's important to represent the experience for its recognition.

In this example, the workshop might ask the writer to define kyopo if this is supposed to be a striking detail. They might say if it's not a striking detail to cut it. They might complain that it's not a familiar detail to them, or they might complain that if it's a familiar detail to the writer, then what's the point? They might complain how "the spell of the story was broken" when they found a word they didn't know and it wasn't defined. Or so on with a thousand other things you could imagine. Again this would be maybe even an appropriate response if the point of the craft is to write for people of a dominant American culture.

It is exhausting to me too to go through all of these examples, but let's take defamiliarization. You can imagine the above possibility would be similar if the writer wanted to familiarize rather than defamiliarize. Say the writer wanted to defamiliarize, though, wanted to take the cultural craft advice. So he went through and defamiliarized, say, the lunch box, described it as a square little jail of food. Defamiliarization is for the familiar, and it wouldn't be a surprise if the workshop told the writer they couldn't understand what the square jail of food was, and encouraged her then not to defamiliarize, pointing out how, for them, the common details of Korean culture are already unfamiliar enough. The different strategies then come into conflict for the writer of color, who might end up simply confused.

What happens then if he can't see, because the workshop doesn't encourage him to see, that the confusion here is over who the craft is for?

* * *

Coming back to the question then of why writers of color often write about race in their craft essays, and perhaps even focus on race in craft essays, my general thought is that writers of color are doing the hard work of (a) reacting to a history of craft as "just craft" and even trying to correct it,

(b) catching writers of color up by explaining the cultural issues that do go mostly unacknowledged and untaught, and (c) making sure that their craft essays reflect their experience and do not make the same mistake. It seems to me that part of what the craft essay must do, at this point, is to talk about how craft and culture can't be separated.

The example of sensory detail is a small example in the scheme of things. How do I write a craft essay about things like how novels often hinge structurally on the past meeting the present without addressing that these concerns are cultural? Without examining how the craft has actually changed my own personal experience with my past and the way that I think about it? Without examining how my cultural experience and my learned cultural experience—my past and my present—informs even my understanding of plot and structure? *And at the same time* acknowledge that this negotiation between cultures is what goes on with craft and that the acknowledgement can help students to understand their own relation to craft as it is taught in creative writing workshops?

Cultural assumptions stand behind what makes many craft moves "work" or not, and for whom they work. There's a lot of work to do, with craft, and writers of color know it.

Part 4

So the time has come to try to put forth some ways to approach these deficits in the workshop. I have a few ideas, but I'm sure I'm only scratching the surface, and maybe not scratching hard enough. I'd love to hear comments from people who talk about the cultural values in the workshop and how to offset the deficit certain writers have to what we call "craft" because of their cultural backgrounds, whether because of their identity or whether they prefer high fantasy or whether they are from our hypothetical q-world.

1   The first way I try to foreground and address these issues is through making the discussion of who the reader is something we need to talk about. It's an obvious thing to do in a nonfiction workshop, when audience is already one of the primary concerns of rhetoric, but it's equally important in other workshops where the "audience" is talked about as "the reader," as if the reader is the same for all writers. Identifying who the reader actually is for a particular writer and critiquing the story by imagining oneself in the shoes of that reader

can help, if it is combined with diverse readings and discussions of craft as cultural. It doesn't help the writer writing outside of the dominant culture to have people read her work as if she's writing inside the dominant culture. Often the result of those workshops is to push the writer to write to the dominant culture instead.

2   Letting the writer talk. Sometimes we need to let the writer speak in workshop, and speak early. One of the things I have taken to doing is, if a discussion of a story's main theme seems important, for example, having the workshop discuss and then having the writer respond right away, before the end of the workshop comes up and we've spent the rest of the class talking about it incorrectly. I think the argument against this is that the writer can learn what the theme is "on the page," and might want to redirect her efforts to making that the main theme, but then we're relying on an often not-so-diverse group of people to say what the main theme "really" is, and also relying on the idea that the writer would want to change it. If it's important for the writer to know she's on the wrong track, then that's a very brief discussion, which the writer can then follow up on, and the discussion can then go on from there to how to help the writer reach her goal (if she doesn't want to change it). The same works for audience. The writer can quickly say whom she intends as her audience, either before or after a brief discussion. The author can speak up to talk about the culture that might inform her choices, or to dispute the colonization, or so on. Fears of the writer taking over the workshop—why do we fear this so much? Let's think about why.

3   I've heard people talk about letting the writer redirect the conversation, but what about asking the writer if the workshop is effectively talking about the story. "Is this a helpful conversation?" "Is talking through a suggestion to move the beginning action into the middle a useful discussion?" "Is our conversation about defamiliarization something we need to save for more general discussion rather than your particular story?" And so forth.

4   I should have put this a lot higher, but acknowledging the culture behind the craft is really what all of these posts are about. It's trying to hide this that makes it so hard for the writer of color to sort through the comments. Acknowledge the culture all the time, including in the bias of the workshop, the makeup of the workshop (usually out of the instructor's hands), etc., and talk about how that affects the ability of

the workshop to talk about a particular piece of writing. I like the idea of writing it into your syllabus.

5   More diversity in the readings (obviously). And talking about how they are diverse and why, and how one writer approaches italics versus another, etc. Maybe try choosing some of the readings during the class, not before. I've been running some of my workshops where I choose the reading after I get the workshop story. A quick read that night and an email out to the class with readings relevant to that particular story. Or letting the students choose the stories, talk about the cultural values to the craft in each of them, etc. Teaching them to be cognizant of the diversity and cultural implications of their choices.

6   This semester I'm teaching a workshop where, in the second half, when we workshop revisions, we are workshopping only by asking questions and asking the author to respond in class. This then lets the author think through her process and her choices, her intents and the culture that goes into them or is maybe imposed upon them. I started doing this from a conversation with Lily Hoang and Matt Bell, as I started to think about how to workshop revisions in a way that was different from the earlier drafts. (It feels less helpful to me to workshop them both the same way, though who knows.) Questions focus on the author's intentions, culture, and intended audience. What we want for conscious thought for why one does what she does—that's craft that's not hidden.

7   I think it can help to encourage both the idea that the workshop leader and participants have particular views (cultural views) of what craft is, and to always remember that, and the idea that students should be able to challenge those views and ask why they exist.

8   Sometimes it can help to talk about cultural failures in the example readings as well as successes. We can read a great story and talk about the culture in which it is great, but also the ways in which it fails when maybe it talks about certain things without considering its own cultural position.

9   One of the things I'd like to try with grading is having the grades be based on self-analysis of how the writer engaged with elements such as plot or structure or showing vs. telling or point-of-view, or etc. Let the student talk about her own use of craft and evaluate based on the articulation of why those decisions were made, personally and culturally.

10 Letting the writer lead the workshop, or offer rules for the workshop. What about switching the classroom so that the writer leads and the instructor fills the imaginary spot of the writer? (I don't know if this would work and have never tried it.) There are plenty of ways to rethink things.

Poetry, Politics, and Letters to the Empire

Craig Santos Perez

Craig Santos Perez is a native Chamoru from the Pacific Island of Guåhan/Guam. He has performed his works all over the world, speaking in lecture halls, high schools, and conferences, where he also discusses his poetry, activism, indigenous studies, militarization, and decolonization. In this essay, which was originally published on the *Poetry Foundation's Harriet* blog in 2012, Perez evaluates poetry as being more than formal craft; it can also be a means to shape public opinion. How can one make the words move beyond the page in order to captivate their social and political community? Perez is the co-founder of Ala Press, co-star of the poetry album *Undercurrent* (Hawai'i Dub Machine, 2011), and author of two collections of poetry: *from unincorporated territory [hacha]* (Tinfish Press, 2008) and *from unincorporated territory [saina]* (Omnidawn Publishing, 2010), a finalist for the LA Times 2010 Book Prize for Poetry and the winner of the 2011 PEN Center USA Literary Award for Poetry. He is an assistant professor in the English department at the University of Hawai'i, Manoa, where he teaches Pacific literature and creative writing. (Introduction written by creative writing student Bri Lucero.)

It's always exciting to me when poets actively engage in politics. I respect poets who are finding new and creative ways to address politics in their poetry (symbolic engagement); and I honor poets who sacrifice their writing time to work within their respective communities or within political institutions (activist engagement), even if their poetry is not necessarily political. Most of all, I am inspired by (and aspire toward) those poets who are able to do both.

For myself, I am always asking: how can poetry effectively address political issues (particularly related to the decolonization of my home island of Guåhan)? At the same time, I ask: how can poetry and poets engage with the public and political sphere beyond the page/book?

Since I live in Hawai'i and not in my home island, I am not able to be physically public in the way I would like to be. Fortunately, there are many passionate poets in Guåhan who are actively engaged in the public sphere. So for me, I need to find other non-physical ways of being public.

Beginning last November, I've experimented with writing political prose poems and submitting them as "Letters to the Editor" to one of the two major newspapers in Guåhan: The Marianas Variety (Marianas is the colonial name of the archipelago of which Guåhan is a part). This is not new as many poets in the Pacific, the U.S., and internationally have realized the importance of the media in shaping public opinion. I see my prose poems in that tradition.

In many ways, I also see these prose poems as "Letters to the Empire," since The Marianas Variety, and the other island newspaper, The Pacific Daily News, are both edited by White-American settlers. Both papers have a long and proud tradition of supporting the continued colonization and militarization of Guåhan. While I know I don't have to convince the readers of this blog about the power of the media to shape public opinion, you can imagine that this power is more pronounced on a small, colonized island where the media becomes an important colonizing agent.

So far, six of these prose poems have been published and are available to read for free online. The subject matter ranges depending on what might have been happening at the time. The most frustrating thing about publishing with The Marianas Variety is that the editor often edited the content—and even the paragraph structure—without permission. For those who work in the prose poem form, you know that changing the paragraph structure is like changing line breaks in a free verse poem! Which is to say, it completely changes the rhythm and pacing.

One thing I like about The Marianas Variety is that their online site actually shows how many people accessed the Letters. The most read letter was accessed by about 900 readers, while the least read letter still reached about 450 readers. To be honest, I haven't read the comments because the comment section in the Marianas Variety is notorious for being trolled by other White-American settlers.

While I can't measure the political efficacy of these prose-poems-disguised-as-Letters-to-the-Editor-of-the-Empire, I think what's most important is that I continue to believe that poetry can make a symbolic difference and that poets can creatively, actively, and publicly engage in politics.

Here are the titles and dates of the published letters for those who are interested:

1 "All Our Generations" 2/2/12
2 "The Promise of Latte Stones" 1/13/12
3 "The Invasion of Guåhan" 1/4/12
4 "Our Sea of Voices" 12/19/11
5 "The Winds of Trade" 12/8/11
6 "Hate Speech Sanctioned?" 10/14/11

Poetry and Catastrophe

Benjamin Paloff

What follows is a review of *Poetry of Witness: The Tradition in English, 1500-2001*, published in 2014 and edited by Carolyn Forché and Duncan Wu, a sequel to Forché's 1993 anthology *Against Forgetting: Twentieth Century Poetry of Witness*. Benjamin Paloff's discussion of both books offers a useful analysis of what a writer should consider when writing in the tradition "of witness." The review was first published in *The Nation* in 2014. Paloff has a PhD in Slavic Languages and Literatures from Harvard University and is the author of two collections of poems, *And His Orchestra* (2015) and *The Politics* (2011), both from Carnegie Mellon University Press. His book *Lost in the Shadow of the Word: Space, Time and Freedom in Interwar Eastern Europe* (Northwestern University Press, 2016) received the American Comparative Literature Association's Helen Tartar First Book Subvention Prize. He has translated several books from Polish and Czech, including works by Richard Weiner, Dorota Maslowska, Marek Bienczyk, and Andrzej Sosnowski.

In 1993, a poetry anthology appeared that seemed to speak directly to the spirit of the times and, in so doing, appeal to an audience far larger than what poetry in English could generally boast. More than 800 pages long and featuring the work of 145 poets, *Against Forgetting: Twentieth-Century Poetry of Witness* was a heady book for a turbulent era, when several ideologies against which Americans had tended to define their own politics for generations, among them Soviet communism and South African apartheid, were unraveling or had collapsed. As Carolyn Forché, the anthology's editor, explained in its introduction, the express purpose of the project was to monumentalize poems about the major atrocities and injustices of the recent past: "Many poets did not survive, but their works remain with us as poetic witness to the dark times in which they lived." The anthology was greeted with enthusiasm, some of it fueled by an inchoate fear that history was accelerating, or may even have ended, and was indifferent to what we deem worthy of remembrance. After all, what is all the hand-wringing about Americans' lack of historical memory, or the mantra "Never forget" applied to everything from nightclub fires to genocides, but a tacit acknowledgment of our own oblivion, and also of how, despite tragedies personal and collective, most of us somehow manage to go on with our lives?

In some respects, Forché wasn't breaking new ground. Poetry has long been enlisted as a tonic to forgetfulness, with poets and critics reminding readers, with more pedantry than irony, that the muse of lyric poetry is the daughter of Mnemosyne, or Memory. What made the project daring was Forché's suggestion that, beyond being a medium for reflecting on historical realities, poetry could also serve a testimonial or evidentiary purpose. Because poems written from "conditions of historical and social extremity" bear the "impress of extremity," we can regard them as "evidence of what occurred." Instead of meditating on the record, poetry could be the record.

Against Forgetting was a powerful inspiration for its early readers, myself among them. It expanded horizons, giving many of us our first glimpse of major poets from Eastern Europe and Latin America, even if the book's capaciousness meant that a glimpse of their faces in the crowd is all we got. Yet as both a collection of texts and a framework for their interpretation, the anthology has not aged well. Although Forché promised "a resistance to false attempts at unification," it is precisely a false unification that her anthology proffered. Poems with no discernible bearing on a historical circumstance were thrust under such weighty rubrics as "Revolution and Repression in the Soviet Union" and "Repression and Revolution in Latin America," with even the headings eliding the particularity of places and events. It was an act of martyrology. No less problematic was the book's unquestioning sense of being on the right side of history, an attitude that in our globalized society has been the source of no end of heartache. Which is why *Poetry of Witness: The Tradition in English, 1500–2001*, a new anthology edited by Forché and Duncan Wu, is so baffling. Not only does it suffer from the conceptual flaws of its antecedent; it compounds nearly all of them.

Despite its breadth, the earlier anthology was insistently Eurocentric; barely more than a half-dozen of its poets wrote in a non-European language. For its part, *Poetry of Witness* dispenses with linguistic diversity altogether, focusing on English-language poetry written in North America and the British Isles. (The recently published anthology *Another English*, edited by Catherine Barnett and Tiphanie Yanique, offers a sense of the excellent poetry being written in English elsewhere.) At the same time, the editorial notes focus, almost exclusively, on war and political turmoil, seeming to suggest that these are the only forms of communal experience worth witnessing.

Even with its narrow historical interests, the poems included in *Against Forgetting* are inconsistent in quality and purpose: poems that are not especially good, but that have some bearing on a momentous and tragic historical event, appear alongside excellent poems that don't seem to qualify as poems of witness at all. *Poetry of Witness* is similarly at odds with itself, as are its editors about its aim, so much so that Forché and Wu each provide an introductory essay that fails to cohere with the other. Of the two, Wu's is the more sober, though he repeatedly runs up against the contradictory notion that, on the one hand, poems are always written as testimonials to the poet's own experience, and on the other, the poet is secondary to the event itself that calls to be witnessed in the poem. At one point, Wu tries to draw a lesson from William Blake's presence in London during the anti-Catholic Gordon Riots in 1780. Instead of focusing on Blake as a "mythmaker or cryptographer," a view that Blake deliberately courted, Wu suggests the poet's work embodies "the terror and excitement that came from watching the world burn down," and concludes that poetry of witness, as a critical lens, "argues that, at the point at which the artist confronts extremity—whether imprisonment, torture, or warfare—his vision is altered irrevocably, turning utterance into testimony." This should be self-evident: as individuals and communities, we are changed by our experiences.

But by privileging historical catastrophe, Wu makes a value judgment that dramatically narrows the definition of art. In Blake's case, it leads him to downplay how the poet's intensive study of drawing, engraving and the Bible shaped his vision not only of the Gordon Riots, but of poetic form and expression in general. To complicate matters, whereas historians disagree as to whether Blake participated in the Gordon Riots, Wu presents the event as the touchstone of Blake's art. When Blake notes the "Marks of weakness, marks of woe" in the faces of strangers in "London," written over a decade after the riots and included in *Poetry of Witness*, are we to suppose that the poet is offering a veiled testimony about an event that took place years earlier, and that may or may not have affected him? The editors' own criteria are applied idiosyncratically and imply that either everything is poetry of witness, or nothing is. The only difference is whether we choose to read with blinkers on.

There is certainly great value in drawing attention to the historical context of a poem. We ignore an essential feature of literature when we lose sight of its power as an artifact of a particular moment, place or era. Still, it is difficult to read *Poetry of Witness* without quickly sensing that the editors are gaming the system to support their narrow preconception of poetry's utility. Prevarications like "perhaps," "might," "could have" and "may be" suffuse the biographical and explanatory notes. Or consider their gloss on Samuel Taylor Coleridge's visionary poem "Kubla Khan": "'Kubla Khan' has been read as apolitical, though the 'ancestral voices prophesying war' suggest some insight into recent history; after all, it is the inherent propensity for conflict, something we now understand as part of our genetic inheritance, that turns revolution (however well motivated) into bloodshed." There is a persistent sense that the editors want the poems they have included to refer to specific instances of political violence or upheaval, even when there is little or no evidence to support their claim, and even when pressing the point diminishes a poem's range of meaning.

I don't mean to suggest that the notion of witness is entirely without merit. Forché and Wu have assembled a good selection of poems about the last century's two world wars, though the editorial decision not to include work by any poet already anthologized in *Against Forgetting* leaves these pages feeling gutted. In the earlier sections, too, there are poems that serve an evidentiary purpose quite naturally. By its nature the occasional poem, such as the famous elegy that Chidiock Tichborne penned while awaiting execution in the Tower of London in 1586, hews closely to its event. The same can be true of epistolary poems, which typically communicate their context directly from author to addressee. Thus the gorgeous poems exchanged in 1598 between John Donne and his dear friend Sir Henry Wotton clearly speak to their time, though their having been arranged out of chronological order diminishes their value as dialogue. And there is real testamentary virtue in the verse chronicle, such as Abraham Cowley's epic on the English Civil War, as well as in *Britain's Remembrancer*, George Wither's account of the 1625 London plague:

> Friends fled each other, kinsmen stood aloof;
> The son to come within his father's roof
> Presumed not; the mother was constrained
> To let her child depart unentertained;
> The love betwixt the husband and the wife
> Was oft neglected for the love of life;
> And many a one their promise falsified
> Who vowed that nought but death should them divide.

Wither was a mediocre and, as he grew older, mad poet, but in his description of how crisis tears away at the social fabric even his most wooden lines are redeemed by their evidentiary power. There is, then, some basis to Forché's public-spirited proposition that poetry can be "a mode of reading rather than of writing, of readerly encounter with the literature of that-which-happened," such that "its mode is evidentiary rather than representational—as evidentiary, in fact, as spilled blood."

Yet even when the testimonial relationship between the poem and the event is unambiguous, there are limits to Forché's willful reading, not least of which is the fact that a poem is not "spilled blood." Reading the poem as evidence of a crime—or, for that matter, regarding youths dancing in a YouTube video as an assault on the Iranian state—is just as likely to land us on the side of the tyrant. Beyond that, many poems composed to mark a specific occasion are pure doggerel. William McGonagall, the nineteenth-century Scottish poet frequently cited as among the worst that English has to offer, was an incorrigible author of the occasional poem and could easily satisfy the editors' definition of poetry of witness. He isn't afforded space in this anthology, but there are many here whose struggles in life meet comparable struggles in language. Take, for example, Sir Roger L'Estrange's fustian in praise of suffering for one's monarch:

> When once my prince affliction hath,
>   Prosperity doth treason seem,
>   And for to smooth so rough a path
>   I can learn patience from him;
> Now not to suffer shows no loyal heart—
> When kings want ease, subjects must learn to smart.

Or else there's Anne Askew's "Ballad Written at Newgate," from shortly before her execution in 1546:

> Not oft use I to write
> In prose nor yet in rhyme,
> Yet will I show one sight
> That I saw in my time.
>
> I saw a royal throne
> Where Justice should have sit,
> But in her stead was one
> Of moody cruel wit;
>
> Absorbed was rightwisness
> As of the raging flood;
> Satan in his excess
> Sucked up the guiltless blood.

Strange and askew, indeed. These lines speak to genuine grief and grievance, but they do so in flat allegory. *Poetry of Witness* is thick with poems of this ilk, accompanied by biographical notes that rival them in length, making for an unpleasant reading experience. More skillful verses, meanwhile, such as John Newton's "Amazing Grace!"—published in 1779—are inspiring in part because they are not about any particular historical circumstance at all. This allows us to infuse them with new meaning—in effect, to identify with them, to see ourselves in the poem—as happened with Newton's hymn in the twentieth century. What, then, do we gain by shoehorning poems into the "poetry of witness" rubric?

Robyn Creswell, in a review of *Poetry of Witness* for the *New Yorker*'s Page Turner blog, argues that *Against Forgetting* is "in some sense" an effort to create "an invented tradition," that is, a way for the present to justify itself by rewriting the past. While accurate, Creswell's assessment is overgenerous. An "invented tradition"—one example is the Scottish clan tartan, with its rigid rules—is typically more consistent than an inherited one, because practices accumulated over time and across space also accumulate variance. *Poetry of Witness* includes many poems with no discernible bearing on the martyrology the editors promote in their notes, so it has neither the sharp focus of an invented tradition nor, except in rare cases, the pertinence of a real one.

There are a great many poems early on in the collection whose only "victim" is the courtier who feels oppressed by his own proximity to power. Sir Thomas Wyatt, one of the most marvelous specimens the language has produced, laments his falling in and out of Henry VIII's favor, "That whoso joins such kind of life to hold/ In prison joys, fettered with chains of gold." And the Roman Catholic priest Robert Southwell, canonized in 1970, wrote some eight years before his execution in 1595:

A prince by birth, a prisoner by mishap;
From crown to cross, from throne to thrall I fell;
My right my ruth, my titles wrought my trap,
My weal my woe, my worldly heaven my hell.

These men faced tragedy in their lives, but they also understood the risks that privileges brought. Surely Wyatt knew the difference between "chains of gold" and those of iron, having experienced both. Yet the effect of mourning so many men of power in the book's first 200 pages is like binge-watching *Game of Thrones*. It has the paradoxical consequence of de-individuating their experiences, effectively trivializing them, at the same time as it emphasizes the editors' near-total disregard for the power these men wielded over the lives of others.

If Forché and Wu aim to keep our sights squarely on forms of political violence and injustice, then what accounts for their inattention to endemic poverty and wealth inequality—unquestionably modernity's most pervasive and most overlooked form of political violence? We have at best the plaints of the rich man or the aging poet, often the same courtier, who finds he is no longer as attractive to the young ladies as he once was. Thus John Wilmot writes, in "The Disabled Debauchee":

> So, when my days of impotence approach,
> And I'm by pox and wine's unlucky chance
> Forced from the pleasing billows of debauch,
> On the dull shore of lazy temperance,
> My pains at least some respite shall afford,
> Whilst I behold the battles you maintain
> When fleets of glasses sail about the board
> From whose broadsides volleys of wit shall rain.

And Sir John Suckling:

> To draw her out, and from her strength,
>   I drew all batteries in,
> And brought myself to lie at length
>   As if no siege had been.
>
> When I had done what man could do
>   And thought the place mine own,
> The enemy lay quiet too,
>   And smiled at all was done.

These biting verses use military metaphors, yet the editors' claim that poets like Suckling "sublimated their experience in songs addressed to women, preferring to speak of love rather than of war" approaches self-satire.

What are we being called upon to witness: an old man's fear of death, a fop's meditations on his waning sexual powers? These are authentic aspects of the human experience, to be sure, and are among the original subjects of lyric poetry, but they add confusion to the anthology's focus on poets speaking truth to power. So does Forché's introductory essay, titled "Reading the Living Archives: The Witness of Literary Art," which seeks to lend theoretical grounding and heft to the project. Forché turns to the likes of Jacques Derrida, Emmanuel Levinas and Maurice Blanchot, French-language philosophers who were among the last century's best thinkers about the intersection of literature and ethics. In Forché's formulation, witness "is neither martyrdom nor the saying of a juridical truth, but the owning of one's infinite responsibility for the *other one*. . . . In the poetry of witness, the poem makes present to us the experience of the other, the poem *is* the experience, rather than a symbolic representation." But this is a profound misreading of these thinkers' work. For Levinas, responsibility is the default position of every relation. It's not something you take ownership of, because it's not something you can ever cast aside: my encounter with you is inherently responsive, whether I behave "responsibly" or not. For Blanchot, witnessing has nothing to do with testimony: all writing is a trace of existence, which is itself an involuntary process of "witnessing." Stripped of Forché's interpretation, these philosophers cannot admit a poetry of witness as she presents it.

The editors of *Poetry of Witness* are knowledgeable and unquestionably sincere in their belief that they are doing something essential not only for poetry, but also for our sense of ourselves in the world. The project was born of a genuine concern that we, as modern-day Americans, are too pampered to understand all the horror our species inflicts on one another. Thus Forché writes in the introduction to *Against Forgetting*: "As North Americans, we have been fortunate: wars for us (provided we are not combatants) are fought elsewhere, in other countries. The cities bombed are other people's cities. The houses destroyed are other people's houses." Yes, but there are plenty of places in North America where the "war on drugs," "war on crime" and "war on poverty" are not metaphors, and where drugs, crime and poverty fight back.

It is in this respect, then, that *Poetry of Witness*, besides being haphazard when it isn't simply dull, is also morally corrosive. By directing our attention to the wrong side of history, it assures its readers that we are on the right side. In touting some of the bad things that happen, it also points to an invisible *them* as the perpetrators. As has been noted by Bernard Stiegler, one of Derrida's most engaging students and himself no stranger to incarceration, "it is not by denouncing the *they* that one avoids the risk of falling into it, and perhaps the opposite is true, as is often seen in times of great reactivity." Poetry, too, can wake us from self-satisfaction in the verdicts we place on history. It requires, however, a very different mode of reading if it is to do so.

Materializing the Sublime Reader

Cultural Studies, Reader Response, and Community Service in the Creative Writing Workshop

Chris Green

"Materializing the Sublime Reader" is written specifically for creative writing teachers, but the content of this essay is equally relevant to students of creative writing. A longer version of this essay appeared in the scholarly journal *College English* in 2001. In it, poet Chris Green interrogates the assumptions made in creative writing about whom literature is written for, questioning the idea that workshop writing must be suited for a "sublime reader" who reads for craft. Green calls us to ground writing in diverse living communities "to examine how texts actually exist and are used in the world beyond the workshop." He writes, "The workshop needs to address lived situations rather than assuming and perpetuating the presence of a falsely sublime (generally a white, educated, middle-class) reader." Green teaches poetry in communities throughout central Kentucky and is Director of the Loyal Jones Appalachian Center (LJAC) and associate professor of Appalachian Studies at Berea College. He is the author of a book of poems *Rushlight*, the monograph *The Social Life of Poetry: Appalachia, Race, and Radical Modernism* (Palgrave, 2009), and co-editor of *Radicalism in the South since Reconstruction*, and editor of *Coal: A Poetry Anthology*.

Introduction: The Writing on the Wall

[The Nuyorican poet] is the philosopher of the sugar cane that grows between the cracks of concrete sidewalks.

—Miguel Algarín, "Nuyorican Language"[1]

When I was reading manuscripts for the *Indiana Review* a few years ago, a dilemma arose. I had run across a stack of poems by death row inmates sent along by their writing instructor. The poems were not models of good writing: cliché after cliché pummeled the reader, couplets brashly rhymed, and abstraction after ineffective abstraction abounded. Yet, I was moved that these men had been able to write poetry and voice the injustices of our judicial system. I began thinking about voice and violence, criminal justice and couplets, creative writing and racial profiling, loss and literacy. I was confronted with the fact that who writes a poem and the circumstances under which they compose affect my critical reaction: their pummeling clichés, one couplet blow after the next, were designed to hammer a reader's denial into wrought awareness, and their abstractions such as "justice" became palpable testimony about the bludgeoning of the American judicial system. Although we did not accept any of the poems for publication, reading them nonetheless led me to ask how my students might write poems that matter as much.

Given the pedagogical configuration of the creative writing workshop as I then ran it, I realized that for the most part, I could only help students write poems that looked good in the workshop. This point was forcibly made to me again, when I read a poem by the El Salvadoran revolutionary Roque Dalton (1935-1975) called "A History of a Poetic":

> That was when he began writing on the walls
> in his own handwriting
> on fences and buildings
> and on the giant billboards.
> The change was no small thing
> quite the contrary
> in the beginning
> he fell into a deep creative slump.
>
> It's just that sonnets don't look good on walls
> and phrases he was mad about before, like
> "oh abysmal sandalwood, honey of moss"
> looked like a big joke on peeling walls.[2]

Under the conditions of composition that Dalton lays out, the types of poem produced in workshop would also be evaluated as less than successful.

Although the examples of death row inmates or Central American revolutionaries might seem extreme, the urgency and purpose of their writing exist no less in each good poem I have read. In this article, I seek to add another vocabulary to the pedagogy of the creative writing workshop: the language of use and action, of practice and implementation—praxis. To be of service to our students and their worlds, creative writing needs to undertake revisions that, due to its institutional history, have not yet been conducted. This article investigates how to reform the discursive walls between creativity and theory and ends by suggesting how we might bring classrooms and communities together.

In order to address students' world experience and prepare them for writing after college, we need to construct a workshop where the class readership acts to represent the rhetorical circumstances of interpretive communities outside the university. Let me offer a metaphor about workshops that I share with my students at the beginning of each class. If we were a group of builders helping each other to design beautiful and effective buildings, we would have a remarkably different set of advice for buildings in different contexts. Compare these three examples: first, in Los Angeles a builder is designing mobile shelters for the homeless out of abandoned shopping carts; second, a builder in Vancouver is building a tree house for family living from recycled plastic; finally, another builder is using native sandstone to build a cabin in the Smokey Mountains. Of course, although all three builders would have to know the basics of construction, how we render questions and evaluations about effectiveness and beauty (about where the bathtub goes or if one can or should be included at all) depend upon the situation.

At question in creative writing classrooms are the limits and possibilities of audience, circumstance, and rhetoric. A single poetry does not exist in America: instead, there are many poetries for many readerships. As the fierce and thoughtful work of multicultural scholars has shown, the differences in readerships and cultural values are not only historically but currently myriad. An effective piece of poetry to one interpretive community will not necessarily seem interesting or well done to another. In addition to writing well and having a broad literary background, our students should learn how to speak to chosen vernacular interpretive communities and their literary traditions.[3] To serve these communities means implementing new theories of consumption and audience as articulated by Jane Tompkins and reader-response theorists who study the engaged rhetoric of communities outside higher education: writers do best when they learn how to write better poems for those communities they wish to serve. Learning how to write a better poem in chalk on a wall will be different from writing a better poem for an Episcopalian church bulletin.

In addition to helping our students learn to write good poems, we can teach them to consider the realities of how writing lives in the world and the realities of living as a writer. I do not refer to a professional career as a writer, but to the study of how writers have followed their vocation.[4] As students learn to address the audiences and traditions in which they wish to function, they also begin to learn how to negotiate the histories and institutions that structure their possibilities as writers. Life as a writer in the social world means more than just writing poems (I am a poet and so will often refer to the writing of poetry, but my points are applicable to other modes as well): it means negotiating the vast, complex, nebulous, tyrannical, ever-present, varied structures and institutions of publication, education, readings, employment, community, politics, and family.

[. . .]

The promise implicitly made to students of discovering voice is often thwarted by how we train creative writers to write for what I am calling the "sublime" reader of the creative writing workshop. This sublime reader, hovering over the workshop, is manifested through the pedagogical instruction that teaches students how to write well and address their work to, as Fenza writes, "the public and the markets that serve the public."[5] The organizers focus on texts and utilize strictures of genre conventions, tone, and diction to prepare the workshop and the students for succeeding with this singular "public." As a result, the workshop feigns the presence of the sublime reader from this market for the adequate preparation of its students. But what if a writer does not wish to prepare a commodity to sell to this disembodied, moneyed "public and the markets that serve" it? Options should be provided.

From the Sublime Toward the Ideal: Audience in the Creative Writing Workshop

There is the falsely mystical view of art that assumes a kind of supernatural inspiration, a possession by universal forces unrelated to questions of power and privilege or the artist's relation to bread and blood.

—Adrienne Rich, "Blood, Bread, and Poetry"[6]

Although article after article has offered new workshop strategies and techniques, the goal and gaze of the sublime reader remains. Before asking how students can better write "good" poems, I propose we look beyond the gaze of the sublime reader and ask how students can write useful poems. Only after the potential use of a poem is established within specific cultural institutions of production, distribution, and consumption can poets then judge how to train themselves to write "good" poems that can act with efficacy within particular cultural situations.

An illustrative example is supplied by Cary Nelson, who began one class by presenting five representative poems from the Great Depression that were "uncivil burlesques" of "American culture."[7] He held "a vote to determine which poem seemed most 'literary' or 'poetic' and which the least." As a whole, the class disregarded the "Ballad of a Lumberjack," which was written in roughly pentameter ballad stanzas with fast-paced, low diction (including words like "em" and "crummy"). Nelson then presented its context and specific audience as a way of evaluating literariness, hoping to get students to engage in a deeper analysis of rhetorical moves the poet made. The poem was "a leaflet distributed during the 1937 Timber Workers strike," in which its seven stanzas "lay out the realities of industrial exploitation." His students agreed that once the poem was seen from the perspective of a striking lumberjack, it was moving, and they proceeded with an involved discussion that discovered how the poem "condensed some fairly complex notions of class difference and rhetorical deception into commonsense language."[8] Issues of class, marginalized voices, and accessible commonsense language are no less with us today, but if a student turned in such a poem to a creative writing workshop, the class would reel. The hundred dictums of "good" or "well-crafted" language would come into play, invalidating the poem.

Responding to the need to allow marginalized voices to be heard, Lynn Domina, in "The Body of My Work Is Not Just a Metaphor," appeals to the creative writing teacher to acknowledge difference through granting students "permission to address one's personal obsessions."[9] Open pursuit of obsession and "risk of revelation" for many students, however, "is exacerbated by their place in society."[10] Domina believes that the creative writing classroom needs to be made a place where all voices can be heard and a place that ensures against, for example, "the lack of a threat of punishment for racial identity."[11] Domina mentions how, in addition to ensuring an audience that provides the basics of respect and consideration, the class might extend an active empathy to its participants, though she does not supply the details:

> To whatever degree possible, the writing classroom must become a community with porous boundaries, such that, regardless of the extent to which a student's audience exists outside the class, he or she can be confident that an adequate audience also exists within the class. By adequate audience, I mean individuals who are willing to attempt, if only for a time, a synoptic stance.[12]

Domina's plea for tolerating difference fails to explain how this synoptic stance is to be gained. Regardless of intent, pedagogical approaches designed to ensure the right to "speak what one knows" do not address the real problem: creative writing remains a text-centered approach that privileges an author/ity that, no matter the good will of its intentions, effaces speech communities with an urgent stake in life beyond the construct of the workshop. The way students are taught to write is unintelligible to the community of experience about which they write.

[. . .]

The question then for instructors is how to widen the possibilities of putting the workshop in service to the student and the speech communities they represent without calcifying success within institutional discursive measures of skill, craft, or authenticity. Regardless of the discipline, theoretical approach, or political bent of the instructor, classes taught under the auspices of university education reorient the students from previous speech communities' substantive practices and uses of poetic discourse to the sanctioned discourse of the university. How students learn to speak in the university is appropriate primarily for similar nationally endorsed systems of authorized professionals, not participation within their originating discursive communities. The community of origin, if discussed at all, is the object of investigation: "they" are talked *about* rather than talked *to*. Members of these communities become "material" rather than an audience.

The Association of Writers and Writing Programs (AWP) has undergone this critique often, leading Fenza to claim, "It's a bit difficult to have 'a university-based subculture' when colleges and universities include students of almost every economic class, region, and ethnicity to be found in North America. . . . Those that attend writing classes hardly become hermetically sealed within a separate zone."[13] Yet this "hermetically sealed" state is precisely the danger the workshop is obliged to overcome, when Fenza calls upon creative writing programs to mold the writer into a professional: "the studies, work, and temperament of the artist must be addressed to [. . .] the markets."[14] Higher education can mean more than effacement and co-optation, but classes need to be structured so that students can transfer skills and knowledge to their various speech communities. Of course, most students come to the university precisely to learn the language that will enable them to become part of the professional-managerial class. They most likely have few doubts about the worth of this goal and probably have given little thought to the cost of their transformations, eager as they are to get on to success. But if they plan to return, they will have been trained to act in a capacity that demands an entire system of support—to function as trained, a pharmacist needs doctors, advanced medications, and drug-stores.

In creative writing, specifically, we must learn to resist the urge to "produce" writers who hope to assume professional positions, for few such professional positions exist. I am not, as some might claim, projecting interventionist politics onto my students; unlike pharmacy school, no sure path into industrial participation exists for writers, and students who come to the creative writing class do not generally do so with hope of professionalizing themselves. When such romantic fantasies exist, honesty with students about the politics of success and competition is key. This candor also leads to the opportunity to talk about the reality of the daily hand-to-mouth work that writers do. We might also learn to serve writers from widespread and even oppositional communities in such a way that their participation in those communities is facilitated. Whether increasing the range of potential speech or implementing new narratological theory, the goal of the writing class is still how to write well, along with all the unspoken ideological baggage that word entails (e.g., objective standards of "good" and humanist assumptions about value and worth). In creative writing, we owe it to our students to examine how texts actually exist and are used in the world beyond the workshop. The workshop needs to address lived situations rather than assuming and perpetuating the presence of a falsely sublime (generally a white, educated, middle-class) reader.

Given that we are now aware of the "sublime" reader, what exactly is an "ideal" reader, and how can a poetry workshop act as ersatz "synoptic" audience? And even if readers act as an ideal audience, under what auspices are they assuming the poem is being encountered? No poem has even been encountered without a context that lent meaning to it and drew meaning from it. Where was the poem encountered? Who found it? What did they do with it? Poems are not read by ethereal readers considering craft. The audience in the workshop should be able to anticipate what interpretive speech community is going to receive the poem, in what form: in this capacity, readers in the workshop can grant useful evaluation. A poem might be too "well crafted," if by "well crafted" we mean "well written": it might easily alienate an audience or violate discursive conventions. We have seen Gwendolyn Brooks make powerful decisions about her poetry by purposely tailoring her work to a specific audience, yet her work appears in the anthology next to "The Waste Land" as unsophisticated and transparent (as if this were a problem), just as "The Waste Land" alienates an audience for whom she often writes. In the end, there are no such things as well-written poems, only contingently useful poems and less useful poems. Multiple interpretive communities with differing rhetorics—and the ideological plight and actual consequence of negotiation between them—clarifies a writer's investment.

How to Craft Audience and Context in the Creative Writing Classroom

No poet, no artist of any art, has his complete meaning alone.
—T. S. Eliot, "Tradition and the Individual Talent"

June Jordan's Poetry for the People offers the best examples I have yet found for leading students to awareness of their placement in our culture and their relationship with others. In her beginning classes, Jordan asks her students when critiquing each other's poems, "How does it fit into or change a tradition of poems?"[15] In addition, students are asked to write poems in which they "explore the relationship between the poet and his or her particular cultural legacy." To clarify this legacy and its difference from others, students take poetic models from their own and other traditions and write poems based upon those models. For instance, poets might write a "'How Do I Love Thee' poem, using Elizabeth Barrett Browning, Queen Latifah, and Toni Braxton as models."[16] At question is the canon, and each class member begins to explore her or his relationship to it: "As new American poets, we consult guest poets and lecturers to help us name, reinvent, and reclaim literary and cultural traditions."[17] Jordan's work provides a worthy beginning upon which to build.

One way to widen the list of rhetorical purposes and techniques might be to have students compile a list of terms that they feel are appropriate to evaluating their poetry. For instance, my class begins with a comparative study of defenses from different periods that serve as models for the students as they write their own: Sidney's "Defense of Poesy," Algarín's "Nuyorican Language" (an introduction to an anthology of Puerto Rican poetry from the streets of New York), and Rich's "Blood, Bread, and Poetry." The students are also required to give group presentations on the Elizabethan historical and literary milieu, Sidney's life, and the material history of Sidney's defense (its audience, its publication history). What becomes obvious from an examination of these defenses is the historical contingency of the use of poetry in terms of power and authority around religion, nationality, class, and gender. A simultaneous inquiry is made through journal entries and exercises into how students see poetry being used in their vernacular cultures, where poets find poems, and how they recognize a poem when they see one. I ask them to respond to queries such as, "When did you first become aware that you loved language?" "Where is language for you the most alive?" and "What places have you witnessed powerful language being used?"

Indeed, poets will talk endlessly about these issues, since they feed the soul of their work. Quincy Troupe tells about the streets of St. Louis and how he trains students to be aware of how language lives, not in poems, but in their lives:

> In order to listen to language people have to lose whatever perceptions of poetry they hold—that's what I had to do. I thought poetry was just something about dried roses and violets until I discovered that it could be about my shoestrings, about the neighborhood, about the sky, about my mother, about being a basketball player or a musician. . . . Often, high school has really turned kids off to poetry because the poetry that was historically given was a poetry that had no connection to the kids' real lived lives.[18]

Indeed, the best training I know is "to listen to language" of "real lived lives."

One way of making the assumed rhetorical operations more explicit would be to have students "translate" poems they read into terms of their own speech communities based on their defense of poetry. Lisa Delpit, in *Other People's Children: Cultural Conflict in the Classroom*, poignantly clarifies the realities of power and language with minority children in the public school system. Although Delpit's exercises are designed to help students learn to function in the "culture of power," her exercise about translations between interpretive communities offers rich potential for creative writing teachers interested in helping their students locate and speak to and from their place in the world. Delpit writes,

> Students begin to understand how arbitrary language standards are, but also how politically charged they are. They compare various pieces written in different styles, discuss the impact of different styles on the message by making translations and back translations across styles, and discuss the history, apparent purpose, and contextual appropriateness of each of the technical writing rules presented by their teacher. And they practice writing different forms to different audiences based on rules appropriate for each audience.[19]

Of course, part of the work of poetry is empathetic study, with the goal of reading a poem in its full life valence, but the exercise leads to a fast-paced discussion of rhetoric and purpose as we discuss what the translations have lost and gained. As the students conduct these assignments, the ongoing process of self-recognition is shared with other students. Students begin to get some sense of their differences and how they can be useful readers to one another.

As we go further into the semester, I ask students to read about the poetics from their tradition; they then discover and write about what terms and approaches seem most relevant to them. For instance, I might suggest reading Fahamisha Patricia Brown's *Performing the Word: African American Poetry as Vernacular Culture*[20] or María Herrera-Sobek and Helena María Viramontes's collection *Chicana Creativity and Criticism*,[21] or, if the student was from eastern Kentucky, George Ella Lyon's "Contemporary Appalachian Poetry"[22] and P. J. Laska's "Poetry at the Periphery."[23] I promote "poetics" because a well-done poetic not only performs a close reading of poetry but also examines how the poetry functions in and grows from a particular place and time. The task of finding relevant material for students, given the sheer diversity of people and of poetry in the United States, can be overwhelming, but it is always stimulating, eye-opening work. A good beginning bibliography of ethnic poetries, traditions, and poetics is provided in *June Jordan's Poetry for the People.*

These exercises establish contact with poets, poems, and poetic traditions of use to the student, enable classmates to aid the other poets in the class on their terms, and show that a common language of craft can be adapted to individual needs. In the workshop, as we focus on each other's poems, I coach students to "look for the poem's heart" and help it live up to the use it seems to be answering. Since students in my class have come to know each other well, I ask the writer to be silent because learning to listen to the heart of their writing is critical to discerning and generating its integrity, rather than forcing it narrowly into their desired goals and purposes. Rather than teaching my students how to wield their wills upon the writing, I teach them how to listen to the nascent spirit in their writing so they might nurture it into a poem they might wield. I have found usefulness in the criterion of evaluation I return to again and again.

I have been struggling to define usefulness for a long time to fellow poets as a means of my evaluations of their work and to other readers when I edit literary magazines. Usefulness can make artists uncomfortable, for they can feel constrained to tangible, socially recognized productivity. I wish to examine usefulness, however, beyond the confines of commodity labor.

Jane Tompkins's *Sensational Designs* makes astute conjectures we might well transfer to contemporary poetry rather than nineteenth-century fiction: "When literary texts are conceived as agents of cultural formation rather than as objects of interpretation or appraisal, what counts as a 'good' [literary device] changes accordingly."[24] After noting the institutional mechanisms that lead to a certain literature becoming recognized as "well done" and entrenched in the canon, her attention turns to asking questions about those texts outside of the canon and on the rhetorical function for the reader: "I ask, 'what kind of work is this novel trying to do?' My assumption in each instance has been that the text is engaged in solving a problem . . . specific to the time in which it was written."[25] Within the concept of use comes the concept of act or event—someone is using the poem, someplace, to do something for some reason. Poets then go beyond writing a good poem and begin to think about how to use a poem, and how to write a poem they can use.

Use, however, is perhaps a term too burned with utility. David M. Stewart, in "Cultural Work, City Crime, Reading, Pleasure," critiques Tompkins's focus on functional utility, which ignores the issues of pleasure, amusement, ecstasy, and desire.[26] His point is well taken, and we have to remember to be careful not to limit use to pragmatic utility but extend our consideration to other varieties: use might be pleasure or horror, stimulation or seduction.

Perhaps more problematic than the term use might be the term *audience.* One of the creative writing workshop's great offerings is to liberate students from social constraints (and audiences) that have silenced them and thus have not allowed the articulation of disruptive truths. In this way, creative writing workshops are a necessary shelter for many writers whose previous cultural experience of writing and poetry was one of silence and control. In this case, the class forms an essential audience, though the reality of language that the writer has lived is a central point. Many writers cannot return to their originary speech community, but their work serves as a powerful tool for those who remain.

Further, poet after poet will point out that they speak to no limiting, material audience and that to do so is to sever the voice from the truths it might speak. Although a writer might address "propriety" or a divinity rather than an immediate audience, the mechanisms of this mode of address are still guided by a set of principles. Whether referring to W. B. Yeats's term "phantasmagoria" or Trinh T. Minh-Ha's "Diseuse, Though-Woman, Spider-Woman, Griotte, Storytalker, Fortune-Teller, Witch,"[27] discourses of ecstasy are still structured by interpretive communities that have widely different methods and goals. Our attention should be routed to helping students honor, examine, research, and practice not only the more readily apparent traditions of a speech community's vernacular conventions but also that community's conventions of ecstatic discourse where individual ego-limits are shed and visceral participation in tradition occurs.

Some might claim that identity in vernacular communities entombs the writer, limiting possibilities: yet until writers begin to explore their intricate, subtle, ambiguous relationship to the place of their identity, the language they are given in school will be a muffling mask rather than a tool of chosen empathetic ecstasy. Awareness of the location and of the possibilities of identity is a place from which a poet's myriad voices (many of which may not be his or her "own" voice) may rise. The poet Ai's dramatic monologues are a powerful case. Similarly, the Chilean writer Marjorie Agosín crosses the boundaries of class, otherness, suffering, and life and death. Her narrators speak from the place of the Chilean mothers of the Disappeared whom she had been interviewing in order to document their experience: "My job, that of making history, of witnessing, of telling, and of rescuing memory became a vocation and an obsession. . . . I felt my body covered with wounds and knew that I would face the challenge of making the dead speak and not to elaborate on the empty space, on the absence of the disappeared."[28]

The complexities of this honorable ecstatic work, as well as the dangers of transgression, are what our students begin to explore as they delve into the integrity, history, and richness of their own speech communities. Some sublime readers come from beyond the marketplace.

From Ersatz Audience to Worldly Writer: Literary and Cultural Studies

> For, as Aristotle saith, it is not gnosis but praxis must be the fruit.
> —Sir Philip Sidney, "The Defence of Poesy"

The next step is to help students begin to see their options for living their lives as writers and how they might guide the path their writing takes in the world. As a writer, I am curious about how other writers have done what they have done. I mean not how they wrote (although this is perhaps the center), but how they lived their lives as writers; how they made things happen; how they began, survived, despaired, strived, thought, made their livings, and died. I want to know about the decisions they had before them and how they found themselves in that place, because I need perspective and help in seeing and guessing beyond the walls of the options my culture gives me, which seem inevitable. You may, if you wish, call this cultural studies. Indeed, it is important to do so.

Cultural studies does more than expand the potential types of texts we might read (movies, ads); in addition, cultural studies considers the text as being in the world, examines how it arrived, asks who uses it and why. These considerations are about the gritty pragmatics of using rhetoric, not just of writing it. Rarely have these questions been asked of poems in the creative writing classroom, focused as we have been upon close reading.

In terms of literary theory, cultural studies examines the pragmatic mechanisms of hegemony through which the possibilities and limitations of an individual's actions are encountered. My focus, of course, is biased toward acts of pragmatic agency that writers might undertake. The important point here is that a workshop contains not only a theory of textuality but also a theory of reception dependent upon what Richard Johnson calls the "circuit of the production, circulation, and consumption of cultural products."[29] In his article "What Is Cultural Studies Anyway?" Johnson points out that if we are to understand how texts act, our focus must not be on the texts themselves but upon the entire cycle of cultural transformation, including the "specific conditions of consumption or reading."[30] For poets this would include, but not be limited to, an investigation of the literary marketplace, publishers, and small magazines. But more importantly, Johnson warns, "We need careful analysis of where and how public representations work to seal social groups into the existing relations of dependence and where and how they have some emancipatory tendency."[31] As the students begin to examine their own and others' "lived culture," these possibilities start to become clear.

In order to do so, writers had best first gain some understanding of their own situatedness, of how poetry and literature work in the communities to which they are connected and in which they have lived. This goal is partially achieved by students investigating their community origins (as already outlined), but to gain critical distance, we also might read poetry from past cultures to provide a background against which our own ideological assumptions may stand out. As suggested by Alan Sinfield in "Against Appropriation," "We should use [literature] to recreate imaginatively an alien society and its informing ideology, and to locate the text within those structures. The scholar may wish to rest there, but the reader who demands modern relevance may use this recreated otherness as a vantage point from which to re-examine and reassess present-day attitudes, allowing the alien perspective to stimulate and provoke."[32] To this end, it is vital for workshops to study the means of publication, cultural utilizations, and relationships between discourses as well as the decisions that authors made based on their intervention into these systems. These matters are appropriate for writers insofar as they allow us to make informed decisions about our own interventions.

Once we attempt to construct the context of reading, we may begin to read poems as events rather than as texts, as something used rather than as something written and read. Our work as readers of poetry from the past is made more complex, and it enables us to be responsible to our own words. To achieve this responsibility, my students delve into poems from a particular historical era, studying the work that poetry performs at every point of the cultural cycle. The approach is easily adaptable to interest, and any historical era could be chosen as a platform of investigation. One might use anti-strip-mining Appalachian literature even as someone else might focus on the Harlem Renaissance or Dudley Randall's Broadside Press and the Black Arts movement.

I set out an examination of the various tiers of Elizabethan poetry selected for differences in class position as well as differences in actual material manifestation. To this end we perform a comparative reading of sonnets from Sidney to the contemporary, investigate the broadside ballads (the writers of which Sidney called the "ape-poets"), look into Ben Jonson's life and literary decisions, and then do a comparative study of criminal poetry from Luke Hutton's Elizabethan book "The Black Dog of Newgate"[33] to Pamela Hadas's series of poems about Belle Star[34] to actual poetry written by death row inmates.

My classes spend about half of our time in workshop, though all classes are held in the round with maximum discussion and participation. In addition to working from two anthologies representing distinct poetic traditions (in this case Hayden Carruth's *The Voice That Is Great within Us*[35] and Ishmael Reed's *The Before Columbus Foundation Poetry Anthology*[36]), the students conduct their own readings and report back to the class (in brief presentations) on two poets they have found to be of value to them. Such a literary approach may seem daunting to those students who have taken the class as an easy A or to those instructors not comfortable with teaching literature from a historical perspective. As a teacher within the university, I work to provide paths for students to use the knowledge they have gathered to strengthen their participation in their communities of choice. In this way may I hope to honor Richard Hugo's words about creative writing's responsibility, "the responsibility of creating and maintaining a place where people can bring the immediacy of their lives and language."[37]

Speech Communities, Commodity Capitalism, and a Role for the University

The question remains of how speech communities come into being and of the efficacy of referencing them as sites for a poet to address. Hayden Carruth, in "How Not to Rate a Poet," reminds us that the object of our investigation is the entire literary process, not only the master writers: "Master artists are not the ones who keep literature going. . . . [L]iterature is kept going by something quite different: the mechanism of a dynamic culture. And this mechanism in a real sense is sustained not by the works of masters but by the works, far more voluminous, of journeymen and apprentices."[38] The difficulty of tracking the relations of material reproduction and lived cultural experience in a country of 284 million people is not to be underestimated, but neither is it to be theorized away. I would like—against the seeming inertia in mass media toward homogeneity—to assert that access to material reproduction, rather than homogenizing and inhibiting the formation of speech communities, offers possibilities for previously unenunciated populations to come into historical self-awareness.

It is tempting to assume that such communities exist as chthonic natural traditions to which we do not belong and about which we talk as outsiders. Rather, communities are fluid and continually in the process of creating their foundations. Not to valorize every meager saddle-stapled volume, but pockets of significant literary action are flashing onto the scene for brief years, sometimes for brief months, before the energies that catalyzed and informed that group of writers fade. What we often see in cases of these evolving speech communities is not subjugation to commodification but a resistance to the logic of that system which attempts to pacify and absorb contradictions in their experience. Neither ought we to limit possible communities in readily available terms of demarcation (ethnicity, race, class, nationality). Undefined communities, which lie outside the language and concepts we currently use, are struggling toward definition and coherence through culture and writing.

[. . .]

I write this article at an opportune moment: wide changes in the role of creative writing and English departments in the university and the community as a whole are not only possible but necessary. Starting with the renovation of the creative writing workshop and ending with the development of service learning programs in the university, these steps, if carried out, promise to awaken our lives, our students, the university, and the communities we touch. There is good work to be done if people are to be brought together around the love of writing and literature, around its possibilities, its limitations, and its actualities. We might, in the process, learn to listen and respond to each other in all our difference, hope, and conflict as we negotiate this world . . . and perhaps write a good poem or two as we are doing so.[39]

Notes

1. Miguel Algarín, "Introduction: Nuyorican Language," *Nuyorican Poetry: An Anthology of Puerto Rican Words and Feelings*, edited by Miguel Algarín and Miguel Pinero (New York: William Morrow, 1975), 9–20.
2. Roque Dalton, *Poems,* translated by Richard Schaff (Willimanntic, CT: Curbstone Press, 1984), quoted in Barbara Harlow, *Resistance Literature* (New York: Methuen, 1987), 1.
3. The term vernacular interpretive community is informed by reader-response theory and Stanley Fish's idea of interpretive community as spelled out in "Interpreting the *Variorum*" (147–80) from *Is There a Text in this Class?* (Cambridge: Harvard University Press, 1982). For our concerns, Fish's approach has two limits: he focuses upon interpretation or meaning in reading, not in actual rhetorical use; and, as a result of his focus upon theory and criticism, vernacular speech communities are excluded from the types of interpretive communities that have been discussed. Indeed, I want to go beyond the word interpretive. Although Fish does ask "What does this text do?" rather than "What does it mean?" the goal is still the same: to interpret. My essay follows Jane Tompkins's revision, which enquires into the real-world rhetorical power of writing.
4. We might note two important facts. First, English programs are adapting to pressures to form more professional and pragmatic degrees in fields such as technical writing. Second, few creative writers do go on to become self-supporting writers. In a 1995 survey conducted by the University of Florida at Gainesville, only some 10 percent of the graduates were employed via writing (mostly technical jobs), whereas some 60 percent made their living through teaching, with half of these being adjunct instructors (Grant). Creative writing programs remain tremendously popular (graduating over 2,000 students in 1998), but they, too, are under pressure to show their pragmatic utility. Community involvement rather than corporate professionalism answers this demand.

5. D. W. Fenza, "Creative Writing and Its Discontents," *The Associated Writing Programs*. Web. Section 4.

6. Adrienne Rich, *Blood, Bread, and Poetry: Selected Prose, 1979-1985* (New York: Norton, 1986), 178.

7. Cary Nelson, "A Theorized Poetry Class," in *Teaching Contemporary Theory to Undergraduates*, edited by Dianne E Sadoff and William E. Cain (New York: MLA, 1994), 185.

8. Nelson, "A Theorized Poetry Class," 185.

9. Lynn Domina, "The Body of My Work Is Not Just a Metaphor," in *Colors of a Different Horse: Rethinking Creative Writing Theory and Pedagogy*, edited by Wendy Bishop and Hans Ostrom (Urbana, IL: National Council of Teachers of English, 1994), 29.

10. Domina, "The Body of My Work," 31.

11. Ibid., 32.

12. Ibid., 33.

13. D. W. Fenza, "Creative Writing and Its Discontents," section 12.

14. Ibid., section 4.

15. Lauren Muller and the Poetry for People Collective, eds., *June Jordan's Poetry for the People: A Revolutionary Blueprint* (New York: Routledge, 1995), 117; examples of student essays follow, 118–23.

16. Ibid., 124.

17. Ibid., 74.

18. Quincy Troupe, "Quincy Troupe," in *The Language of Life: A Festival of Poets*, edited by Bill Moyers (New York: Doubleday, 1995), 423.

19. Lisa Delpit, *Other People's Children: Cultural Conflict in the Classroom* (New York: New Press, 1995), 44.

20. Fahamisha Patricia Brown, *Performing the Word: African American Poetry as Vernacular Culture* (New Brunswick, NJ: Rutgers University Press, 1999).

21. Maria Herrera-Sobek, and Helena Maria Viramontes, eds., *Chicana Creativity and Criticism: Charting New Frontiers in American Literature* (Irvine, CA: Arte Publico Press, 1988).

22. George Ella Lyon, "Contemporary Appalachian Poetry: Sources and Directions," *Kentucky Review* 2 (1981): 3–22.

23. P. J. Laska, "Poetry at the Periphery," in *Appalachia/America: Proceedings of the 1980 Appalachian Studies Conference*, edited by Wilson Somerville (Boone, NC: Appalachian Consortium Press, 1981), 190–99.

24. Jane. P. Tompkins, *Sensational Designs: The Cultural Work of American Fiction, 1790-1860* (New York: Oxford University Press, 1985), xvii.

25. Tompkins, *Sensational Designs*, 38.

26. David M. Stewart, "Cultural Work, City Crime, Reading, Pleasure," *American Literary History* 9, no. 4 (Winter 1997): 676–701.

27. Trinh T. Minh-Ha, *Woman, Native, Other* (Bloomington: Indiana University Press, 1989), 121.

28. Marjorie Agosín, "How to Speak with the Dead? A Poet's Notebook," *Human Rights Quarterly* 16, no. 1 (February 1994): 219–20.

29. Richard Johnson, "What Is Cultural Studies Anyway?" *Social Text* 15 (1986–87): 47. For an excellent discussion of the permutations of cultural theory in the composition class, see James A. Berlin's "Composition Studies and Cultural Studies: Collapsing Boundaries," in *Rhetoric in an Antifoundational World* (New Haven: Yale University Press, 1998), 389–410.

30. Johnson, "What Is Cultural Studies," 46.

31. Ibid., 52.

32. Alan Sinfield, "Against Appropriation," *Essays in Criticism* 31 (1981): 182.

33. Luke Hutton, "The Black Dog of New Gate," in *The Elizabethan Underworld*, edited by Arthur Balentine Judges (New York: Octagon Books, 1965).

34. Pamela White Hadas, "The Bandit Queen Remembers," in *Beside Herself Pocahontas to Patty Hearst* (New York: Knopf, 1986).

35. Hayden Carruth, *The Voice That Is Great within Us* (New York: Bantam, 1983).

36. Ishmael Reed, ed., *The Before Columbus Foundation Poetry Anthology* (New York: Norton, 1992).

37. Richard Hugo, "Creative Writing: The New Responsibility," *AWP Newsletter* (April 1980), 9.

38. Hayden Carruth, "How Not to Rate a Poet," in *Effluences from the Sacred Cave: More Selected Essays and Reviews* (Ann Arbor: University of Michigan Press, 1983), 11.

39. My thanks go out to Dale Bauer for her keen suggestions and ever-present enthusiasm. Thanks also to Kathryn Flannery, who granted me space to adapt cultural studies and Elizabethan literature to creative writing.

Chapter Reflection

Questions for Discussion

(Some of the following questions were generated by creative writing student Bri Lucero.)

1   What connections can you draw between what Salesses refers to as "pure craft" and what Green refers to as the "sublime reader"?

2   What responsibility does a writer have to their society, if any? Do writers have a responsibility to respond to the political issues of their time? How does the context of a writer's life affect one's answer to this question?

3   What privileges must one take into account when writing creatively about social issues? Who has the right and ability to write about whom? Is it possible to tell another's story in a way that honors that person and their story? What does the writer of a poem or story of witness need to consider in terms of ethics, power, and responsibility? Are there subjects, phenomena, or events that are off-limits to a literary artist? What is the role of censorship in how we think about these questions?

4   Compare what it means to write poems and stories, as opposed to articles or videos, to amplify a political message? What are the benefits and consequences of using one genre or another? How do various media platforms alter the way a political piece is interpreted by its audience?

Writing Prompt

What ecological, social, political, or ideological problems matter most to you? Select one of these issues. What knowledge and understanding do you need in order to write about this issue? What reading communities do you want to engage in representing this issue? Try writing a story, essay, script, poem, song, and so forth that tangentially, obliquely, or directly engages one of the issues on your list.

Suggestions for Further Reading

1 Cushway, Phil, and Michael Warr. *Of Poetry and Protest: From Emmett Till to Trayvon Martin*. Norton, 2016.

2 Danticat, Edwidge. *Create Dangerously: The Immigrant Artist at Work*. Princeton University Press, 2010.

3 Damon, Maria, and Ira Livingston, ed. *Poetry and Cultural Studies: A Reader*. University of Illinois Press, 2009.

4 Gass, William H., and Lorin Cuoco. *The Writer in Politics*. Southern Illinois University Press, 1996.

5 Yu, Timothy. "Engagement, Race, and Public Poetry in America." *Jacket2* (Mar. 2015). Web. And *Race and the Avant-Garde: Experimental and Asian American Poetry Since 1965*. Stanford, 2009.

2
Identity

Stop Pigeonholing African Writers

Taiye Selasi

Taiye Selasi was born in London, educated at Yale and Oxford, and is currently living in Rome. Her novel *Ghana Must Go* (Penguin, 2013) is set in Accra, Lagos, London, and New York and was published in 13 countries. Named one of *Granta*'s "20 Best Young British Writers," Selasi has published essays and short fiction, including the "The Sex Lives of African Girls" which was published in *The Best American Short Stories 2012*. The following was published in *The Guardian* in 2015. "Stop Pigeonholing African Writers" is about artistic freedom, audience expectations and biases, identity, diaspora, the ways texts are categorized and marketed, and more. Selasi introduces the idea of "pigeonholing," a topic that all of the essays in this chapter discuss, noting the dimensions of this tendency and its ramifications.

African literature, as it's called, is enjoying a bit of a moment, with the western media regularly heralding splashes, rebirths, dawns. When I published my novel *Ghana Must Go* in 2013 I joined a list of writers that, on the face of things, appears encouragingly long. There are my fellow Nigerians Chinelo Okparanta, Chimamanda Adichie, Helen Oyeyemi, Helon Habila, Chris Abani, Teju Cole; the Kenyans Yvonne Owuor, Binya Wainaina, Mukoma Wa Ngũgĩ; the Ethiopians Maaza Mengiste, Dinaw Mengestu; the Sierra Leoneans Aminatta Forna, Olufemi Terry; the Zimbabweans Petina Gappah, NoViolet Bulawayo. It seems that African literature is the literary dish *du jour*, like the Indian (more Lahiris!) and Middle Eastern (more Hosseinis!) dishes before.

Of course, one could argue that 50-odd writers emerging from a continent of 1.1 billion people represent more of a trickle than a wave. So, too, might one question the media's fondness for these little ethnic trends. (When did the white male novelist's moment begin, and when will it end?) One might pause to wonder what so-called African novels have in common: does the commercial category function as a creative one, as well? The Scottish-born novelist Aminatta Forna has asked why her novel *The Hired Man*, set in Croatia, is sometimes found in the "African section" of bookshops. What of Helen Oyeyemi's *Boy Snow Bird*, set in New England? (Oyeyemi is British;

her family moved to the UK when she was four.) Or Teju Cole's *Open City*, much of which takes place in Manhattan? Are these African works?

When I warn against grouping African writers together, it is not because I lack pride in the continent's literary tradition, but rather that I am conscious of the west's tradition of essentialising African subjects. As Evan Mwangi put it in the Kenyan Daily Nation, artists who resist such categorisation do so because "they shouldn't be vacuum-packed as ethnic writers in the metropolitan academy, which has perfected these tendencies whenever it encounters any writing that is not white".

More interesting to me than the media's approach to African writers is the discourse among those writers themselves. It was 1963 when Chinua Achebe, reflecting on a conference of African authors, wrote: "There was [one] thing that we tried to do and failed—and that was to define 'African literature' satisfactorily. Was it literature produced in Africa or about Africa? Could African literature be on any subject, or must it have an African theme?" The same year Nigerian poet Christopher Okigbo (in)famously announced himself a writer, simply a writer, not an African one. Thirty years later, the first African winner of the Booker prize, asked to describe himself, said: "I think Ben Okri is a writer who works very hard to sing from all the things that affect him. I don't know if he's an African writer. I never think of myself in terms of any classification. Literature doesn't have a country."

It may not, but publishers do. And two decades on, the same tensions have arisen again, exacerbated by the fact that so much African literature is published outside Africa. If no one can quite say what African writing is, many have views on what it should be: what it must say, what it mustn't say, who can write it, who should read it. At the heart of this increasingly noisy debate lie, I think, three central questions: who is an African writer, what should she write and for whom is she writing?

1 Who is an African writer?

In 2013, Tope Folarin won the 14th Caine prize for African writing, the first American-born writer to do so. His victory suggested that Africans in the diaspora now qualified as African writers, a question of distracting importance. The weekend before the ceremony, the Ethiopian-American writer Maaza Mengiste wrote a marvellous piece for *The Guardian* called "What makes a 'real African?'." She noted: "On the shortlist of five, three writers live in the US and at least one has US citizenship. The Caine prize, some have argued, should be only for 'real' African writers. But who is to judge what makes a 'real African'?" I saw myself in her words:

At a recent conference on African literature . . . I sat on a panel with two other female writers. A question was asked almost immediately: do you consider yourself an African writer? It seems that every new writer with any remote connection to the continent of Africa, either willingly or unwillingly, has first to wrestle with this question of identity before talking about what should matter most: their book.

African writers are not the only victims of such questions—which, among other absurdities, assume that their identities are open to assessment by absolute strangers. In Vikram Chandra's well-known essay "The Cult of Authenticity" (2000), he writes about a friend who attended a Delhi University syllabus revision committee:

> [My] friend suggested *Midnight's Children* and she was shouted down. Salman Rushdie isn't Indian, the majority of the professors asserted. Amitav Ghosh, however, was found to be sufficiently Indian, and so his *Shadow Lines* was accepted into the canon. The issue was decided not on the basis of the relative merits of the books, but on the perceived Indianness of the authors, and by implication, the degree of their assimilation by the west.

Writing over 10 years apart, Mengiste and Chandra alert us to the same trend: the prioritisation of perceived cultural allegiance over creative output. The most scathing critique of the African writer is not that she is insufficiently talented, but that she is insufficiently African.

Why? It is no secret that Africa (like India) is the starting point of a modern diaspora. There are an estimated 1.6 million African immigrants in the US, a number that has doubled every decade since 1970. That many in this number should consider themselves both American and African doesn't seem so controversial. Their African-ness may be peculiar to the diasporic experience, and their American-ness peculiar to the immigrant one, but they are legitimate identities, no less comprehensible for being multiple. Asked whether she considers herself Ethiopian or American, Mengiste said: "That's like asking whether I am my mother's child or my father's." She is Ethiopian and American. I am Ghanaian, Nigerian and cosmopolitan. We belong to Africa's diaspora. We don't need a panel discussion to suss out who we are.

But the wider literary establishment has trouble with writers who belong to diasporas. It doesn't know where to put us. It can be unclear which team we are playing for: home or away, or neither? Our art is subjected to a particular kind of scrutiny; it is forced to play the role of anthropology. What

Chandra described feeling in 2000, I lament in 2015; replace "Indian-ness" with "African-ness" and "Indians" with "Africans", and Chandra's words fit my woes to a tee:

I noticed the constant hum of this rhetoric, this anxiety about the anxiety of Indianness, this notion of a real reality that was being distorted by "third world cosmopolitans", this fear of an all-devouring and all-distorting west. I heard it in conversations, in critical texts, in reviews. And Indians who wrote in English were one of the prime locations for this rhetoric to test itself, to make its declarations of power and belonging.

With African writers, as with Indian, the critical issue is control: who gets to control what diasporic writers write, which is to say, what global readers read.

2 What should the African writer write?

In November last year, I joined Chinelo Okparanta, author of the collection *Happiness, Like Water*, on a panel called "In This Way Comes Morning: New Writing of the West African Diaspora". It was the second of a series. (Note: where the other six readings matched writers on the basis of their writing, for example Claire Vaye Watkins and Ruth Ozeki on "Weaving Fact into Fiction", we were paired for our African-ness alone.) At the reception, Okparanta spoke of a reader who criticised her story "Runs Girl" for its depiction of a Nigerian hospital plagued by power outages. Okparanta, who lives in Maryland, spent weeks with her aunt in a Port Harcourt hospital; she explained that her description was accurate. The reader was implacable. "You're writing poverty porn," he insisted.

It's a popular accusation these days. In May 2013, Bulawayo, who lives in California, published *We Need New Names*, a heartbreaking portrait of a Zimbabwean girl. The novel was shortlisted for the Man Booker prize, and appeared on many best books of the year lists—rightly so. I was shocked when, in his Guardian review, the Nigerian author Helon Habila (who lives in Washington) accused Bulawayo of "performing Africa". By this he means "to inundate one's writing with images . . . that evoke, to borrow a phrase from Aristotle, pity and fear, but not in a real tragic sense, more in a CNN, western-media-coverage-of-Africa, poverty-porn sense". Habila ticks off the tragic images found in Bulawayo's text—Aids, political violence, street children—then quips: "Did I mention that one of the children is pregnant after being raped by her grandfather?"

I was baffled. Anyone who knows even a bit about Zimbabwe's recent history will affirm that Aids, political violence and street children were devastating features of its decline. Bulawayo, born and raised in Zimbabwe, has written a beautiful novel that tells some very ugly truths about things that she has seen first-hand. These are not truths about Africa the monolith, as Habila claimed, nor about the state of Zimbabwe in general, but truths of the life of one Zimbabwean character, Darling, and the worlds she inhabits. When my mother, a pediatrician and public health specialist in Ghana, read *We Need New Names* she said: "We need this book." She has spent decades advocating for the rights of African children, examining how dysfunctional African governments disproportionally affect children, especially girls. For her, Bulawayo had told an important story honestly.

Of course, at no point in his review did Habila argue that Bulawayo is wrong about the ills plaguing Zimbabwe. His issue is not with her accuracy but what he imagines to be her animus, a "palpable anxiety to cover every 'African' topic; almost as if [she] had a checklist made from the morning's news on Africa". I share Habila's contempt for western depictions of Africa; the news coverage of the Ebola epidemic is just one recent infuriating example. I understand that it is not enough to say, simply, that a story is true; a work of art exists in context and the context here is a culture that habitually promotes demeaning portrayals of Africa. What I don't understand is what Habila and others would have the writer do. If poverty and violence exist in the country in which a novel is set, should the African novelist simply Photoshop them out? More than 50% of Africa's population lives in poverty. Should their stories be erased from Africa's literature?

Last year, Mũkoma Wa Ngũgĩ reviewed a new collection, *Africa39: New Writing from Africa South of the Sahara*, in the Los Angeles Review of Books. "To understand the aesthetics and political distance African literature has travelled between *Things Fall Apart* and *Africa39*," he wrote, "one would have to think of it in those terms of mourning and melancholy, of inherited traumas and memories, which define the new African literary generation."

I was nodding along enthusiastically, taken by Wa Ngũgĩ's notion of "a state of melancholy", when I reached this: "To my ear, Chimamanda Ngozi Adichie's story in *Africa39*—set in the United States—suffers from an African, middle-class aesthetic that was also present in her latest novel, *Americanah*. This is an aesthetic that is so concerned with not telling a single story of poor, fly-infested Africans that it goes overboard into the academic halls of Princeton, of mansions, housemaids, and casually worn and perhaps ill-gotten wealth."

Damned if you do, damned if you don't. While Bulawayo and Okparanta are criticised for airing Africa's dirty laundry, Adichie is faulted for focusing on its finer linens. Why? An African middle class—small though it is, corrupt though it is often assumed to be—unquestionably exists. There *are* mansions and housemaids in certain parts of Nigeria, and African students at Ivy League schools, as Wa Ngũgĩ, a professor at Cornell, surely knows. In what way has Adichie gone "overboard"? How does her story "suffer" from being set in a world that exists? *Americanah* is celebrated in part because it paints so fabulously *real* a portrait of two contemporary Nigerian lovers. From Ifemelu's childhood home in working-class Lagos to Obinze's stint cleaning toilets in London, there is no single class aesthetic on display.

To what is Wa Ngũgĩ objecting? If the African novelist is not meant to describe the experiences of impoverished Africans or those of privileged ones, is there some working-/middle-class sweet spot for which she should aim? Or is the problem not what she writes but for whom she is imagined to write it? Wa Ngũgĩ and Habila assume that Adichie and Bulawayo are writing for someone, either concerned not to tell that someone "a single story of poor, fly-infested Africans" or else "palpably anxious" to do the same. Neither critic imagines that the novelist has immersed herself fully in the world and the work of her fiction, attending with such care and wisdom to her characters that they cannot possibly be read as representations.

The African novelist is rarely granted the privilege of writing, as Toni Morrison famously put it, the novel she wanted to read. Instead, the novelist is assumed to be or accused of writing for the west, producing explanatory ethnographic texts dolled up as literary fiction. It's a curious allegation, one that denies both the agency and artistry of the writer while threatening to obscure, I think, the actual source of the unease.

3 For whom is the African writer writing?

In November last year, Adaobi Nwaubani published an article entitled "African Books for Western Eyes" in *The New York Times*. Nwaubani is the first contemporary African writer to have got an international book deal while still living in her home country. Her article expresses, among other things, frustration with Africa's publishing industry, a sentiment I share.

I am often asked why *Ghana Must Go*, a story about a Ghanaian-Nigerian family, was not published in Ghana or Nigeria. The answer is: we tried. Ghana, where my parents live, has no credible local publisher. To launch the novel in Accra, as I was determined to do, we had to go it alone. After an attempt to form a partnership with a bookshop failed (not wanting to pay the customs fees, they abandoned the shipment of books at the port), we organised two public events. After the book sold out, my mother ordered more directly from Penguin and sold them from her clinic.

I know of what Nwaubani speaks when she writes: "Any Nigerian in Anchorage who so wishes can acquire my novel. But here in my country [my] book is available only at a few bookstores." Nigeria, which last year surpassed South Africa as Africa's biggest economy, could subsidise a stable publishing house, distributing books to the entire continent. It is maddening that it doesn't. It is unacceptable that African novelists cannot easily or profitably publish in African countries. But it does not follow that African novelists are writing for the west.

Can we really not imagine that the African novelist writes for love: love of craft, love of subject? Do we really believe that she is not an artist but an anthropologist, not a storyteller but a native informant? Would we really suggest that she hasn't the right to engage a global audience? Many African novelists publish in the west because no alternative path to global readership exists. Even if it did—even if, say, I could have published in Ghana—I'd still want our books to travel the world. Touring *Ghana Must Go*, I had the most magical encounters with readers: Indian-Americans in New Jersey, Chinese-Americans in San Francisco, Nigerian-Americans in Texas, British West Africans in London, Turkish and Croatian immigrants in Germany, who recognised themselves in my characters. Are these readers "the west"? Did I write "what the white people wanted to read"?

The Nigerian author Okey Ndibe has said: "We used to spend so much time agonising over the question of whether we were writing for the west. In retrospect I see our error. In Nigeria we grew up reading the west. The west was talking to us. Why shouldn't the west read Nigeria? Why shouldn't we talk back?" With his trademark ease Ndibe put his finger on my disquiet: the limitations imposed on African writers by their colleagues. Habila and Wa Ngugi would have read in Henry James' Art of Fiction, "We must grant the artist his subject . . . our criticism is applied only to what he makes of it." Beyond examining what the artist has made of her subject (street children, Princeton grads), the critics render inappropriate the subject itself. Nwaubani, in turn, is content to define 'appropriate ways' to describe those subjects. "A story about an African wife in the 1980s, for instance, should not show her comfortable with having only one child," she writes. But who is this "African wife"? From which country does she hail? To what socioeconomic class does she belong? A generic "African wife in the 1980s" may belong in a sociological study but has no place in a novel of nuanced characters.

Taken together, these critiques become a set of edicts: here are the subjects you can write about (not too much poverty! not too much privilege!), here is the appropriate way to write about them. My problem with these rules is how they threaten to silence voices. The voice of the street child in Zimbabwe, the Nigerian grad student at Princeton. . . . We need more stories about more subjects, more readers in more countries. Not fewer.

It is precisely because there are so few novels by African writers in global circulation that we ask those novels to do too much. No one novelist can bear the burden of representing a continent and no one novel should have to. The list at the beginning of this piece represents five of 55 countries, with no francophone, lusophone or, say, Central African writer in sight. Those on it are more or less socioeconomically homogenous: born, raised or granted degrees by universities in the west, and now living in or "between" western cities and African capitals. This is a problem. African books for global eyes must be written by a broader range of Africans, including those writing in non-European languages. Diasporic novelists such as Mengiste and Wa Ngũgĩ are doing wonderful work in bringing African writers who work in indigenous languages to global attention. With them, I share the heartbreak in Nwaubani's words: "Some of the greatest African writers of my generation may never be discovered."

We—African novelists, western publishers, global readers—must attend to this. We need more writers from more countries, representing more class backgrounds. We need more names.

Perhaps, then, we might grant more freedom to the ones we already have. As Henry James reminds us: "A novel is in its broadest definition a personal impression of life; that, to begin with, constitutes its value, which is greater or less according to the intensity of the impression. But there will be no intensity at all, and therefore no value, unless there is freedom to feel and say." The diasporic novelist, as much as any other, must be granted that freedom.

Aesthetics Contra "Identity" in Contemporary Poetry Studies

Dorothy J. Wang

The title of Dorothy J. Wang's book *Thinking Its Presence* was adopted by the Creative Writing and Race conferences held in Montana and Arizona since 2014—conferences that, in John Keene's words, "grapple . . . with the discourses and ideology of whiteness as normativity, and the systems and structures that have made it so, institutionalized racism, and, in particular, the unnameable thing in our society, the ideology of white supremacy." Wang's book has been important to this conversation because it makes the case "that aesthetic forms are inseparable from social, political, and historical contexts." Wang's book *Thinking Its Presence: Form, Race, and Subjectivity in Contemporary Asian American Poetry* won the 2016 Best Book in Literary Criticism Award, sponsored by the Association for Asian American Studies (AAAS). What follows is the book's introductory chapter. An American Council of Learned Societies (ACLS) 2017 Frederick Burkhardt Residential Fellow, Dorothy J. Wang is an associate professor of American Studies at Williams College.

A Few Snapshots of the Current State of Poetry Reception

In the January 2008 issue of *PMLA*—the official publication of the Modern Language Association (MLA) sent to more than thirty thousand members in one hundred countries[1]—a cluster of essays by eight distinguished literary critics appeared under the title "The New Lyric Studies."[2] The pieces took as their jumping-off point the eminent poetry critic Marjorie Perloff's MLA presidential address, "It Must Change," given in December 2006 at the annual convention in Philadelphia and later reprinted in the May 2007 issue of *PMLA*. In that talk, Perloff asks, "Why *is* the 'merely' literary so suspect today?" (original emphasis), contending that "the governing paradigm for so-called literary study is now taken from anthropology and history."[3]

Because lyric has in our time become conflated with the more generic category of poetry,[4] the *PMLA* forum serves to address not only the state of lyric studies but, more broadly, the state of poetry studies today. Nine critics may seem a small number—hardly representative of the larger numbers of academic poetry critics in the country—but because of the influential reputations of the critics involved (Perloff and Jonathan Culler in particular);[5] because the MLA, despite the ridicule to which it is sometimes subjected, is the largest, most powerful and influential professional organization for professors and academic critics of literature; and because the *PMLA* reaches a wider and broader audience than any other literary-critical journal,[6] the views of these particular critics are highly visible and influential and cannot be easily discounted or dismissed. The MLA is one of what Edward Said calls the "authoritative and authorizing agencies" of culture in the Arnoldian sense (*WTC*, 8). Individual articles in *PMLA* may be overlooked, but statements by high-profile members about the state of the field of literary criticism—especially when marked by an adjective such as "New"—are often noticed and by a not insignificant number of readers.

In quite a few respects, the arguments made in "The New Lyric Studies" were varied: from Culler's making the case for the specialness of lyric—with its "memorable language" and its being "characteristically extravagant"[7]—to Rei Terada's calling that we "[be] release[d] from lyric ideology" and "let 'lyric' dissolve into literature and 'literature' into culture"[8] (Robert Kaufman, the requisite Marxist contributor, splits the difference by claiming, via Adorno and Benjamin, that lyric is special precisely because it operates ideologically by the same "version of aura or semblance" that the commodity form does[9]); from Stathis Gourgouris's and Brent Edwards's urging that lyric scholars engage with truer and more incisive forms of interdisciplinarity;[10] to Oren lzenberg's assertion that "it makes good sense to bring literary study into closer proximity with the disciplines that give accounts of how the mind works," such as "the philosophy of mind, philosophical psychology, and metaphysics that deal with the nature of mental phenomena and their relation not so much to the determinations of culture as to the causal structure of reality."[11] Virginia Jackson and Yopie Prins both argue for more and better historicization: Jackson—pushing against the tendency to make poetry and lyric abstract, idealized, and transhistorical-urges that we "trace . . . the history of lyricization"; Prins, that we examine "the cultural specificity of poetic genres" and the history of poetics and prosody.[12]

Yet despite the various methodological, disciplinary, and aesthetic inclinations of the respondents, there are moments of agreement, some expected and others less so, sometimes cutting across the familiar "literary versus cultural" divide within literary studies. Not surprisingly among scholars committed to the "literary," Culler, like Perloff, makes the familiar validating move of tracing the history of lyric back to the Greeks. Gourgouris, too, bolsters his arguments by appealing to the authority of ancient Greece (not so unexpected given that he works on Greek literature), taking Perloff slightly to task for too narrowly conceiving of *poietike,* which she translates as "the discipline of poetics." But Gourgouris—who makes the point that Perloff "does not inquire if 'poetics' can be conducted nowadays in a fresh language"—does agree with her claim that literary studies has taken a wrong turn, though for him the reasons are internal to the field and not, as Perloff suggests, because interdisciplinarity, in the form of anthropological and historical paradigms, has been a bad influence. Gourgouris writes in "*Poiein*-Political Infinitive,"

> For a decade or more since 1990, the microidentitarian shift in theory precipitated a failure of self-interrogation, especially regarding the paradoxes of the new disciplinary parameters that emerged out of the practice of interdisciplinarity. As a result, literary studies (and other disciplines) suffered, not so much a defanging, as Perloff implies, but rather carelessness, perhaps even arrogance—one is a symptom of the other—which led the discipline to abandon self-interrogation and instead hop on the high horse of identity politics. In other words, if Perloff's scenario for the relegation of literary studies to a secondary practice is legitimate, the devaluation is not external but self-induced. (224)

This moment is surprising in that Gourgouris, who strongly advocates for, in effect, a "truer" form of interdisciplinarity—one that "requires, by definition, the double work of mastering the canonical and the modes of interrogating it" (225)—and who emphatically states that "[p]oetry cannot be understood except in relation to life" (227), places the blame for the fall of literary studies so firmly and unquestioningly on "the high horse of identity politics"—presumably not "relat[ed] to life"—the end result of "carelessness" and the abandoning of "self-interrogation." Indeed, "identity" has already been referenced as a dirty word earlier in the quote when Gourgouris speaks of the "microidentitarian shift in theory" and its having "precipitated a failure of self-interrogation." Let me delay my discussion of this critique of "identity politics" for now and turn to another moment of agreement in *PMLA.*

On page two of his essay "Poems Out of Our Heads," Oren Izenberg—before asserting that literary studies be brought in closer proximity with

more scientific "disciplines that give accounts of how the mind works"—
makes common cause with Perloff, quoting her:

> I share much of Perloff's resistance to viewing poetry as "symptoms of cultural
> desires, drives, anxieties, or prejudices" and to the sometimes haphazard
> forms of interdisciplinarity that this view fosters. (217)

This move is also somewhat surprising, for aesthetic and methodological
rather than disciplinary reasons: not only has Izenberg been harshly critical
in print of the Language poets, of whom Perloff has been a pioneering and
fierce champion, but his privileging of analytic philosophy's methods do
not align with Perloff's more Continental proclivities and her more literary
historical approaches to poetry.[13]

Thus, whatever other aesthetic, methodological, and disciplinary
differences may separate them, Gourgouris, Izenberg, and Perloff do
converge when thinking about one of the reasons—if not the major reason—
for the fallen state of literary studies: forms of sloppy (careless, haphazard)
thinking, slightly differentiated but fundamentally linked, that privilege,
variously, the sociological over the literary (Perloff); identity politics over
rigorous self-interrogation (Gourgouris); the cultural over the literary or
philosophical or something called "reality" and its "causal structure"
(Izenberg). In other words, scholarly overconcern with the cultural, including
the political—dismissed as unspecified "anxieties" and "prejudices"—has
seduced serious literary scholars away from the proper study of the literary,
specifically poetry. Perloff posits this binary quite starkly in her presidential
address:

> Still, I wonder how many of us, no matter how culturally and politically
> oriented our own particular research may be, would be satisfied with the
> elimination of literary study from the curriculum. (656)

Despite her use of the first-person plural pronoun, Perloff suggests that such
"culturally and politically oriented" research is precisely the research that
"use[s] literary texts" instrumentally, as "windows through which we see the
world beyond the text, symptoms of cultural drives, anxieties, or prejudices"
(654). She ends her address by forcefully exhorting,

> It is time to trust the literary instinct that brought us to this field in the first
> place and to recognize that, instead of lusting after those other disciplines
> that seem so exotic primarily because we don't really practice them, what we
> need is more theoretical, historical, and critical training in our own
> discipline. (662)

More rigorous training in the discipline of literary studies—though oddly, a discipline rooted in an "instinct" that brought "us" into the field in the first place (who is included in this "us" and "we"?)—is posited as the antidote to the deleterious cultural and political turn, seen as a "lusting after" the "exotic."

For Perloff, this either-or choice obtains not only with literary methods and disciplines but also with individual authors and texts themselves. In her spring 2006 "President's Column" written for the *MLA Newsletter*, she writes more explicitly and directly of what choices are at stake:

> Under the rubrics of African American, other minorities, and post-colonial, a lot of important and exciting novels and poems are surely studied. But what about what is not studied? Suppose a student (undergraduate or graduate) wants to study James Joyce or Gertrude Stein? Virginia Woolf or T.E. Lawrence or George Orwell? William Faulkner or Frank O'Hara? the literature of World Wars I and II? the Great Depression? the impact of technology on poetry and fiction? modernism vis-à-vis fascism? existentialism? the history of modern satire or pastoral? Or, to put it in the most everyday terms, what of the student who has a passionate interest in her or his literary world—a world that encompasses the digital as well as print culture but does not necessarily differentiate between the writings of one subculture or one theoretical orientation and another? Where do such prospective students turn?[14]

What is one to make of this suggestion that Joyce and Woolf and Faulkner or any of the other canonical authors listed are not being studied because curricula are crammed full with the works of, say, Chinua Achebe and Gwendolyn Brooks?[15] (Since Perloff does not mention the names of minority or postcolonial writers—only that "a lot" of their work is "surely" being studied—one can only guess which writers she is referring to.)[16] What is most noteworthy in this passage is not that Perloff opposes the "important and exciting novels and poems" of "African American, other minorities, and postcolonial" writers against the great works of Joyce et al. (Joyce himself a postcolonial writer) but that, rather, she explicitly sets up an opposition, "in the most everyday terms," between the "literary" and the writings of these racialized[17] and postcolonial subjects who are members of "subculture[s]."[18]

For Perloff, the problem is not the death of literary print culture at the hands of the digital, as some critics lament—she is forward-thinking in championing new technologies and rightly sees no contradiction between the literary/poetic and the digital, or even between the literary and the cultural (there is no problem in studying a topic as sociological as "the Great Depression")—but that the works of "African American, other minorities, and postcolonial" writers leave no room in the curricula for those works that satisfy "the student who has a passionate interest in her or his literary world."[19] Perloff explicitly frames the choice as one between "passionate" and "literary" writing by famous named authors, all white, and an undifferentiated mass of unliterary writing by nameless minority authors.[20] Perhaps because she is writing in the more informal context of an organizational newsletter, Perloff feels freer to be more explicit about what exactly threatens the "literary" than in her MLA presidential address "It Must Change," where she uses more generic terms such as "culturally and politically oriented" research—though we can fairly accurately guess what the indefinite pronoun "It" in the title refers to.

My critique here is directed not at Perloff's views as an individual scholar but at an ideological position that she articulates in her MLA presidential address and the newsletter—one widely held in the academy but not usually so straightforwardly stated. Indeed, I admire the forthrightness with which Perloff expresses what many literary scholars think and feel but do not say except, perhaps, between the enclosed walls of hiring meetings: the frightening specter that, because of "politically correct" cultural-studies-ish pressures in the academy, presumably the detrimental legacy of both 1960s activism and the culture wars of the 1980s, worthy, major, and beloved works of literature—whose merits are "purely literary"—are being squeezed out of the curriculum by inferior works penned by minority writers, whose representation in the curriculum is solely the result of affirmative action or racial quotas or because their writings have passed an ideological litmus test, not literary merit. This sentiment is usually expressed in a manner much more coded though, nonetheless, clearly understood.

What makes it particularly disappointing that Perloff is the one using the powerful forum of the MLA presidency to express these conventional (and literary-establishment) views on minority writing and race is that for decades, she has fought hard to open the academy to unconventional modes and forms of poetry, which were often not considered poetry or even literature, at a time when there was no institutional reward for doing so. She was one of the first, and certainly the most prominent and vocal academic literary critic, to champion the Language poets and is almost single-handedly responsible for their now having become officially canonized and holding appointments at various prestigious English departments across the nation, such as the University of California, Berkeley, and the University of Pennsylvania. Anyone who works on avant-garde poetic writing in this country owes a debt to her—including myself.[21]

In the particular 2008 issue of the *PMLA* in question, it is left to Brent Edwards—the only critic in the group of eight respondents who writes on ethnic literature (and is himself African American)—the task of explicitly making the argument for the social in his response, "The Specter of Interdisciplinarity," to Perloff's "It Must Change" address and her posited binary of the "cultural" and the "political" versus the "literary":[22]

> Perloff uses "merely" [in her rhetorical question "Why *is* the 'merely' literary so suspect today?"] to suggest that the literary, even if threatened or "suspect," can nevertheless be considered in isolation, as the core of a disciplinary practice. (189)

> In whatever form, literary criticism must not relinquish its unique point of articulation with the social. (191)

To reinforce this latter point, Edwards turns to the work of the black Martinican poet Monchoachi—"a pseudonym . . . the name of an infamous Maroon who led a violent insurrection against French slavery in Martinique" (191)—active in the *creolité* movement in the Francophone Caribbean:

> It is suggestive to read Monchoachi's speech [made in 2003 on accepting the Prix Max Jacob] in juxtaposition to Perloff's, at once for his "social interpretation" of the role of poetry, his different call for a "return," and his implicit departure from some of her framing gestures, perhaps above all her turn to Greek sources as foundations for the discipline of poetics. (191)

On the previous page, Edwards spoke of "the unique experimental character of postcolonial poetics," adding that "[s]till, only a handful of scholars have begun to theorize the relation between postcoloniality and poetics in a broader sense." That Edwards turns to a Francophone postcolonial poet, rather than an African American one, and speaks of the "comparative literature of the African diaspora," rather than US ethnic literature, is understandable, given the minefield that awaits anyone, especially a minority scholar, who dares to invoke the term "identity" (much less "race" or "identity politics") in a US context. This treacherous terrain is a synecdoche of the fraught nature of any discussion about race in the larger national context—even, or especially, in this "post-race" era.

As it turns out, of the nine or so poets discussed with more than passing reference by Perloff and the eight respondents, Monchoachi is the only nonwhite writer and the one with the least name recognition among American academics.[23] In other words, even as the nine literary critics here evince a variety of aesthetic proclivities and allegiances (traditional versus avant-garde, major versus minor, and so on), methodological approaches (literary criticism, analytic philosophy, Frankfurt School), disciplinary stances (intra- versus inter-), and ideological commitments (classical, Marxist, postmodern, among others), the poets they choose to speak about constitute a much more homogeneous and narrow group. This is not an insignificant observation: the selection of which authors critics consider worth devoting time and energy to study speaks volumes about whom they consider truly literarily important. And, despite what we would like to believe, the occlusion of minority poets here is not unrepresentative of aporias in the field of poetry studies at large, even with the work of those (nonminority) critics of modern and contemporary poetry who have sought to link aesthetics and politics—Rachel Blau duPlessis, Michael Davidson, Alan Golding, David Lloyd, Cary Nelson, Aldon Nielsen, Jerome McGann, Susan Schultz, Donald Wesling, and Shira Wolosky, to name a few.[24]

Here, I must confess that, even as I tallied the list of poets in the previous paragraph, I felt guilty—or was it pre-accused?—of having taken precisely the sort of instrumental approach opponents of "identity politics" decry: of having come down on the side of the political and the social and the cultural against the "literary." I felt and feel this indictment even though I am someone who has spent my life, academic and otherwise, devoted to poetry; someone who is the daughter of two English professors—a Romanticist and a Victorianist—and someone who feels that there is indeed something distinctive and valuable about literature and literary criticism and that literary critics make a mistake when they become would-be analytic philosophers or scientists or legal scholars or economists.[25] I, too, feel wonder at "how and why the art called poetry exert[s] such a magic spell"[26] and believe that what literary and poetry critics have to contribute to the field of knowledge is an attunement to and understanding of language and the various literary forms it takes. I, too, agree that we must have "theoretical, historical, and critical training in our own discipline" (including prosody and poetics—knowing what an ode or a terza rima is—and, in Gourgouris's words, "mastering the canonical and the modes of interrogating it" [225]).

But—and this is a big but—I do not at all see why we must make an either-or choice between reading Beckett *or* reading Aimé Césaire, between calling out and into question "cultural desires, drives, anxieties, or prejudices"—the supposed realm of the cultural, the social, and the political, cordoned off from the pure realm of the literary—*or* analyzing metonymy, chiasmus, sprung rhythm, lineation, anaphora, parataxis, trochees, and so forth. The posited choices are false ones.

As Shira Wolosky, a scholar of nineteenth-century American poetry (and of Paul Celan), writes, "The notion of poetry as a self-enclosed aesthetic realm; as a formal object to be approached through more or less exclusively specified categories of formal analysis; as metahistorically transcendent; and as a text deploying a distinct and poetically 'pure' language: these notions seem only to begin to emerge at the end of the nineteenth century, in a process that is itself peculiarly shaped in response to social and historical no less than aesthetic trends."[27]

That critics of avant-garde writing fall into these traps is perhaps even more perplexing given that they have long had to fight off the same sorts of dismissive arguments about "literary value" and "literariness" that are now made about minority writing. But being marginalized in one arena, as avant-garde poets and critics have been, does not guarantee that one understands forms of marginalizations in other arenas—here, specifically racial.

What seems to me so drearily familiar in this exchange in *PMLA* is how much the readers both intuit and are expected to intuit, in a myriad of ways, spoken and unspoken, precisely what the terms invoked "really" mean and what is at stake here, at stake not just in the debates about the state of the profession but in the very conditions—the framework and terminologies—of the forum itself. In other words, what is even more operative here than what is explicitly stated is what is *not* stated, what does not *need* to be stated, or what needs to be stated only by shorthand: "identitarian," "identity politics," "cultural," "social," "political," "anxieties," "prejudices," "exotic," "carelessness," "haphazard" versus "literary," "classic," "classical," "discipline," among other terms. These terms (as does the term "avant-garde") act as placeholders for larger assumptions and beliefs, many of which have largely become normative in shoring up the supposed opposition between the cultural against the literary.

For, even as we have entered the twenty-first century—with a black man in the White House for two terms, avant-garde Language poets now holding major posts at our most prestigious universities, a globalized world with non-Western countries "on the rise," new forms of technology and media cropping up faster than we can assimilate them (including new forms of digital poetries and archives and forums of literary criticism)—many members of our profession continue to rely upon assumptions, beliefs, categories, and norms that operate unquestioningly in English departments across the country.[28] So it is that critics who might diverge quite strongly in their poetic allegiances, or who might disagree about how disciplinarity has or has not played itself out, can easily come to agreement across the aesthetic and institutional divides about what threatens the literary and the poetic. (Yes, the MLA and *PMLA* represent a certain "official" or perhaps institutionalized segment of poetry critics, but their influence has no close rival in the field.)

And I do not think that the views expressed in "The New Lyric Studies" are idiosyncratic or marginal to literary studies, despite, as noted earlier, the important work of a dozen or so poetry critics who do attend to the inseparability of the aesthetic and the sociopolitical. The conceptions and reception of minority poetry are concerns that are not quirky and individual matters of, say, "taste" but deeply ideological, institutional, and structural ones—framed and reflected by the curricula of departments of English, disciplines and units within colleges and universities, (in)visibility within the pages of *PMLA*, and decisions made by the NEH, and so on.

The framing of the state of decline of poetry studies as an opposition between social context and the literary is, of course, not new. Debates about poetry's role and relevance in society, "form" versus "content," and so on, extend back through the history of poetry—to the Greeks, surely, but more significantly and urgently for those of us in the modern era, to the Romantics (German and especially British, who witnessed firsthand capitalism's brutal triumph and the concomitant splitting off from the sullied market-driven world a realm of "pure" artistic sensibility). To understand how little we have traveled, imagine how William Blake and Percy Shelley might feel about their poetry's being discussed in purely "literary" terms. As Raymond Williams reminds us:

> What were seen at the end of the nineteenth century as disparate interests, between which a man must choose and in the act of choice declare himself poet or sociologist, were, normally, at the beginning of the century, seen as interlocking interests. . . . [A]s some sort of security against the vestiges of the dissociation, we may usefully remind ourselves that Wordsworth wrote political pamphlets, that Blake was a friend of Tom Paine and was tried for sedition, that Coleridge wrote political journalism and social philosophy, that Shelley, in addition to this, distributed pamphlets in the streets, that Southey was a constant political commentator, that Byron spoke on the frame-riots and died as a volunteer in a political war; and further, as must surely be obvious from the poetry of all the men named, that these activities were neither marginal nor incidental, but were essentially related to a large part of the experience from which the poetry itself was made.[29]

Since the revolutionary and world-changing period we now call Romantic, urgent grapplings with the question of the aesthetic's relation to the social and the political have made themselves felt in distinct and vibrant poetic movements and groupings: various Modernist movements (Italian and Russian Futurism, Dada, Surrealism, Harlem Renaissance, among others), the Frankfurt School, Negritude, Black Arts, Language poetry, to name the most noteworthy. In the English literary tradition alone, poet-artists and poet-critics such as William Blake, Percy Shelley, Ezra Pound, Allen Ginsberg, Amiri Baraka, Adrienne Rich, and Harryette Mullen, to name but a few, have thoughtfully and incisively interrogated the intersection of the aesthetic and the social.[30]

But what *is* new in the discussions of the last two decades or so—in the aftermath of the various political movements of the 1960s and 1970s, which inevitably led to furious "culture wars" about the literary canon in the 1980s—has been the firm clicking into place of the terms "identity," "identitarian," and, most overtly, "identity politics" as the antithesis of (opposite to and opposing) literary value and critical rigor. So it is that one can group the terms "identitarian," "identity politics," "cultural," "social," "political," "anxieties," "prejudices," "exotic," "carelessness," and "haphazard" together and know exactly what is being invoked (that is, demonized).

In the US academy and society at large, the words "identity," "identitarian," and "identity politics" are often automatically conflated. Used synonymously, all three function as a reductive shorthand to refer to an essentializing and unthinking "identity politics"—almost always regarded, explicitly or not, as the provenance of minorities with grievances. "Identity politics" is a straw-man term. This is what I meant earlier when I called many of the words used by half of the *PMLA* critics "placeholders": they index something understood by readers as troubling but whose precise contours are amorphous and indistinct—and, I would argue, ultimately incoherent and indefensible. Indeed, if one were to put pressure on Gourgouris's singling out of the "high horse of identity politics," one might ask him, "Who exactly are the practitioners of this 'identity politics' in the academy? What specifically do they believe? Is 'identity politics' really the demon that has overtaken the study of literature and wrecked the disciplines of poetry studies and theory?"

This negative reaction to the term "identity" finds consensus across ideological and aesthetic differences, though for reasons varying in degree of nuance. And here we come to my second snapshot: While Gourgouris teaches in the Classics Department at Columbia and has translated the fairly mainstream poetry of Carolyn Forché into Greek, another scholar, Steve Evans, a major critic of more formally "radical" poetry (and of capitalism), has noted a not-dissimilar reaction among young avant-garde poets toward "identity," but for more complex and radical reasons than are evident in Gourgouris's *PMLA* piece. In "Introduction to *Writing from the New Coast*," an essay originally written in 1993 to introduce a collection of new experimental writing (and later reprinted in a 2002 anthology of essays on avant-garde poetics of the 1990s), Evans takes up Yeats's declaration that "the only movements on which literature can found itself . . . hate great and lasting things":

> It is my contention that such a hatred as Yeats speaks of does animate the present generation [of post-Language avant-garde writers] although it is a hatred so thoroughgoing, so pervasive, and so unremitting as to make the articulation of it seem gratuitous, even falsifying. It is the hatred of Identity. . . . It is the hatred of those who have learned that, given current conditions, there exists not a single socially recognized "difference" worth the having.[31]

Evans is specifically talking about the conditions under capitalism in which everyone and everything are done violence to and flattened—what he describes as "capital's need to manufacture and mark 'difference' (commodification) while preserving and intensifying domination (its own systemic identity)" (14):

> As social space is forced to yield more and more of its autonomy to "the market"—where the mundane logic of the commodity dictates that nothing appear except under the aspect of identity—even progressive demands for the recognition of ethnic, linguistic, and sexual difference are converted into identity claims and sold back to the communities in which they originated at a markup. (14-15)

This sentence is a forceful rejoinder to critics, like Gourgouris, who indict those—one assumes members of various minorities—who supposedly make "identity" claims. Evans perceptively points out that, under late capitalism with its commodity logic, genuine claims of difference are "sold back" to the communities in which they originated "at a markup": for example, repackaged either as the illegitimate accusations of "identity politics" or in the form of an "inclusive" "multiculturalism" that exacts its own hidden high price.[32]

Yet, while I agree with Evans that no one and nothing escape Capital's maws, I cannot help feeling a lingering disquiet about the broad sweep of his claim that, under capitalism, "only one meaningful distinction remains—the distinction between identities-in-abeyance (markets awaiting 'penetration') and Identity as such (penetrant capital)" (15)—and for these reasons:

First, despite the fact that under capitalism "there exists not a single socially recognized 'difference' worth the having," the reality is (and I do not think Evans would disagree) that there are those who must unequally bear the burden of the material and psychic marks of these differences' continuing to be enforced and perpetrated, even if these differences are illusory.

Second, even within the airless and closed system of capitalism, there do exist varying ethical and political responses, specific ways to acknowledge and respond to the ongoing reality and effects of "socially recognized differences," even if they are produced under capitalism's corrupt aegis and are ultimately illusory—both the differences and the responses.

Third, such broad economically based analyses such as Evans's have the unfortunate outcome of producing their own flattening of differences and identities, even as Evans explains that "this generation's hatred of Identity"

> does not mean that all traces of the abstract idiom of "otherness" and "difference" developed in the poststructuralist and multiculturalist discourses have been, at a single stroke, erased from this emergent discourse [avant-garde poetries of the 1990s]. (15)

While Evans surely understands that those who find themselves on the wrong side of otherness and difference know that there is more at work and at stake than abstract idioms, he somehow fails to acknowledge the privilege that allows him—someone who is not an ethnic, linguistic, and/or sexual minority—to make such sweeping pronouncements with ease.

In this regard, Evans is not atypical of many smart and hip white male theorists and practitioners of avant-garde poetry who make cogent critiques about institutionalized forms of knowledge, power, and class (and poetry's relation to them) but do not seem to take into account their own (racial) privilege. Kenneth Goldsmith, the most famous of the Conceptual poets and a Perloff favorite, writing two decades later in *Uncreative Writing*,[33] evinces an even more myopic cluelessness about the privileges of his own subject position, as he lobbies for "uncreative writing":

> Uncreative writing is a postidentity literature. (85)

> If my identity is really up for grabs and changeable by the minute—as I believe it is—it's important that my writing reflect this state of ever-shifting identity and subjectivity. (84)

Goldsmith's token acknowledgment that "[t]he rise of identity politics of the past have [*sic*] given voice to many that have been denied. And there is still so much work to be done: many voices are still marginalized and ignored"[34] does not negate the raced, gendered, and classed tone-deafness and thoughtlessness of his somewhat glib claim that identity is "up for grabs and changeable by the minute."

As with Goldsmith's espousal of "postidentity literature," so with Evans's "hatred of Identity," there is the danger that, despite Evans's clarification about "multiculturalist discourses," such a broad use of the term "Identity" inevitably conjures for readers the specter of race and, especially for less discerning ones, an essentializing and unthinking racial "identity politics"— not the least because, as I have said, in the US context, "identity" and "identity politics" are often automatically conflated and associated with the aggrieved and "unearned" demands of racial minorities.

The reality is that we currently live in a system in which socially recognized differences operate. If they exist at all, conversations on race in this country suffer from, variously, inhibition, defensiveness, a paucity of signifiers, a narrow range of possible preordained positions, caricatures of thought on all sides—in short, a spectacular failure of memory and imagination. Thus, in invoking "Identity," even with his multiculturalist caveat, Evans puts into play in the mind of readers the bugaboos of "identity politics" and racial essentialism and all the knee-jerk, unexamined responses, assumptions, expectations, categories, and beliefs about race that swirl around the terms "identity" and "identity politics." Even used neutrally or "benignly"—as in discourses of "multiculturalism" and "diversity"— these terms are viewed as code words, and woe to the minority critic who foolishly invokes the term "identity"—or worse, "race." In polite company, some things are better left unsaid.

At the same time, we academics, whatever our political affiliations, understand that one black critic should be included at the party—in this case, a soiree of *PMLA* respondents. Brent Edwards, whether he wants to or not, serves a preordained role in the system: as the exceptional exception, hailing from an Ivy League institution, of course, but also the representative, in both senses of the term, of the social in the realm of the literary, the one who is given the unspoken (and unenviable) distinction of speaking for and about minority critics and poets.

Charles Bernstein is correct in seeing links between multiculturalism's so-called inclusiveness and a barely concealed (neo)liberal politics:

> I see too great a continuum from "diversity" back to New Critical and liberal-democratic concepts of a common readership that often—certainly not always—have the effect of transforming unresolved ideological divisions and antagonisms into packaged tours of the local color of gender, race, sexuality,

ethnicity, region, nation, class, even historical period: where each group or community or period is expected to come up with—or have appointed for them—representative figures we can all know about.[35]

That Edwards chooses to discuss a Francophone black Caribbean rather than an African American poet makes, as I mentioned earlier, perfect sense—and one does not need to ascribe a personal motive to Edwards to see that. As the token black critic in the *PMLA* forum, why should he also have to take on the burden of having to convince other critics that a particular American black poet is really as "literary" and "rigorous" and worthy of study as, say, Robert Frost (or Susan Howe)? This is the Catch-22 situation in which minority literary scholars all too often find themselves trapped.

While "hard-core" or "real" literary and poetry critics talk about questions of etymology, prosody, and form, minority poets and poetry are too often left out of the conversation about the literary (or simply left out). How is it possible that among nine poetry critics, speaking about poets across centuries and "The New Lyric Studies," not a single poet of color writing in English is cited? How is this possible when and especially when—if we are to take such claims as Perloff's seriously—hordes of minority and postcolonial writers are taking over our literature courses? This occlusion is, as we have seen, as true of critics emphasizing literary issues, whether traditional or avant-garde, as those interested in history (and historicizing) and ideology.

My third snapshot of the current reception of minority poetry is a more experimental counterpart, if you will, to "The New Lyric Studies": The "Rethinking Poetics" conference, held in June 2010 at Columbia University, was a three-day gathering, convened by the Penn-Columbia Poetics Initiative and organized by Bob Perelman, one of Language poetry's major figures and a University of Pennsylvania professor, and Michael Golston, who teaches avant-garde poetry and poetics at Columbia University and wrote his dissertation under Perloff. Like the *PMLA* forum and as its title indicates, "Rethinking Poetics" was conceived of as a "rethinking" of poetry and poetics, though more specifically by way of contemporary avant-garde writing (a.k.a. non-official-verse-culture poetry) rather than through a specific category of poetry such as lyric.[36] Prominent figures from Language and post-Language poetries participated or were in attendance: Susan Howe, Charles Bernstein, Bruce Andrews, Joan Retallack, Craig Dworkin, Juliana Spahr, Lisa Robertson, among others. "Rethinking Poetics" did include minority American poets and critics, though predominantly African American ones: of forty-one speakers—poets and/or academics—four were

African American (including Brent Edwards), one Native American, and two Latino/a.[37] There was not a single self-identified Asian American included, despite the fact that New York City is the home to several prominent and established avant-garde Asian American poets, most notably John Yau and Mei-mei Berssenbrugge.

The minority invitees were tastefully dispersed across such panels as "Ecologies of Poetry" (the Native American poet was slotted here), "Globalism and Hybridity," and "Social Location/Ethics," though not in the crucial "Poetics as a Category" panel, which, not surprisingly, was all-white. Again, as in *PMLA*, the minority poets and critics served a certain preordained function: as representative tokens of the gathering's inclusiveness and open-mindedness, but their presence did not give rise to either a serious grappling of issues of race in American poetics and poetry— eco-poetics, by contrast, got its own panel—or an acknowledgment that minority poets and critics have something to say about avant-garde poetics "as a category."

In other words, neither "The New Lyric Studies" nor the "Rethinking Poetics" conference actually did a rethinking of the fundamental category of American poetry, including the intrinsic role of race in that category's formation[38] (that is, the inseparability of minority poetry and American poetry). This oversight is especially indefensible in the US context, given how crucial—indeed, fundamental—the question of race has been to the formation of the US nation-state and to the very notion of what is "American": our history, ideologies, myths, psyches, and, of course, our art forms, especially our literature.[39] The primacy of race in the US imaginary and reality is not simply a question of sociological "content" but has been, and continues to be, determinant of the forms of our textual productions— including our sacred foundational documents, the Declaration of Independence and the US Constitution.[40]

Poems are never divorced from contexts and from history, even as they are, among other things, modes of thinking philosophically through an engagement with formal constraints.[41] Likewise, what constitutes the social, the cultural, and the political must be analyzed for their linguistic and structural forms. Poetry works by conscious and unconscious means and arises from the complex interplay between the poetic imagination and the larger world. To be an American poet or poetry critic and *not* think about this larger world and its history seems like an incredible act of repression. "[W]hatever is said / in the world, or forgotten, / or not said, makes a form," reminds Robert Creeley.[42]

Race and American Poetry

That well into the second decade of the twenty-first century, we as literary critics are still perpetuating the either-or binary of the social versus the literary in the pages of our most prominent professional organization's journal says as much about the state of American poetry studies as it does about the larger US inability to face its history and the consequences of that history, especially in relation to issues of race. Race seems to me the most salient, contested, and painfully charged social difference in the American context,[43] and one that imbues—and must be disguised by—the more generic terms "cultural" and "political" when they are raised in opposition to the "literary." That said, I understand clearly that issues of race are inseparably intertwined with issues of class, and that class, too, produces painful differences. But in the minds of those who decry "identity" and "identity politics," it is race, not class, that drives the engine of "identity" and "identity politics," though this belief will not likely be explicitly articulated for fear of seeming to appear "racist."

To discuss American poetry and not discuss a single American minority poet-or include only the token one or two-speaks volumes about both a delusive blindness and a double standard in poetry studies. Because minority subjects and cultures are viewed in the American imaginary as occupying the realm of the bodily, the material, the social, they are often overlooked when considering questions of the literary and the cultural (in the sense of cultural value and high culture).[44] Form, whether that of traditional lyric or avant-garde poems, is assumed to be the provenance of a literary acumen and culture that is unmarked but assumed to be white.[45]

And if minority writers are acknowledged as producing literature at all, it is a literature that functions mimetically and sociologically as an ethnographic window into another "subculture"—or, in Founder Thomas Jefferson's words, a poetry of the "senses only, not the imagination."[46] Elaine Showalter, a major critic of women's writing who taught for two decades at Princeton University, expresses a not atypical view of minority literature's character:

> During the 1960s and 1970s, teaching literature became an explicitly political act for radical and minority groups in the university. English departments were the places where feminist and African-American critics first began to initiate courses and put pressure on the curriculum to include black and women writers. Their efforts heralded a paradigm shift in canon formation and literary studies generally, and a repudiation of formalism in favor of a

more engaged and partisan reading that saw the goal of literary study as the formation of personal identity and political struggle. . . .

But the theory revolution of the 1970s quickly shifted attention away from the mimetic use of literature.[47]

Note Showalter's smooth elision of "radical" and "minority." And while her facts are not quite accurate about English departments' being the first sites of struggle—they were arguably the sites of the most bitter struggles, given how resistant English departments in general were (and in too many instances, still are) to the inclusion of minority writers into the curricula[48]— she expresses the not uncommon view among English professors that minority literature "repudiates formalism," is "partisan" (in contrast to racially "unmarked" canonical literature, which presumably is unpartisan) and mimetic, and emphasizes the "formation of personal identity" as a "goal" of literary studies.[49]

In assuming the interchangeability of "minority" and "mimetic" forms, Showalter may not know her American literary history very well. Modernist writers such as Jean Toomer and Langston Hughes and the Filipino poet Jose Garcia Villa were experimenting with form well before the 1960s and 1970s. The mixed-race poet Sadakichi Hartmann, whose mother was Japanese, was writing Symbolist poetry at the end of the nineteenth century (he also served as a secretary to Walt Whitman).[50] Even during the "radical" 1960s and 1970s, Black Arts writers, such as Amiri Baraka, and Asian American writers, such as Mei-mei Berssenbrugge,[51] were acutely interested in pushing the limits of the English language—a project that did not contradict (indeed, helped to further) the struggle to attain the full equality that had been promised all Americans, not just white men of property, since the eighteenth century. (Baraka, as LeRoi Jones, was, of course, centrally involved with downtown avant-garde culture in New York City in the 1950s, and close to poets in various avant-garde and countercultural movements.)

Baraka is a perfect example of a formally innovative and politically engaged poet who almost always gets typecast as a "radical" minority writer and is marginalized by both mainstream and avant-garde poetry groupings. As a key figure in the New York City literary scene in the 1950s and 1960s, Baraka has incorporated all sorts of formal and political concerns in his poetry and in his work in various communities. His writing has had crucial links to American Surrealism, Black Mountain, the New York School, the Bears, Black Arts (which he largely founded), jazz poetry,[52] jazz criticism, leftist poetry, avant-garde poetry, minority poetry, and minority and avant-garde fiction. He is perhaps the most polyvalent American poet and critic of the twentieth century. Baraka's work has been endlessly inventive over the decades, never standing still, yet he is for the most part largely categorized as an "angry," "radical" black poet stuck in the 1960s and Black Nationalist and Marxist thinking.

The problematic nature of the rhetoric and forms of how minority poetry gets discussed is a function of several factors—of which the endemic American inability to deal head-on with the legacy and reality of racial oppression and disparities is one. First, there remains a lingering tendency within literary studies and in the wider reading public to view prose as the bearer of social analysis, and poetry, especially the lyric, as the genre addressing more personal, private, and "purely" literary concerns. Even as illustrious a critic as Bakhtin, despite some later revising of his ideas, held this bias.[53]

Second, since the racialized poet, subject, and person is often apprehended in terms of the bodily,[54] the material, and the political, her poetry is inevitably, though often not consciously, posited in opposition to the abstract, the intellectual, the literary. Minority writing, including poetry, is inevitably read as mimetic, autobiographical, "representative," and ethnographic, with the poet as native informant (for example, Chinatown tour guide), providing a glimpse into her supposed ethnic culture. Since poetry remains, even in the twenty-first century, the epitome of high literary culture, minority poetic production is often treated as a dispensable add-on to this long tradition— the recent inclusion of minority poets in poetry anthologies such as the *Norton Anthology of Poetry* functions largely as a concessionary bone (market-driven) in this so-called multicultural age.

Third, since the terms "minority" and "poetry" are conceived of in the academy as intrinsically opposed—content versus form, sociological versus literary, and so on—minority poetry is often seen as belonging more properly to the provenance of cultural studies or ethnic studies. As we can see in the *PMLA* presentation of "The New Lyric Studies," the place at the table for minority poetry in discussions about, say, meter or poetic form, is barely there, if it exists at all—and this holds true, again, for critics of both mainstream lyric poetry and avant-garde work. When critics read "real poets" such as Jorie Graham or John Ashbery, they almost always examine the "poems themselves," paying attention, for example, to their use of tone or parataxis. When they read a literary work, fiction or poetry, by an Asian American writer, they almost inevitably assume that the work functions as a transparent window into the ethnographic "truth" of a hyphenated identity and an exotic "home" culture—in other words, as if there were no such thing as the mediatedness of language.

On the other side of the aesthetic spectrum, critics of avant-garde Asian American poetry (such as that by Tan Lin or Mei-mei Berssenbrugge) tend, in their analysis of the poems, to completely ignore the ethnicity of the poet,[55] even when the poet makes clear that racialized/ethnic identity is not a trivial concern in the work. Ironically (and self-contradictorily), critics of avant-garde poetry, who privilege a focus on form and who usually excoriate thematic readings of poems, will dismiss the relevance of race in the work of, say, Berssenbrugge, by recourse to the very sorts of thematic rationales they abhor: in this case, by citing the lack of racial themes or markers. But a perceptive reader, especially an experienced reader of formally innovative writing, would know to look closely at what the poem's form, and not simply its content, tells us.[56]

Asian American Poetry and the American Body Politic

I turn now from the broader category of "minority poetry" to the particular case of Asian American poetry, which, like Latina/ o and Native American writing, is seen as marginal to the category "minority literature"—and is thus doubly marginalized within the academy (triply, if one takes genre into account). Most critics use the term "minority" to mean "African American," as typified by the previous Showalter quote and demonstrated by the demographic representation of the *PMLA* and the "Rethinking Poetics" groupings. If discussed at all, Asian American writing is treated as ancillary in the current academy and viewed as being of interest mainly to Asian American students; unlike African American literature, Asian American literature is almost wholly studied by specialists of Asian American literature, who are almost all of Asian descent. If Asian American literature is included in American literature courses at all, it is represented by the token inclusion of Maxine Hong Kingston's *The Woman Warrior* or, perhaps, Jhumpa Lahiri's and Chang-rae Lee's fiction (both having been anointed in the pages of the *New Yorker*). The poetry is almost never taught-except perhaps in specialized Asian American literature courses, but even then not so much.

Indeed, most critics of American literature or poetry can hardly name one Asian American poet, or at most one or two, and view the work as being tertiary to the American literary canon. This is the case even though Asian American poetry has been written for more than a century by an array of authors whose ethnic origins, genres, and styles are widely varied. In terms of its breadth of aesthetic styles and time span, Asian American literature as a category is certainly more variegated and wide ranging than, say, Modernist writing. All too often in English departments Asian American literature seems to be taught not so much as a body of work with literary merit but as texts that Asian American undergraduates can "relate to."[57]

So why focus on such a "narrow" stratum of American poetic writing? My answer: because of Asian Americans' unique form of racial interpellation— inextricably linked to the view of them as culturally and linguistically unassimilable—Asian American writing offers a particularly illuminating "limit case," for thinking not only about the relationship between a poet's interpellation (including racialization) in American society and her relationship to the English language but also, more broadly, about the assumptions and preconceptions undergirding our notions of poetry, English-language poetry, American literature, "Americanness," the English language, and questions of literary value, among others.[58]

To explain what I mean requires a knowledge of history.

Like all groups of minority Americans, Asian Americans have experienced unique forms of racial interpellation within the United States, but unlike other minority groups, "Orientals," "Asiatics," and "Asians" in particular came to exemplify a racialized form of *constitutive and immutable* alienness from what it means to be "American."

A little over thirty years after the arrival of Chinese immigrants to this country in the mid-nineteenth century, this perception of utter foreignness, nonassimilability, and un-Americanness—which, to a greater or lesser degree, has persisted to this day, albeit in slightly variant guises—had already hardened into pernicious, and legalized, form. The Chinese Exclusion Act, passed in 1882 and not repealed until 1943, was the first and only immigration exclusion law in American history to exclude a specific named group on the basis of race.[59]

In fact, the Chinese were seen as more unassimilable than even ex-chattel slaves. As Supreme Court Justice Harlan wrote in 1896 in his oft-lauded dissent in *Plessy v. Ferguson*, arguing against the logic of the majority opinion upholding "separate but equal," "There is a race so different from our own that we do not permit those belonging to it to become citizens of the United States. Persons belonging to it are, with few exceptions, absolutely excluded from our country. I allude to the Chinese race."[60]

Yet, as US history has unfolded, this interpellation of Asians and Asian Americans as perpetually and constitutively foreign, alien, and threatening to the very idea of "Americanness" itself has also become intermixed with or, some may think, supplanted by what is mistakenly viewed as more benign or even "positive" images of as "model minorities"[61] and "honorary whites." In reality, these hollow honorifics (stereotypes) "reward" Asian Americans precisely for their compliance, docility, submissiveness—and function to generate more (nameless, faceless, and interchangeable) workers in our capitalist economy and ensure their invisibility and voicelessness within the American national and political body.[62] "Honorary whites" are, of course, not "real" whites and are granted none of the benefits of white privilege; at the same time, Asian Americans also experience the drawbacks of not being perceived as "real" or "true" minorities either.[63]

For all minority groups in this country, two facts obtain: First, the processes of racialization have entailed the pressure to assimilate, the struggle to prove one's true "Americanness," and have been enforced by forms of violence and domination. Second, proving one's "Americanness" has always been inextricably tied to the imperative to master English[64] and to erase any foreign tongues and accents.[65] But, Asian Americans in particular have been singled out in US history as *constitutively* and immutably foreign and "nonnative" to American culture and the body politic[66]—threatening to the very idea of "Americanness"[67]—a pernicious and unwavering ideological characterization that has been inseparable from the belief that "Orientals" are also *constitutively* nonnative speakers of English and thus can never overcome, no matter how hard they try, this deficit to the English language because it is foundational.[68] Even Asian Americans who are fourth-generation American, with a perfect command of English, are often asked if English is their native tongue.[69]

One might ask, "What is the link between the perception that Asian Americans are not 'real' Americans and are nonnative speakers of English, and the belief, largely unconscious, that Asian American poets are not 'real' poets?" It is clear that this perception of Asian Americans as utterly alien to Americanness and to the English language—a view that persists even in this "post-racial" era—cannot *not* be a factor in the reception of Asian American poets.

Given these assumptions and stereotypes, an Asian American poet, whether knowingly or not, often faces a particularly vexed and compensatory relation to the English that is always already not hers, and to an English literary tradition in which poetry continues to be seen as the genre most tied to high culture, literary tradition, formal mastery, and "native tongue"—a literary tradition from which minority writers were largely excluded for centuries and into which they were granted entry only recently, after the furious canon wars of the 1980s, and only begrudgingly—in limited and policed fashion—allowed to occupy circumscribed academic and aesthetic Bantustans because of the generosity of enlightened liberals. While many writers feel an "anxiety of influence" in relation to a dominant literary tradition, for Asian American writers, the usual questions of literary culture, tradition, and reception confronting an individual writer take on an added, if not more intense (and intensely painful), urgency and burden for all the reasons detailed.

How then does an Asian American poet situate herself in an Anglo-American poetic tradition when she is marked as constitutively alien and unassimilable and excluded from the category of "native speaker" of English? How does an Asian American poet labor under and contend with the foregone conclusion that her English will never be "good enough"?

It is my contention that the answers surface as much in the formal structures as in the thematic content of Asian American poetry.

Many of the poets in this study focus obsessively on the question of language and writing, even as their poems deal with a wide range of concerns. Of course, to some extent all poets are hyperaware of the act of writing itself, but for Asian American poets, this relation to the writing—and wished-for mastery—of English takes on a heightened sense of self-consciousness because of their constitutive exclusion from the category of native speaker. When Li-Young Lee says, "Everything is language,"[70] he may be speaking primarily as a poet, but one has the strong sense that his poems' obsessive concern with getting names and naming right is more than just a function of his simply being interested in words.

Since Asian American poetry occupies a unique place in the American national body and literary imaginary—as a body of American writing that inextricably ties the racial group seen as having the most alien/alienated relationship to the English language and the most exalted and elite English literary genre[71]—it can be argued that Asian American poetry is not only not marginal to thinking about American poetry and poetics but is *especially* resonant for thinking about such literary and literary historical concerns.

There is also a strong case to be made for studying a sizable but largely neglected body of American writing: Asian American poetry. While Asian American fiction has had some visibility with the reading public, primarily through the popularity of two works—Amy Tan's *The Joy Luck Club* and Maxine

Hong Kingston's *The Woman Warrior*—few Americans, including literary scholars of American literature, are familiar with Asian American poetry.

While I am highly aware of the many contradictions of and tensions within the category "Asian American," I also understand the practical realities and strategic necessity of such a term. Just as in the 1960s and 1970s, various Americans who (or whose ancestors) emigrated from China, Japan, the Philippines, Korea, Vietnam, and other Asian countries shared an experience of racism and discrimination in American society—of being seen as "gooks"[72] and "all looking alike"—and, thus, found political power in coming together as "Asian American," so in the twenty-first century, the presence of the categories "Asian American studies" and "Asian American literature" in the academy enables Asian American literature to be taught at all. Indeed, one could make a strong case that without these institutional slots, even *The Woman Warrior* would rarely be taught, whether in classes on American literature or contemporary fiction. The same was the case with the categories "women's studies" and "African American studies": the institutional existence of these disciplines was necessary so as to get writing by women and blacks into the door and onto curricula. These writings did not just magically appear in universities—their presence was the result of hard-fought battles and struggles taking place over many years, and still being fought today, with professional and personal costs to minority professors and students.[73] In other words, in order to interrogate the category "Asian American," one needs the category to begin with.

Asian American literature occupies the paradoxical position of being both emergent—many English departments across the country are just now filling their first positions in Asian American literature long after they have hired specialists in African American literature and women's literature—and disappearing at the same time: not a few English departments at prestigious institutions across the country are now turning toward "transnational" or "global" or "diasporic" conceptualizations and contextualizations of Asian American writing, moving away from having to deal with issues of US racial politics—and racism.

When confronted with how little college and graduate students and faculty colleagues know about either Asian American history or literature, I often have to remind them that in the last century the United States fought four wars with Asian countries (the Philippines, Japan, Korea, and Vietnam,[74] with many millions killed), that an Asian country was the only one in history to have had a nuclear bomb (two, in fact) dropped on it, that the only group of potential immigrants to the United States to have been specifically identified and systematically excluded on the basis of race was Chinese (government enforcement of the Chinese Exclusion Act in 1882 necessitated the creation of the precursor—and foundation—of our current US Citizenship and Immigration Services, an agency within the Department of Homeland Security),[75] and that the only group of American citizens ever interned in concentration camps on the basis of their ethnicity was Japanese Americans. One is almost surprised at how consistent and continuous the yellow-peril rhetoric has been over the past century and a half, from Chinese exclusion to, now in the twenty-first century, the "rise of China."

I am not saying that there is an easy one-to-one correlation between how Asians and Asian Americans have been apprehended in American history, society, and in the public imaginary and how their writers have been received in the literary realms, but I am confident that the common (mis)perception that Asian Americans are perpetual foreigners bearing a constitutively nonnative relationship to the English language cannot have *not* influenced the ways in which Asian American writing has been read—or rather, misread.

For example, in 1982, when Cathy Song became the first Asian American poet to win the Yale Younger Poets Prize for her first book, *Picture Bride*, the selecting judge, poet Richard Hugo, described the Honolulu-born, Wellesley-educated poet as one who "accommodates experiential extremes with a sensibility strengthened by patience that is centuries old, ancestral, tribal, a gift passed down."[76] One wonders if Hugo would have invoked the "ancestral, tribal" and "centuries-old" patience and sensibility of a white American Yale Younger winner or focused on the poet's "accommodating" nature and the "experiential."

One would think that things are different now, in the wake of multiculturalism and the changes wrought by the canon wars. Yet almost thirty years later, when Ken Chen won the same prize in 2009, reviewers' responses to his work split into two distinct and opposed categories. As Chen puts it in an e-mail, "My book confuses them [reviewers] bc [because] they either think it's all Asian all the time and ignore the rest or they only focus on the avant-garde formal stuff and ignore the content."[77] As an example of the former, the reviewer on the Poetry Foundation's Harriet blog reads Chen's volume *Juvenilia* almost wholly thematically:

> The speaker's upbringing is marked by his parent's *[sic]* disaffected marriage ("faces that would not kiss in life") and eventual separation. The inability to communicate, an affliction that spans across generations for this Chinese American family, manifests itself as a mysterious illness on *[sic]* the young speaker who sees his relatives succumb to the ills of unhappiness bottled up within.[78]

This sort of reception is not atypical. Reviewers and scholars, when writing about Asian American poetry, almost never pay attention to linguistic, literary, and rhetorical form (perhaps because of their ingrained perception of Asian Americans' generations-old "inability to communicate"?)—an oversight that is all the more puzzling when the object of attention is a poem, whose very being depends on figures of speech, meter, rhythm, and other formal properties. This seems to be the tendency, though less pronounced, even when the critic works within the field of minority literature or is a minority person himself (as is the case here).

Anyone who has written even a few lines of poetry knows how crucial a decision it is that someone chooses to write a poem—and not, say, a journalistic essay or political manifesto—and how essential are the myriad formal decisions made at every turn in a poem: where to break the line, what rhythmic or metrical pattern (or none) will govern, what will constitute the unit of the stanza, how the poem will look on the page, and so on. It is not only a matter of conscious authorial choice but no less of the submerged or unconscious structures of language that make themselves felt in the particular language of individual poems.

Certainly in the United States, where race has been absolutely fundamental to the formation of national identity and national history and to the texture of everyday life, one's racial identity—or presumed universality in being racially "unmarked"—must play a role, consciously or unconsciously, in the formation of the American poet, black or yellow or white. Racial interpellation is absolutely inescapable in the formation of American subjectivity, not just the subjectivity of "visible minorities."

Thus, the occlusion or ignoring of race by critics and poets at the avant-garde end of the critical spectrum is equally as disturbing as the fetishization of racial and ethnic content and identity by more mainstream poetry critics. Critics of avant-garde writing, despite their openness to radical new poetic forms, often fall into the same traps as more formally conservative critics when thinking (or, more accurately, not thinking) the link between poetry and the subjectivity—which includes the racialized subjectivity—of the poet. They overwhelmingly tend to ignore race by focusing exclusively on formal properties or other themes in the writing (for example, emotion or science in Berssenbrugge's poetry); to explicitly oppose political and social "content" (including racial identity) against formal literary concerns; or to distinguish between "bad" ethnic poetry (autobiographical, identity-based) and "good" poetry (formally experimental) that just happens to be written by a person of color.[79]

An example of the third route appears in the review of Chen's *Juvenilia* in *Publishers Weekly*. While not writing for an avant-garde publication, the anonymous reviewer nonetheless privileges certain kinds of formal experiment and expresses a firm view of what constitutes bad ethnic writing:

> The latest Yale Younger Poet writes about his Chinese-American heritage; he draws on classic Chinese poets, such as Wang Wei and Li Yu. Yet his verse and prose stand at the farthest possible remove from the memoirlike poems, and the poems of first-person "identity," that have characterized so much recent verse about U.S. immigrant life. Instead, Chen is "experimental" in the best and broadest sense of the term: each new page brings an experiment in self-presentation, in sentence, syntax, or (long) line.[80]

Here, good minority poetry is set against bad minority poetry, which focuses on "identity" (that hated concept, again), and to be experimental in the "best and broadest sense of the term" is, implicitly, not to discuss race or ethnic identity.

One could make the case that the categories "experimental," "innovative," and "avant-garde" are often implicitly coded as "white"—as Harryette Mullen and a few other experimental minority poets and scholars have argued—and that not only do the few minority writers included in experimental anthologies and conferences tend to function as tokens (Mullen describes the situation as "aesthetic apartheid")[81] but also, as we see in the case of Baraka's poetry, certain modes of experimentality, such as jazz poetics, are excluded from definitions of the avant-garde and "experimental." The criteria of what counts as avant-garde, even in the twenty-first century, is judged according to High Modernism's purely formalist repertoire: disruption of syntax, fragmentation of the line, and so on.[82]

We should interrogate this monolithic view of what constitutes the avant-garde and what criteria of linguistic experimentation passes the test. In "Language and the Avant-Garde," a chapter of his book *The Politics of Modernism*, Raymond Williams writes,

> Thus what we have really to investigate is not some single position of language in the avant-garde or language in Modernism. On the contrary, we need to identify a range of distinct and in many cases actually opposed formations, as these have materialized in language. This requires us, obviously, to move beyond such conventional definitions as "avant-garde practice" or "the Modernist text."[83]

We can see that, just as much as the term "identity politics," the term "avant-garde" comes with its own set of (racialized) assumptions and implications.

Experimental minority poets are often included in the avant-garde fold either because their work and stylistic choices are universalized as part of an avant-garde movement ("she's just like us, but, oh, isn't it great that she also happens to be black?") or because they are seen as "exceptions" to the general tendency of minority poets to write badly and to focus mistakenly on identity politics (or is it that they write badly *because* they focus on issues of race and identity?). As I have demonstrated, racial identity often becomes conflated with the strawman term "identity politics."

In the last section of *Thinking Its Presence: Form, Race, and Subjectivity in Contemporary Asian American Poetry*, I examine the work of Mei-mei Berssenbrugge and Pamela Lu, whose poetry manifests virtually no ethnic themes or markers at all. By looking at this avant-garde writing, I put to a more strenuous test my argument that it is in the formal and rhetorical manifestations, particularly the linguistic structures, of the poems that one sees evidence of the impress of social and historical influences. For instance, Berssenbrugge's having been born in Beijing to a Dutch American father and a Chinese mother, with Chinese as her first language, but then raised in New England, have made her acutely aware of the contingency and relationality of not only human identity but also language and natural phenomena. This awareness deeply informs her poetic lines, which are rife with a syntax of contingency and conditionality (frequently marked by use of the subjunctive mood and/or the conditional mode). One example: "She wonders what the body would reveal, if the cloud were transparent" (from "Honeymoon," published in *Empathy*).[84]

In making a claim for the link between a minority avant-garde poet's work and her racialized ethnic subjectivity, I make a critical intervention in current discussions about avant-garde writing. Whether critics focus solely on ethnic content in more mainstream Asian American poetry or whether critics ignore issues of race in avant-garde Asian American poetry and privilege the "purely" literary or formal (against the ethnic), the full complexity of Asian American poetry—and minority American poetry—has not been acknowledged. These critical approaches profoundly impoverish our understanding of the complex multidimensionality and contradictions of American and English-language poetry.

Thinking Its Presence

In *Thinking Its Presence: Form, Race, and Subjectivity in Contemporary Asian American Poetry*, I argue against such reductive modes of reading

Asian American poetry. The book builds its case by focusing with great particularity on the writings of five contemporary Asian American poets who range in age from their early forties to late sixties[85]—Li-Young Lee, Marilyn Chin, John Yau, Mei-mei Berssenbrugge, and Pamela Lu—and whose poems represent a spectrum of literary styles, from expressive lyric to less transparently representational and more formally experimental. For each poet's body of work, I consider, through detailed readings, a formal crux or mode (metaphor, irony, parody, a syntax of contingency, the subjunctive mood) whose deployment is central to his or her poetic project and whose structure articulates and enacts in language the poet's working out of a larger political (in the broadest sense of that term) and/ or poetic concern or question.

These specific formal aspects of the poems simultaneously reflect and manifest aesthetic influences[86]—compositional decisions, structures of language (conscious and unconscious), the shadow of literary precursors, and so on—but also, importantly, the influence of socio-political forces and historical context, such as geographical location, current events, and his or her socialization in the world as a person of a particular, race, gender, sex, class, and educational level.[87] This is as true for "mainstream" lyric poets as it is for "avant-garde" poets. And it is as true for white poets as for minority ones.

Even supposedly as "hermetic" and "enigmatic" a poet as Paul Celan—who certainly knew firsthand what it meant to be a minority (and racialized) poet in a hegemonic European language—understood that "the poem does not stand outside time. True, it claims the infinite and tries to reach across time—but across, not above." This from a speech he gave in 1958, thirteen years after the end of the Nazi death camps.[88]

By doing intensive and serious readings of these particular Asian American poets' use of language and linguistic forms—what Susan Wolfson calls "theory in action"[89]—I aim to show how erroneous we have been to view Asian American poetry through a simplistic, reductive, and essentializing lens: as a homogeneous lump of "nonliterary" writing by "Asians." As with white poets' work, each Asian American poet's practice is different from another's, and how language is deployed in his or her work is particular to that writer.

Thinking Its Presence: Form, Race, and Subjectivity in Contemporary Asian American Poetry joins in its analytical framework methods and areas of study usually considered disparate, if not mutually exclusive: formal analysis, literary history, reader reception, race studies, avant-garde writing. By juxtaposing form, sociohistorical context, and poetic subjectivity, it questions customary methodological, literary-historical, and disciplinary practices and assumptions—such as the supposed dichotomy between cultural-studies approaches and formal literary analysis. Must a poetry or cultural critic be forced to choose between an interest in form (with its implied anti-cultural-studies stance) and the desire to understand the historical conditions, social and aesthetic, of the production of a poem? In the twenty-first century, is it not time to rethink these ingrained poetic and literary-critical categories and assumptions?

The phrase "thinking its presence" in my book's title comes from Mei-mei Berssenbrugge's poem "Chinese Space" (from her 1989 volume, *Empathy*) and evokes both the ineffability of certain phenomena and their very real materiality and presence. Being able to cognitively grasp ("think") these phenomena—in this case, politics, history, race, and their effects on subjectivity and language—does not in any way reify or essentialize or make reductive the not always definite (note the indefinite pronoun "its"[90]), often mysterious, but very real relation between and among the social (racial), subjective, and poetic. As Boris Ejxenbaum writes in "Literary Environment," "The relations between the facts of the literary order and facts extrinsic to it cannot simply be causal relations but can only be the relations of correspondence, interaction, dependency, or conditionality" (61).

Paying close attention to what poems tell us—not so much in their stated content but in their formal manifestations—is itself a praxis-based methodology of theorizing. As poems in their linguistic specificity are powerful means of philosophically thinking about the world through language, so my close readings are, in their detailed unfolding, a theoretical engagement with the poem and the social world.[91] For example, in the poetry of Li-Young Lee, the structure of metaphor, with its almost-but-not-quite equivalences, isomorphically captures both the poet's Romantic struggles to have an unmediated connection to his authoritarian, Chinese, Presbyterian-minister father; to God; to his Chinese ancestry and language; and to the felt pressure to assimilate to American culture in rural Pennsylvania and to the English language.

Let me make clear that I am not positing a simplistic causal or reductive link between the world—in this case, being "Asian American"—and the poem (Ejxenbaum again: "The relations between the facts of the literary order and facts extrinsic to it cannot simply be causal relations" [61]). Nor am I arguing that Li-Young Lee is deploying an "Asian American" (or even Chinese American) way of using metaphor, that there is an "Asian American" way of writing poetry, that there is a reifiable Asian American "essence" that can be found in various formal elements and structures, or that there is one "Asian American" or "Chinese American" essence or link joining the work of Asian American poets (or even the half dozen Chinese American poets in my study). In other words, as a category, "Asian American literature" encompasses texts that are as heterogeneous and varied as those in other conventional literary categories, such as "women's literature" or "African American literature" or "American literature" or "Victorian literature."[92]

Thus, the use of participial phrases in the poetry of Mei-mei Berssenbrugge works differently and springs from different sources than the use of such phrases in the work of Myung Mi Kim (or Robert Lowell). The lived experiences of all three poets as poets of particular social and historical formations are as much a part of their poetic subjectivities as are their readings in the poetic tradition, and these influences emerge in the form of language in the poem. Each poet's life history is particular to her—as is her poetic practice—but that is not to say that certain shared general experiences do not obtain (for example, the Great Depression) and make an impact on one's subjectivity and work, even though that impact will be expressed in ways specific to each poet. For the racialized poet, a significant part of her lived and psychic experience is the fact of having moved in the world and been apprehended as a racialized subject. Given the importance of race and racialization in the formation and history of these United States, one could argue that for *American* poets, white or minority, to ignore such fundamental sociopolitical issues consistently and broadly over time constitutes serious acts of omission.

While the precise nature of the link between the world and a poetic text can never be fully explicated, what is clear is that the path to understanding that relation can come only through close readings of particular poems themselves—and an understanding of the poet's and text's place, both temporal and spatial, in historical context. Whether reading the poems of Li-Young Lee or Gerald Stern, Mei-mei Berssenbrugge or Leslie Scalapino, one must pay careful attention to the nuances and specificities of the poet's particular use of language and the sociopolitical environment, whose particular residues (some different, some shared) have suffused each poet's subjectivity and influenced the production and reception of poems.

I cannot emphasize this point enough. For in bringing race into the critical conversation about avant-garde writing—in particular, by positing a link between racial subjectivity and the forms of poetry—one runs the risk of being accused of conjuring up a link that is not there (or artificially "imposing" the issue of race onto "racially unmarked" writing, usually by smuggling in some reductive essentialist version of racial identity).

A typical objection might run: "If John Yau and T. S. Eliot in their poetry both question a stable and transparent subjectivity, then why is what Yau is doing specifically 'Asian American' or 'Chinese American'"? The fallacious assumption here is that because Yau and Eliot both seem to be making similar poetic (and metaphysical) moves, these moves are formally and substantively identical. But Eliot and Yau are *not* actually doing the same thing in their poetries. Given how radically different their persons, subjectivities, histories, contexts, and so on are, there is no way that their projects of destabilizing subjectivity are the same. Nor can the resulting poems be the same.

Poetic subjectivities and poetic practices are not interchangeable. It would be just as wrong to claim that Eliot's and Yau's are interchangeable as it would be to claim that Yau's and Tan Lin's are interchangeable. Sadly, though, our idea of ethnic Americans is often to (unconsciously) render them as abstract, one-dimensional, homogeneous, and interchangeable.

While it may initially appear that Yau and Eliot are doing the same thing with the subject, their reasons for doing so stem from different contexts and are specific to, and part of, their own histories, subjectivities, and poetic projects.[93] Thus, it would be misguided to claim that Yau's emphasis on destabilized identities itself is specifically "ethnic" or "Chinese American" or is necessarily limited to Chinese American subjects.

The variegated and complex particularities of Yau's experiences as a racialized person cannot be reified into some practice or thing called "Chinese American." There is no one stable Asian American or Chinese American identity or subjectivity or point of view or poetic practice. The subjectivity of an ethnic American is not a thing or a content. Of course other poets who are not Chinese American—such as T. S. Eliot—destabilize the subject, too. Eliot's reasons, conscious or unconscious, for his poetic choices will be different from Yau's.

To underscore how the element of race skews these discussions about poetry; how it elicits reductive, contradictory, conflationary thinking; how it throws the burden of proof over and over again back onto the critic who raises the issue of race, one need only do two thought experiments.

The first would be to continue with the comparison of Yau's and Eliot's poetry, but to switch the burden of proof from Yau's minority poetry to Eliot's canonical poetry and to change the extratextual feature from race to some nonracialized experience or feature—for example, Eliot's experiences in Europe in World War I. How likely would a critic of Modernist poetry be given a hard time for claiming that these experiences influenced the fractured subjectivities and the broken lines in *The Wasteland*? How likely would this appeal to the extratextual be shot down for being extratextual? How likely would this critic be rebutted with the argument that, because no unproblematic correlation between Eliot's extratextual experiences and his poetry can be proven, then the fractured lines and subjectivities in *The Wasteland* were not influenced at all by Eliot's wartime experiences in Europe?

And, to push the point further, how likely would it be that someone would then say to that critic, "Well, John Yau also fractures subjectivity and breaks lines in his 'Genghis Chan' poems, and because Yau does the same thing as Eliot, but Yau never lived in Europe during the war, then Eliot's having lived in Europe was not a necessary influence on *The Wasteland*. And not only was it not necessary but it was not an influence at all"?

The second thought experiment: remove race from the equation completely and compare not a white and a minority poet but two white poets—say, Eliot and Stein—using the same scenario of a critic's claiming that Eliot's experiences in wartime Europe had influenced the form of *The Wasteland*. How likely would this critic of Modernist poetry be rebutted by the counterargument that since Stein also fractured poetic subjectivities and lines, but did not have the same experiences as Eliot in Europe, then Eliot's particular war-time experiences were not a "necessary" influence on the lines in *The Wasteland*— again, not only were not necessary but were not a factor at all?

The arguments in *Thinking Its Presence: Form, Race, and Subjectivity* in *Contemporary Asian American Poetry* about the interplay between racial subjectivity and poetic writing depend crucially upon paying close attention to the language and structures of the individual poems of particular poets, including—or especially—minority poets. This praxis-based critical argumentation, in which the poems themselves suggest theoretical orientations, resists abstract generalizations that can easily oversimplify (and render reductive and one-dimensional) arguments about racial subjectivity and minority poetry. Let us pay nuanced attention to what the language and forms of poems—*all* poems in the American body—tell us.

Notes

1. See http://www.mla.org/about, which gives facts about the MLA and its membership.
2. "The New Lyric Studies," *PMLA* 123 (2008): 181–234. Note the definite article.

3. Marjorie Perloff, "It Must Change," *PMLA* 122–3 (2007): 655, 654.

4. See, for example, Virginia Jackson, "Who Reads Poetry?," *PMLA* 123, no. 1 (2008): 181–87; and *Dickinson's Misery: A Theory of Lyric Reading* (Princeton, NJ: Princeton University Press, 2005).

5. All of the critics were asked to participate because they have a reputation in literary studies, many in the study of poetry, and all teach at elite institutions: University of California, Berkeley; University of Chicago; University of California, Irvine; Tufts; University of Michigan; Columbia University; and Cornell University.

6. Beyond the thirty thousand MLA members who automatically receive a subscription with their membership, other literature and language professors in the country and worldwide read the journal. It is the one literary journal that most broadly crosses various literary specializations.

7. Jonathan Culler, "Why Lyric?," *PMLA* 123, no. 1 (2008): 201–06, quotes on 205.

8. Rei Terada, "After the Critique of Lyric," *PMLA* 123, no. 1 (2008): 195–200, quotes on 196, 199.

9. Robert Kaufman, "Lyric Commodity Critique, Benjamin Adorno Marx, Baudelaire Baudelaire Baudelaire," *PMLA* 123, no. 1 (2008): 207–15, quote on 211.

10. Stathis Gourgouris, "*Poiein*-Political Infinitive," *PMLA* 123, no. 1 (2008): 223–28; Brent Edwards, "The Spector of Interdisciplinarity," *PMLA* 123, no. 1 (2008): 188–94.

11. Oren Izenberg, "Poems Out of Our Heads," *PMLA* 123, no. 1 (2008): 216–22, quotes on 217.

12. Jackson, "Who Reads Poetry?," *PMLA* 123, no. 1 (2008): 181–87, quote on 183. Yopie Prins, "Historical Poetics, Dysprosody, and The Science of English Verse," *PMLA* 123, no. 1 (2008): 229–34, quote on 233.

13. See Izenberg, "Language Poetry and Collective Life," *Critical Inquiry* 30, no. 1 (2003): 132–59; reprinted as chapter 4 of his *Being Numerous: Poetry and the Grounds of Social Life* (Princeton, NJ: Princeton University Press, 2010).

14. Marjorie Perloff, "Creative Writing' Among the Disciplines," *MLA Newsletter* 38, no. 1 (2006): 4, http://www.mla.org/pdf/nl_spring06pdf.pdf.

15. One need only look at the curricula and major requirements in various English departments across the country to know that this description does not accurately reflect the current state of affairs in literary studies.

16. The terms of Perloff's characterization underscore my earlier point: "African American, other minorities, and postcolonial" are lumped in one abstract homogeneous category—"one subculture . . . and another"—while the "great" writers are individually named and represent a range of genres, styles, genders, sensibilities, and nationalities.

17. Though the only minority group she specifies is African American.

18. The prefix "sub-," of course, holds various, often simultaneous, meanings, such as "a part of," "subordinate to," and/or "inferior to." The *OED* lists this as the first meaning: "In prepositional relation to the noun constituting or implied in the second element, with the sense 'situated, existing, or occurring under, below, or at the bottom of.'" *OED* online, 3rd ed., June 2012, http://www.oed.com.

19. This rhetoric of a zero-sum game or a scarcity model in literature departments and universities echoes the rhetoric used historically and currently in debates about "illegal aliens," most notably Chinese and Mexican. Thanks to David Eng for this point.

20. One is reminded of Said's description of culture as "a system of discriminations and evaluations-perhaps mainly aesthetic, as Lionel Trilling has said, but no less forceful and tyrannical for that-for a particular class in the State able to identify with it. . . . For it is true that culture is, on the one hand, a positive doctrine of the best that is thought and known, it is also on the other a differentially negative doctrine of all that is not best" (*WTC*, 11–12). "All that is not best" is relegated to what Perloff calls "subculture(s)", with all the less-than-elevating resonances that the prefix "sub-"carries (including subpar).

21. In my case, it was her indirect influence—by way of her student Craig Dworkin—that led me to begin reading experimental (minority) writing.

22. I recognize that several of the other contributors—Terada, Kaufman, Jackson, and Prins—do not fall neatly on either side of this implied binary of "the literary versus the social," but it is also true that Edwards is the only one who explicitly speaks out against Perloff's binarization. One might have thought that Kaufman, a Frankfurt School devotee, would have, or Jackson and Prins, with their strong historical commitments.

23. The other eight writers discussed are canonical, most considered "major" names—Baudelaire, Beckett, Cavafy, Dickinson, Frost, Lanier, Melville, Tolstoy (as evidenced by their being recognizable simply by their last names)- although Sidney Lanier, cited by Prins for his nineteenth-century work on prosody, is considered a minor poet, and Melville, cited by Jackson, is more famous for his prose than poetry. Emily Dickinson is the sole female poet in the group. The only twentieth-century American poet discussed (by Culler) is Robert Frost. Thus, of the four American poets named more than in passing, two—Melville and Lanier—are certainly not more important as poets, one could argue, than Langston Hughes or Amiri Baraka or, if one goes international (as many in this group of critics do, and as Perloff has often exhorted American literary critics to do), Aimé Césaire.

24. The number of poetry critics focusing *primarily* or *solely* on minority poetry remains dismally small: the most notable are Aldon Nielsen, Fred Moten, Nathaniel Mackey, and Brent Edwards-all writing on African American and African diasporic poetry. Within the group of critics analyzing minority poetry, the number of those focusing on formal concerns is even smaller. In the United States, we have not had a poetry critic of the stature and influence of Raymond Williams to elevate the study of culture and society. Williams, who, despite his shortcomings in acknowledging the full significance of gender and race in British culture and literature, set a standard for both his close attention to literary language, deep knowledge of history, and his keen awareness of sociopolitical forces and structures.

25. It baffles me why a not insignificant number of literary scholars evince little feeling for or interest in literature or literary language—and I do not exempt scholars in Asian American studies and ethnic studies from this criticism. Literary examples can sometimes feel like add-on accessories to theoretically driven arguments that do not need such examples to exist. Why study literature specifically then? Why not just go out and do, say, economics or law instead? My hunch is that mastering the English language and having purchase on its illustrious literary tradition are still seen as signs that one has achieved full assimilation as an American. For immigrants and even more so for children of immigrants (like myself)—particularly for Asian Americans, who are viewed as perpetually "alien" and non-or un-American-the route of literary studies as a means to becoming "fully American" exerts a forceful pull (as it did for an earlier generation of Jewish literary scholars, such as Harold Bloom and Stephen Greenblatt-though for them, only through the study of what Bloom calls the "strong poets," like Shakespeare). It is interesting to note that not a few of the contemporary major poetry scholars who resist discussing ethnicity and identity in relation to poetry are themselves the children or grandchildren of ethnicized European immigrants (e.g., Perloff, Bloom, Altieri). See Marjorie Perloff, *The Vienna Paradox: A Memoir* (New York: New Directions, 2004); Antonio Weiss, "Harold Bloom: The Art of Criticism No. 1," *Paris Review* 33, no. 118 (1991): 178–232. See also Stephen Greenblatt, "The Inevitable Pit: Isn't That a Jewish Name?," *London Review of Books* 22, no. 18 (2000): 8–12.

26. Perloff, "It Must Change," 656.

27. "The Claims of Rhetoric: Towards a Historical Poetics (1820-1900)," *American Literary History* 15, no. 1 (2003): 15. See also her *Poetry and Public Discourse in Nineteenth-Century America* (New York: Palgrave Macmillan, 2010). In an earlier article on Paul Celan, Wolosky writes,

"But the resistance to history, whether as sociological context or political commitment, . . . is itself, as [Hans Magnus] Enzensberger warns, a historical phenomenon that occur in historical contexts." From "The Lyric, History, and the Avant-Garde: Theorizing Paul Celan," *Poetics Today* 22, no. 3 (2001): 652.

28. These tendencies echo and continue New Criticism's strictures against appealing to anything besides the "poem itself," the well-wrought urn. For proponents and practitioners of New Criticism-which, not coincidentally, came into being during the first Red Scare of the 1920s and reached its heyday during the second Red Scare of the 1940s and 1950s-any attempt to bring the social into a reading of a poem was viewed, of course, as "propagandistic," akin to declaring oneself as a "Red Communist." (Despite the political implications of Derrida's and Foucault's work, deconstruction and other forms of poststructuralist high theory have done little to change most poetry critics' assumptions about the separation of the poetic and the social.) Though some extratextual concerns (e.g. gender, class, the environment) are perfectly acceptable for critics to discuss, race remains the one social issue that elicits the most intensely heated reaction when raised. Again, this is as true among those who write on avant-garde poetry as those with allegiances to more traditional forms. In other words, the divide between the poetic and the social feels most unabridgeable when "social" means racial.

29. Raymond Williams, *Culture and Society 1780-1950* (1958; repr., New York: Columbia University Press 1983), 30–31. It is not a coincident that many of the poetry critics who do address the linking of aesthetic and political concerns are, or started as, Romanticists (Jerome McGann, David Simpson, Donald Wesling, Susan Wolfson, for example).

30. Not to mention scores of poets writing in other languages and other literary traditions: Leopardi, Baudelaire, Pasternak, Mayakovsky, Neruda, Césaire, and so on.

31. Steve Evans, "Introduction to *Writing from the New Coast*," in *Telling It Slant: Avant-Garde Poetics of the 1990s*, ed. Mark Wallace and Steven Marks (Tuscaloosa: University of Alabama Press, 2002), 13, 25. Evan's piece originally appeared as the introduction to Oblek No. 12: Writing from the New Coast (Spring/Fall 1993): 4–11.

32. Charles Bernstein similarly punctures the hollow claims of "diversity": "Within the emerging official cultural space of diversity, figures of difference are often selected because they narrate in a way that can be readily assimilated-not to say absorbed-into the conventional forms of the dominant culture" ("State of the Art," in A Poetics, 6).

33. Kenneth Goldsmith, *Uncreative Writing* (New York: Columbia University Press, 2011).

34. Later in the chapter, Goldsmith uses the same somewhat condescending (and familiar liberal) tone to write, "Surely one of the most inspiring identity-based narratives in recent history is that of Barack Obama" (ibid., 86).

35. "State of the Art," 4. Bernstein's analysis is on target, but such an attitude can also run the risk of sounding dismissive of all or most minority cultural production for being "packaged tours of the local color of . . . race [and] . . . ethnicity." In other words, the line between Bernstein's and Perloff's and Gourgouris's views may be finer than might first appear.

36. Or, some would argue, a narrow slice of the contemporary avant-garde scene: mainly founders, fellow travelers, and followers of Language poetry and two particular brands of post-Language writing: Conceptual writing and Flarf. See Kenneth Goldsmith's characterization of these two types of writing, which "fus[e] the avant-garde impulses of the last century with the technologies of the present," in his introduction to the July-August 2009 issue of Poetry that he guest-edited on the topic.

37. Though "Latino/a" includes Mónica de la Torre, who emigrated from Mexico as an adult, and Rodrigo Toscano, who does not identify as a Latino poet.

38. The question of race and poetry dates back to the founding of the United States: Thomas Jefferson in his Notes on the State of Virginia (published in London in 1787, the same year that the US Constitution was adopted) writes, "Misery is often the parent of the most affecting touches of poetry. –Among the blacks is misery enough, God knows, but no poetry. Love is the peculiar cestrum of the poet. Their love is ardent, but it kindles the senses only, not the imagination. Religion indeed has produced a Phyllis Whately [sic]; but it could not produce a poet. The compositions published under her name are below the dignity of criticism. The heroes of the Dunciad are to her, as Hercules to the author of that poem. . . . The improvement of the blacks in body and mind, in the first instance of their mixture with the whites, has been observed by every one, and proves that their inferiority is not the effect merely of their condition of life" (from section 14, "The Laws"). Note the particular oppositions Jefferson sets up in this passage. Thomas Jefferson, *Writings: Autobiography/Notes on the State of Virginia/Public and Private Paper/Addresses/Letters*, ed. Merrill D. Peterson (New York: Library of America, 1984), 266–67.

39. Six of the nine PMLA critics work primarily on American poets: Edwards, Izenberg, Jackson, Kaufman, Perloff, and Prins. Terada and Culler write mainly on literary theory, though both cite American poets in their essays. Gourgouris works on theory as well as Greek literature.

40. See, for example, Pauline Maier, *American Scripture: The Making of the Declaration of Independence* (New York: Vintage Books, 1997).

41. Charles Bernstein insists that "poetry be understood as epistemological/ inquiry" ("Artifice of Absorption," 17–18).

42. From his poem "The Finger," in *Selected Poems* (Berkeley: University of California Press, 1996), 131.

43. One longtime US congressman agrees: after serving thirty-one years in the House, Barney Frank (Democrat from Massachusetts) said in an interview with New York magazine, "I still think race has been the most important problem for us to deal with." Jason Zengerle, "In Conversation: Barney Frank," *New York*, April 23, 2012, http://nymag.com/news/features/ barney-frank-full-transcript-2012-4/.

44. Said's description of humanistic study in American universities thirty years ago has, sadly, yet to become dated. "[E]verything that is nonhumanistic, nonliterary and non-European is deposited outside the structure" (*WTC*, 22).

45. Literary forms themselves are also thought to be timeless and universal, existing outside history.

46. Jefferson, *Notes on the State of Virginia*, 267.

47. Elaine Showalter, *Teaching Literature* (Malden, MA: Blackwell, 2003), 23.

48. Even as late as 1993, when I was an MA student in the Writing Seminars at John Hopkins University, the only minority text taught in that curriculum was Ralph Ellison's Invisible Man.

49. Note that Showalter's evolutionary narrative of progression from bad mimetic methods of reading "identity" literature by minorities to more sophisticated and revolutionary modes of theory reads almost as a mirror image of Gourgouris's postlapsarian narrative of the fall from self-interrogating (presumably theory-laden) literary critical methodology into careless identity-political approaches.

50. See Juliana Chang, *Quiet Fire: A Historical Anthology of Asian American Poetry, 1892-1970* (New York: Asian American Writers' Workshop, 1996).

51. See "Inventing a Culture: Asian American Poetry in the 1970s," chap. 3 in Yu, Race and the Avant-Garde, 73–99.

52. One could productively ask why jazz poetics, for example, does not count as avant-garde among poetry critics. An analogy in the music world: Cecil Taylor and Sun Ra are seen as belonging almost wholly in the (black) jazz world, not as having contributed to the new "classical music" of the twentieth and twenty first centuries-descendants of Arnold Schoenberg, Pierre Boulez, John Cage, and György Ligeti, say—while Philip Glass and John Adams, in many ways, less formally experimental than Taylor and Sun Ra, are seen as part of that lineage. This is so even though Taylor was classically trained at the New England Conservatory and was influenced by modernist and postmodern classical composers, such as Ligeti and Xenakis, as much as he was by black jazz artists.

53. See Donald Wesling, *Bakhtin and the Social Moorings of Poetry* (Lewisburg, PA: Bucknell University Press, 2003).

54. While black or brown or yellow skin may be read as a signifier, a formal sign, it is a sign that it is always affixed to a predetermined content, an essence, which remains static.

55. See, for example, Natalia Cecire, "Sentimental Spaces: On Mei-mei Berssenbrugge's 'Nest,'" *Jacket2*, May 23, 2011, https://jacket2.org/article/sentimental-spaces; Jennifer Scappettone, "Versus Seamlessness: Architectonics of Pseudocomplicity in Tan Lin's Ambient Poetics," *boundary* 2 36, no. 3(2009): 63–76; Charles Altieri, "Intimacy and Experiment in Mei-mei Berssenbrugge's Poetry," in *We Who Love To Be Astonished: Experimental Women's Writing and Performance Poetics*, ed. Laura Hinton and Cynthia Hogue (Tuscaloosa: University of Alabama Press, 2002), 54–68; Linda Voris, "A 'Sensitive Empiricism' Berssenbrugge's Phenomenological Investigations," in *American Women Poets in the 21st Century: Where Lyric Meets Language*, ed. Claudia Rankine and Juliana Spahr (Middletown, CT: Wesleyan University Press, 2002), 68–93.

56. "Content never equals meaning," Charles Bernstein reminds us ("Artifice of Absorption," 10).

57. When I taught Asian American literature at a private midwestern university, where students had held a hunger strike to get Asian American subjects included in the curriculum, my English department colleagues seemed to regard my role in the department as providing another form of student services to Asian American students. In my six years there (2000–06), not one senior colleague besides my "official" mentor ever inquired about my intellectual work. An anecdote might explain why senior Modernist there, who taught and wrote mainly on Virginia Woolf (and in the past, Pound), once asked me, "Why do you put yourself in a box?" When I responded, "Which box?"-I was not sure what she meant since what I work on, minority experimental poetry, is on the margins of various fields and categories-she replied, "The Asian American box," then quickly added, "I can't help it; I just love literature."

The hinged juxtaposition of her two remarks reveals the not uncommon view of the opposition between the narrow, artificially constructed, and nonliterary Asian American "box" to the universal category-clearly not a box-of "literature" (to which Woolf obviously belonged). The irony, of course, is that this English professor did not see herself as occupying any "boxes": whether that of a single-author focus, the literature of a slender chronological period, or women's literature. Though she might not have publicly described African American literature as occupying a box (she had once said to me that African Americans had "suffered more" than Asian Americans, and, thus, their literature was more worthy of study), it was clear that it was the *racial* aspect of Asian American writing-more specifically, its being a secondary ethnic literature, like Native American or Latino/a writing-that made its status as a literary category seem narrow, artificial, and unimportant, indeed, not literature at all. Other categories that were equally "narrow" and artificial in terms of breadth of time period (Modernism) or object of study (a single Modernist author) or social grouping (women) were not indicted as being boxlike.

As with avant-garde critics who deplore thematic justifications for readings of poetry yet use a thematic rationale-here, a negative rationale: the absence of racial markers in the poetry's content-to explain why they do not discuss race in their readings of minority poets, this former colleague saw no contradiction in expressing contempt for extraliterary modes of evaluation and categorization ("extraliterary" here meaning racial-in this case, presumably Asian American "identity") while simultaneously using extraliterary criteria ("degrees of suffering" in so-called real life) to discriminate which minority texts are "real" and worthy of study. One can hardly imagine this same scholar arguing that one should study Woolf and not Pound because Woolf "suffered more," or privilege the study of women's literature over Southern literature because, historically, women have suffered more than Southerners.

58. Equally helpful for rethinking these categories, assumptions, and preconceptions is to examine the contours of the reception of Asian American writing.

59. "The case that upheld the Chinese Exclusion Act to this day remains good law," writes legal scholar Ian Haney Lopez in his *White by Law: The Legal Construction of Race*, rev. ed. (New York: New York University Press, 2006), 28. The issue of class was intermingled-the main target of exclusion was Chinese laborers; merchants and students were exempted.

60. Harlan goes on to write, "But, by the statute in question, a Chinaman can ride in the same passenger coach with white citizens of the United States, while citizens of the black race in Louisiana, many of whom, perhaps, risked their lives for the preservation of the Union, who are entitled, by law, to participate in the political control of the State and nation, who are not excluded, by law or by reason of their race, from public stations of any kind, and who have all the legal rights that belong to white citizens, are yet declared to be criminals, liable to imprisonment, if they ride in a public coach, occupied by citizens of the white race." *Plessy v. Ferguson*, 163 U.S. 537 (1896).

61. Compared to "unmodel" minorities-black, Latino/a, Native American-who do not "work as hard."

62. For example, Asian men are praised for not being "angry" like black men, and Asian women for being demure, rather than "brash" and "domineering" like black women. A typical stereotype of Asian

Americans is that they are apolitical. These stereotypes shore up and also generate political realities. Concrete facts document the nonvisibility of Asian Americans in various realms of power: for example, the racial demographics of the US Supreme Court; the numbers of Asian Americans who are CEOs or heads of colleges and universities.

63. Not "real" or "true" compared to African Americans, in particular—who, given their history of chattel slavery and the cultural products that emerged from that painful history, are perceived as being more "authentically" and "interestingly" minority because "they suffered more"—a view (as noted earlier) that I have heard expressed, or implied by academic colleagues numerous times. Comparative minority hierarchies are often invoked not only for suffering but also for cultural products. Asian Americans are perceived as not having produced what the dominant culture views as black culture's tantalizing musical and linguistic forms such as blues, jazz, and Black English—products of ethnic culture that can be touristically enjoyed, consumed, and in some cases, tapped in to mediate feelings of cultural and historical guilt. Baraka in his book *Blues People* refuses to let us forget the larger, inseparable—and inseparably brutal contexts and histories of African Americans from which this music springs. LeRoi Jones (Amiri Baraka), *Blues People: Negro Music in White America* (1963; repr., New York: Perennial, 2002).

64. Or in the case of African Americans, "standard" English.

65. As we know, not all accents are created equal. A British or French accent is an added bonus, whereas a Mexican or Chinese one devalues the person bearing it and functions as a mark of shame.

66. Even so nonconformist a spirit as Henry David Thoreau-the epitome of American independent thinking and free-spiritedness-in his famous essay on civil disobedience, "Resistance to Civil Government" (1849), cites the example of Asians to mark a group utterly foreign from him (and by implication, other Americans). In critiquing the herd-following, passive and cowardly behavior of his fellow townspeople in Concord, Thoreau writes, "I saw . . . that they were a distinct race from me by their prejudices and superstitions, as the Chinamen and Malays are." In *Walden* (1854), he writes of the contrast between "Jonathan" (the average American Joe of the nineteenth century) and the "effeminate natives of the Celestial Empire, which Jonathan should be ashamed to know the names of." Henry David Thoreau, *Walden and Civil Disobedience* (New York: Penguin 1986), 79–80, 406.

67. Nightmarish visions of "Asiatic hordes" and the Yellow Peril extend far back in American and European history and continue today in the second decade of the twenty-first century, as China "threatens" to "take over the world," like a modern-day Genghis Khan.

68. While African Americans, Latino/as, and Asian Americans all came to this country from other foreign countries-under vastly different circumstances, to be sure-and share a history of racism and of being viewed as an inferior Other, blacks and Latino/as are not viewed as irredeemably foreign in the same way Asian Americans are. African Americans were cut off centuries ago from their "home" country and their African languages; while they face the continual pressure to speak "like a white person," English is still presumed to be their native tongue. And while Latino/as are denigrated and racialized as Spanish-speaking "illegal aliens," Spanish is nonetheless a European language (and Mexico and Puerto Rico, say, are not viewed as real economic threats in the way that China and Japan are and have been). Although comparing degrees of racial exclusion and discrimination on a scale of suffering is problematic, detailing historically and differentially the experiences and assumptions various racial groups have been subjected to-their comparative racializations—is both illuminating and necessary for understanding American history and American literary history. Only by these historical differentiations can one begin to understand the ideological logics and specific workings of white settler colonies such as the United States.

69. And not just by uneducated and "ignorant" people. I was once asked by an Ivy League professor of philosophy whether English was my native language, though he had heard my completely American accent and knew I was an English professor; before I could even respond, he answered his own (rhetorical) question: "I think not."

70. From a 1996 interview with Tod Marshall, reprinted as "Riding a Horse That's a Little Too Wild for You," in *Breaking the Alabaster Jar: Conversations with Li-Young Lee*, ed. Earl G. Ingersoll (Rochester, NY: BOA Editions, 2006), 139. In an earlier interview that same year (reprinted as "Art and the Deeper Silence," in ibid., 82), Lee declared, "(S)yntax is identity"-a fact many nonnative speakers of English experience empirically (and not without varying degrees of shame) on a day-to-day basis.

71. One could argue that poetry is the one genre barred to those with a nonnative relationship to English (or any other language). English literary history would seem to demonstrate this idea: while Joseph Conrad and Vladimar Nabokov are the premier examples of first-rate nonnative prose writers in English, one is hard-pressed to name a poet of equivalent caliber who came to English as a second language.

72. A term that originated in the US imperialistic war in the Philippines and was used to refer to different Asian "enemies" in the subsequent wars in Japan, Korea, and Vietnam. During the Vietnam War, the "mere-gook rule" (or MGR) was followed in the US military. According to investigative

journalist Nick Turse, MGR was "[t]he notion that Vietnam's inhabitants were something less than human. . . . This held that all Vietnamese-northern and southern, adults and children, armed enemy and innocent civilian-were little more than animals, who could be killed or abused at will." Nick Turse, *Kill Anything That Moves: The Real American War in Vietnam* (New York: Metropolitan Books-Henry Holt, 2013), 50. General Westmoreland tells director Peter Davies in his 1974 film *Hearts and Minds*, "The Oriental doesn't put the same price on life as does the Westerner. Life is plentiful, life is cheap in the Orient." Quoted in ibid., 50.

73. "The realities of power and authority-as well as the resistances offered by men, women, and social movements to institutions, authorities, and orthodoxies-are the realities that make texts possible, that deliver them to their readers, that solicit the attention of critics," writes Said (*WTC*, 5).

74. In a 2010 radio interview, Noam Chomsky stated, "The U.S. in the Philippines probably killed a couple hundred thousand people. It was a vicious brutal war with all kinds of atrocities." He went on to speak at length about the Vietnam War: "[T]he [Iraq] invasion itself, awful as it was-practically destroyed Iraq-never even began to come close to what happened-what we did to Indochina. What we did to Indochina is pretty astonishing. And it's remarkable how it's suppressed to this day. Take Cambodia. That's the latter part of the war after, long after South Vietnam was practically wiped out. In 1970, . . . Nixon, then President, told. . . . Henry Kissinger that he wanted large-scale bombing of Cambodia so Kissinger obediently sent the message to-I think it was General Haig at the time-to the military, with classic words. He said, 'Massive bombing campaign of Cambodia. Anything that flies against anything that moves.' I don't think there's a comparable call for genocide anywhere in the archival record-at least I haven't seen one. And it was implemented. But a lot of this remains in the sort of semi-understood consciousness of plenty of people." "Noam Chomsky: The American Socrates on an Upbeat," interview with Christopher Lydon, Radio Open Source, October 28, 2010, http://www.radioopensource.org/noam-chomsky-the-bright-side-of-the-american-socrates/. Chomsky's views are corroborated by Nick Turse in *Kill Anything That Moves*. Turse writes, "This was the real war, the one that barely appears at all in the tens of thousands of volumes written about Vietnam. This was the war . . . in which My Lai was an operation, not an aberration. This was the war in which the American military and successive administrations in Washington produced not a few random massacres or even discrete strings of atrocities, but something on the order of thousands of days of relentless misery-a veritable system of suffering" (22–23).

75. See Mae Ngai, *Impossible Subjects: Illegal Aliens and the Making of Modern America* (Princeton, NJ: Princeton University Press, 2005); and Erika Lee, *At America's Gates: Chinese Immigration During the Exclusion Era, 1882-1943* (Chapel Hill: University of North Caroline Press, 2007).

76. Cathy Song, *Picture Bride* (New Haven, CT: Yale University Press, 1983), x. Stereotypes of "Oriental" spirituality, timeless patience, and the endless ability to suffer, while seemingly much more "positive" than Westmoreland's abhorrent views, nonetheless still function to render one- or two- dimensional, actual Asian (American) lives and beings. See, for example, Jane Iwamura, *Virtual Orientalism: Asian Religions and American Popular Culture* (Oxford: Oxford University Press, 2011).

77. Personal e-mail, February 27, 2011.

78. Rigoberto González, "Shout Out to Ken Chen," http://www.poetryfoundation.org/harriet/2010/04/shout-out-to-ken-chen/; Ken Chen, *Juvenilia* (New Haven, CT: Yale University Press, 2010).

79. See, for example, Charles Altieri, "Images of Form Vs. Images of Content in Contemporary Asian American Poetry," *Qui Parle* 9, no. 1 (1995): 71–91. He compares the work of Marilyn Chin, with her "images of content," unfavorably to that of John Yau, with his "images of form."

80. From the review of Chen, *Juvenilia, Publishers Weekly*, April 19, 2010, http://www.publishersweekly.com/978-0-300-16008-6. The reviewer does at least note Chen's use of language, though one cannot help noticing that classical Chinese poets—long-dead "great" writers—are juxtaposed to the mundane accounts of "U.S. immigrant life." Race and the realities of contemporary American society are, it seems, just not as sexy as Wang Wei and Li Yu.

81. Harryette Mullen, "Poetry and Identity," in Wallace and Marks, *Telling it Slant,* 27–31, quote on 31. Also reprinted in Harryette Mullen, *The Cracks Between What We Are and What We Are Supposed To Be: Essays and Interviews* (Tuscaloosa: University of Alabama Press, 2012), 9–12. Citations are to the Wallace and Marks volume.

82. Thus, attempts by, for example, the poet Marilyn Chin to bring classical Chinese forms into Asian American poetry would not count as "experimental."

83. Williams, *The Politics of Modernism*, 79.

84. Mei-mei Berssenbrugge, *Empathy* (Barrytown, NY: Station Hill Press, 1989). Sections of the poem are also included in her *I Love Artists: New and Selected Poems* (Berkeley, CA: University of California Press, 2006).

85. I choose to use the broader term "Asian American"—to designate the project even though all of the poets in my book are Chinese American. The reasons for this particular grouping of poets are various: I have specific cultural and historical knowledge of Chinese and Chinese

American history and some familiarity with the Chinese language-all factors that contribute toward situating my readings and making them more nuanced; Chinese American writers have produced the largest and oldest body of literary work among Asian American writers over time (primarily a function of the demographics of immigration: Chinese Americans have been in this country the longest as a group and are the largest Asian American subgroup); and finally, as with all critics, I simply have my own proclivities and tastes. In addition, one major criterion I set for choosing poets to include was that a poet have published three or more books of poetry (Pamela Lu constitutes the only exception—her *Pamela: A Novel* is sui generis; it functions as a hinge between twenty- and twenty-first century Asian American writing).

I see no fundamental differences between the issues faced by Chinese American poets and those faced by other Asian American ones. Just as Asian Americans tend to be seen as "all looking alike" in the popular imaginary, Asian American writers are generally viewed as monolithically and homogeneously "Asian" in the academic and literary realms. Understanding the shared and similar history of racial interpellation and mistreatment in the United States and of efforts by those in the Asian American movement of the late 1960s and early 1970s to forge strategic alliances and political identities based on those shared histories, I am convinced that my choice of the more general term "Asian American" is apt-even necessary-for the logic and larger implications of my arguments.

86. I would go further and argue that language works toward constituting and creating the poet's subjectivity; language, in a sense, makes the poet. Or, as Marilyn Chin envisions it in her poem, "Rhapsody in Plain Yellow," the poet becomes language: "Say: I am the sentence which shall at last elude her." *Rhapsody in Plain Yellow* (New York: W. W. Norton, 2002).

87. That said, I agree with the Russian formalist critic Boris M. Ejxenbaum that "(l)iterature, like any other specific order of things, is not generated from facts belonging to other orders and therefore *cannot be reduced* to such facts" (original emphasis). Nonetheless, this observation does not negate the reality that facts belonging to other orders do exert pressures. Boris M. Ejxenbaum, "Literary Environment," in *Readings in Russian Poetics: Formalist and Structuralist Views,* ed. Ladislav Matejka and Krystyna Pomorska (1971; repr. Normal, IL: Dalkey Archive Press, 2002), 61. The essay was originally published in Leningrad in 1929.

88. Paul Celan, "Speech on the Occasion of Receiving the Literature Prize of the Free Hanseatic City of Bremen," trans. Rosemarie Waldrop, in *Paul Celan: Collected Prose* (Riverdale-on-Hudson, NY: Sheep Meadow Press, 1986), 34.

89. Susan Wolfson, *Formal Charges: The Shaping of Poetry in British Romanticism* (Stanford, CA: Stanford University Press, 1997), 1.

90. One might ponder the relationship between the "It" here and the "It" in Perloff's "It Must Change."

91. My basic methodology of close reading is one that is deeply informed by the extratextual (social, historical, political) contexts that influence the formation of a poem. Like the critic Jerome McGann, I am well aware of the history and assumptions of this methodology.

92. One certainly can debate the coherence and logic of literary frames based on temporal segmentation or national boundaries or gender or race, but one cannot fault "Asian American literature" for being a more incoherent or artificially constructed category than these others. I understand that there might be some paradox in my arguing for paying close attention to the formal and aesthetic properties of texts grouped together under the nonliterarily organized category "Asian American," but this is no more or less a paradox than that confronting literary scholars who study "Restoration drama" or "Southern literature." They, too, come up against the tension between aesthetic styles, with their formal particularities, and the larger category's rubric of organization-in this case, temporal, period or region.

93. Thus, to argue that a particular aspect of a poet's worldly experience (e.g. Yau's having grown up Chinese American in Brookline, Massachusetts, the son of Shanghainese immigrants) is an influence on the poetic text is not to "reduce" the poem to that one extratextual aspect or to claim that that one aspect is the sole cause of a particular formal feature.

The Others

Porochista Khakpour

Porochista Khakpour is an essayist and novelist. Born in Tehran, Khakpour is the author of two novels: *The Last Illusion* (Bloomsbury, 2014) and *Sons and Other Flammable Objects* (Grove/Atlantic, 2007), which was a *New York Times* "Editor's Choice," *Chicago Tribune* "Fall's Best," and 2007 California Book Award winner. Her third book, *Sick* (Harper Perennial, 2018), is Khakpour's first memoir. In 2011, Khakpour guest edited the journal *Guernica*'s first Iranian-American issue. The following is the introduction to that issue. "The Others" reflects on what it means to curate such an issue—what it means to read and edit with racial, ethnic, and national categories. "As long as we have books," Khakpour observes, "there will be multitudes of homelands, multiplying at the rate of writers writing."

There was a time, not long ago, when I was downright allergic to journal issues devoted to ethnic and/or racial grouping—about as aesthetically relevant as clusterings based on eye color or mole placement, I insisted. To be put in a box based on something you did not choose seemed uninspired, reductive, and even dangerous. Plus, I had personal reasons: categorization and its many cons had haunted me since I came to this country as a wee preschooler. With looks described as exotic at best and a hyperethnic multisyllabic name regarded as unattemptable at worst, I was coronated an ambassador of my particular brand of other just by virtue of being someone else's first. When I was four, I decided to be a writer *precisely because* the realm of the imagination freed me from confinement regarding how and to whom I was born. But by the time the writing touched any remote professionalization (college workshops, for instance) I was again asked to "write what I know" by wide-eyed, smiling professors—whose "knowing better" was nestled somewhere between an oily *did* and flaky *didn't*—and sheltered students who seemed torn between "coo" and "ew" when it came to me. By a combination of dead-end fatalism and pure accident, I went there (or at least I attempted to), merging the writing of the many whats that I knew with my interests in art, language, and slightly experimental forms (outcome: my first novel). It was only through doing it that I found I actually did have some genuine interest in who and what I was (outcome: years of personal-essay writing on Iranian-American issues).

The seesaw between Iranian and American appeared to have arrived at a miraculous balance. "Iranian-American" was not a label I could necessarily nest in, but at least one I could take a breath at. Even with its pigeonholes and pitfalls, traps and hurdles, stereotypes and caricatures and clichés, it was something I could live with, and this was more than I had ever had. So my disregard for ethnicity-focused anything was ultimately tempered by some authentic self-discovery, some admitted abnegation, and a consequential phobia of hypocrisy—and only really intensely inflamed by those starless lows of overwhelming suspicion and cynicism at everything and everyone American.

But I never lost my skepticism altogether thanks to fixtures of the identity-brand curse, from classic Orientalism 101 to auto-exoticization. As the "Iranian-American" ascended as an entity in the '00s, the discourse churned out by seemingly intelligent American outlets often had the cultural cachet and anthropological depth of a slightly browner *Not Without My Daughter*. When was the last time you saw a book by an Iranian author that *did not* feature on its cover a Persian carpet, pomegranates, faux Middle Eastern arabesque fonts, or a woman in some sort of headscarf? Big publishing and mainstream media in the U.S. seemed just as eager as the Islamic Republic to cast highly photogenic women in veils-and-lashings tearjerkers; they relegated their writers, particularly women, to victim ingénues. Yes, these are true stories, but only one type of story, which is particularly frustrating when so many others remain untold.

Just thirty years after the Iranian Revolution sent many Iranians, like my family members, fleeing *en masse*, Iranian Americans are finally approaching some visibility, thanks to sheer numbers and inevitable assimilation—and, of course, the Islamic Republic's penchant for newsworthiness. As a result, there emerges the problem of how to "come out" here. Perhaps no milestone heralds arrival like last summer's announcement that Ryan Seacrest Productions will follow up its Kardashian franchise with the first-ever reality TV show about Tehrangelenos, L.A.'s sizable Iranian diaspora, called *The Shahs of Sunset*, set to premiere in 2012—interestingly press-released in the same season as a CNN poll that declared half the American public sees Iran as an enemy. Indeed, who can blame a public that possesses the capacity only to stomach us as villains or "reality karachters" when the media so seamlessly abandoned Green Revolution hopes for the shadow of that eminently more spectacular, never-ending menace, our greatest nightmare—mine and yours, I'd wager—war with Iran?

What's a people to do? My only hope is that we Iranian-Americans, in all our separate parts, will prove not only unpalatable but indigestible. If I could have it my way, I'd freeze the world at this moment, where we hover between semi-obscurity and total visibility. I wish that no one had the concept Iranian-American—which might sound pessimistic, but just ask any of your local neighborhood Others what identification has done for them lately.

Given these qualms and reservations, you might wonder: could *Guernica* have made a worse choice for the curator and editor of their first Iranian-American issue? But in putting this issue together, I found that the contrarian instinct in me was useful for soliciting a broad spectrum of writers and writings for a reader unfamiliar with the work of diasporic Iranians. Instead of showcasing commonalities in crude clumps and bulging brands, I wanted to present a collection that's testament to the fact that ethnic origin is where oneness ends. In this way, the grouping is intentionally unsettling. It reaches way past my personal tastes and preferences—and hopefully the tastes and preferences of any one person—as any good anthology should.

I wanted geographic diversity (West and East coasts, plus the Southwest, with writers submitting from Tehran to London), an array of generations (our youngest writer is thirty; our oldest, sixty-five), and a range of experience, from lesser-known up-and-comers to heavily championed veterans (from zero books to six books). I wanted the recognition of legacy (Nahid Rachlin, our first Iranian-American published fiction writer who held Stanford's Wallace Stegner Fellowship in fiction before the Revolution) and a subversion of expectations (Hooman Majd, a celebrated nonfiction writer whose excellent reportage and commentary have deservedly landed him many talk-show-pundit stints, here writes in a genre he has rarely published in, which agents and editors originally steered him away from: his first love, fiction). I wanted aesthetic eclecticism, from Amir Parsa's genre-defying, acrobatic prose to Azadeh Moaveni's intensely observant narrative nonfiction. I wanted comedy (Iraj Isaac Rahmim's rollicking fantasies in modern-day Tehran) and tragedy (Sholeh Wolpé's poignant coming-of-age fairy tale gone awry). I wanted a range in their very Iranianness and Americanness: Sayrafiezadeh's and Fathi's pieces show no traces of their Iranian roots, while over a third of the others go back entirely to Iran. I wanted the mythic Iran of Roger Sedarat's ghost horses set against the more familiar, gritty realism of life in the country today. I wanted to capture the extraordinary scope that defines this young-diaspora-with-an-ancient-culture's literature.

And of course, if I dare pigeonhole/stereotype/caricature myself for a moment, there is something so Iranian in trying to evade identification, something I was reminded of when I emailed my participants asking them to share their thoughts on the label "Iranian-American." As I suspected, only about a third of the writers felt okay with it. Sayrafiezadeh wrote, "It was very liberating for me to finally cease referring to myself as Iranian-American. In other words, to stop defining myself by how others see me. I am an American writer and America is my subject." Majd: "I most definitely do not feel, nor believe myself to be, hyphenated. I am American sometimes, Iranian others, but always just (hopefully) human. I suppose my work reflects who I am— Iranian sometimes, American others—but not always married to either." Fathi: "I do see myself as an Iranian-American, totally shaped by the mixing of both cultures, but it's harder for me to see my poems, the poems themselves, as reflecting a distinctly Iranian-American heritage." Moaveni admits that if she were awakened in the middle of the night and asked this question, she "would say that I consider myself an Iranian writer working in English," while her work belongs to "a fairly specifically American genre of memoir-as-reportage, which hasn't really developed with such verve in other countries." Rahmim jokes about his Jewish-Iranian-Texan-American status, saying, "I am generally not a fan of the hyper-categorization that we come across these days, which seems, often, used to separate us rather than draw others in and allow them to experience our experiences—an act of generosity that, I think, all writers should aspire to." And it took Amir Parsa no fewer than 951 words to articulate and even begin to dissect his own French/German/English/Spanish/Farsi-writing Iranian/Parisian/Brooklynite existence.

I often think of the great Jean Rhys quote "reading makes immigrants of us all," and the many temporary homes I've found in all the books from around the world that I've loved. In that way, we writers are the creators of entirely unique homes. "Every time you write," I tell my students, "you reinvent the universe. No two worlds are identical to any two writers." As long as we have books, there will be multitudes of homelands, multiplying at the rate of writers writing. Although operating under the same hyphenated label here might suggest too many relatives talking over each other in one stuffy living room, I hope you can appreciate this as an invitation to many different homes with different ambiances and temperatures and furniture and architecture, with different families and different gods, whether in the heavens or simply behind the pen.

In the Same Breath
The Racial Politics of *The Best American* Poetry 2014

Isaac Ginsberg Miller

"In the Same Breath" is an essay by Isaac Ginsberg Miller that first appeared in the *American Poetry Review*. The essay reports on the 2014 edition of the *Best American Poetry Series*, an annual anthology that has been published for over 25 years. The book series is edited by David Lehman, and a guest editor is selected each year to curate the anthology. Terrance Hayes was the guest editor for the 2014 edition. In what follows, Miller analyzes Lehman's and Hayes's editorial perspectives. Isaac Ginsberg Miller is a PhD student in African American Studies at Northwestern University. A Callaloo Fellow, Isaac has taught with Urban Word NYC, InsideOut Literary Arts Project, Youth Speaks, and the James and Grace Lee Boggs School. Isaac's writing appears in publications such as *English Journal*, *Colorado Review*, and *Callaloo*. His chapbook *Stopgap* won *The Sow's Ear Poetry Review* Chapbook Contest, and will be published in 2019.

In the opening pages of Claudia Rankine's tour de force *Citizen: An American Lyric*, she writes:

> "You are in the dark, in the car, watching the black-tarred street being swallowed by speed; he tells you his dean is making him hire a person of color when there are so many great writers out there.
>
> You think maybe this is an experiment and you are being tested or retroactively insulted or you have done something that communicates this is an okay conversation to be having.
>
> Why do you feel comfortable saying this to me?"[1]

In this moment the reader is presented with an overwhelming sense of paradox. We assume that the identity of the speaker mirrors that of the author, a Black woman, a prominent writer and professor, a Chancellor of the Academy of American Poets, and yet, still, Rankine's speaker is assumed to be a willing participant in a conversation premised on her erasure. Welcome to the "post-racial" era, which Rankine inhabits and excoriates with tremendous power and precision. As Rankine demonstrates, the world of poetry—often assumed to be a bastion of acceptance—is not immune to the subtle forms of racism that can offer inclusion and dehumanization in the same breath.

I reflect on this tension while reading the 2014 edition of the anthology *The Best American Poetry*. This year's anthology, published by Scribner in September, is edited by Terrance Hayes, a recent MacArthur "genius grant" recipient, National Book Award winner, and faculty member in the Cave Canem fellowship for African American poets. The range, prowess, and sheer pleasure of the poems that Hayes selected for this year's anthology is remarkable. *The Best American Poetry 2014* is a sampling of visionary work gathered at a watershed moment in the history of American poetry, in which there exists a growing racial, ethnic, and gender diversity at the highest levels of a field traditionally dominated by white men. However, while the poems selected by Terrance Hayes (as well as his inventive and playful introduction) offer us a hopeful vision for the future of American poetry, the anthology's foreword, written by David Lehman (the founder and series editor of *The Best American Poetry*), retreads an all-too-familiar argument that the future of literature is imperiled by writers and readers who have become fixated on issues of identity.

Lehman's foreword is ostensibly framed around the longstanding conflict between the sciences and the humanities, which Lehman claims has resulted in the increasing marginalization of humanities-based disciplines. He writes: "In 2013, front page articles in *The New York Times* and *The Wall Street Journal* screamed about the crisis in higher education especially in humanist fields: shrinking enrollments at liberal arts colleges; the shutting down of entire college departments; the elimination of courses and requirements once considered vital."[2] In response, Lehman argues for the continued relevance of the humanities, especially English, by quoting his mentor Lionel Trilling: "The classic defense of literary study holds that, from the effect which the study of literature has upon the private sentiments of a student, there results, or can be made to result, an improvement in the intelligence, and especially the intelligence as it touches the moral life."[3] I agree that literature can have this capacity, but which literature, written by whom, studied by whom, and in what ways? Literature cannot inculcate critical thinking skills if it is studied uncritically. However, Lehman claims that "It is vastly more difficult today to mount such a defense after three or more decades of sustained assault on canons of judgment, the idea of greatness, the related idea of genius, and the whole vast cavalcade of Western civilization."[4] Lehman is implying that those who critique the literary canon as being Eurocentric and patriarchal are in fact responsible for a decreasing interest in the study of literature. Of course, the opposite argument can be, and has been, made: that opening the study of literature to include a broader diversity of writers from different races, classes, genders, and sexual orientations increases the level of interest in literature because a wider range of people see themselves reflected in the work. As Jaswinder Bolina recently wrote about critics who bemoan the decline of poetry: "The thing that's more troubling is that their nostalgia is for a time when self-expression was available to too few, when education and publication were far more limited than they are today. The times and places poetry mattered in the way its critic-defenders mean were those in which freedom of expression wasn't the default for all."[5]

The broadening of poetry's authorship is not only expanding its audience, but also enhancing the integrity, rigor, and scope of the field. Many of the poems included in *The Best American Poetry 2014* are illustrative of the groundbreaking work being done by poets from communities who in the past have been excluded from publication and critical attention. Rather than recognizing this shift, Lehman continues his argument via the words of Heather Mac Donald, who he says "writes more in sorrow than in anger that the once-proud English department at UCLA . . . has dismantled its core, doing away with the formerly obligatory four courses in Chaucer, Shakespeare, and Milton." Lehman, quoting Mac Donald, states that these stalwarts of the Western canon have been replaced by "alternative rubrics of gender, sexuality, race, and class." This all serves as setup for one whopper of a claim. Lehman writes, in reference to UCLA:

> The coup, as Mac Donald terms it, took place in 2011 and is but one event in a pattern of academic changes that would replace a theory of education based on 'a constant, sophisticated dialogue between past and present' with a consumer mind-set based on 'narcissism, an obsession with victimhood, and a relentless determination to reduce the stunning complexity of the past to the shallow categories of identity and class politics. Sitting atop an entire civilization of aesthetic wonders, the contemporary academic wants only to study oppression, preferably his or her own, defined reductively according to gonads and melanin.'[6]

One would expect that after unleashing this statement, Lehman would pause to explain or expand on exactly what he is hoping to accomplish by including it. No, he continues on his meandering discussion of the conflict between the sciences and the humanities before eventually handing the reins over to Terrance Hayes, whose introduction to the anthology appears next.

We should not let Lehman off so easily. His decision to quote Mac Donald's assertion that "Sitting atop an entire civilization of aesthetic wonders, the contemporary academic wants only to study oppression, preferably his or her own, defined reductively according to gonads and melanin" is, to say the least, baffling. Mac Donald's *Wall Street Journal* op-ed (from which this quote was taken) was reprinted from *City Journal*, the publication of the neoconservative think tank The Manhattan Institute for Policy Research, where Mac Donald is a fellow.[7] Mac Donald, an influential conservative commentator who regularly gives public talks, appears on television, and testifies before governmental committees, is the author of such books as *Are Cops Racist? How the War Against the Police Harms Black Americans* and articles including "The Illegal-Alien Crime Wave."[8] Mac Donald has advocated for racial profiling (of African-Americans[9] and Muslims[10]), and justified the use of torture by the US military.[11] Mac Donald has argued for the benefits of mass incarceration vis-à-vis reducing the crime rate[12] and stated that as a result of welfare policies "generations have grown up fatherless and dependent."[13] In her article "Is the Criminal-Justice System Racist?" Mac Donald refuses to acknowledge the existence of structural racism, what author Michelle Alexander calls "The New Jim Crow,"[14] and instead argues that the reason Black people represent a disproportionate percentage of the American prison population is that they commit a disproportionate number of crimes.[15]

Recently, Mac Donald wrote an article criticizing what she claims to be biased national media coverage of 18-year-old Michael Brown's killing by Ferguson, Missouri, police officer Darren Wilson, writing that, "A videotape captured the 300-pound Brown committing a strong-arm robbery minutes before his encounter with the police."[16] Mac Donald also writes that "Ferguson's population is two-thirds black, but five of its six city council members are white, as is its mayor. Conclusion: this racial composition must be the product of racism. Never mind that blacks barely turn out to vote and field practically no candidates." Again, structures of racism, poverty, segregation, mass incarceration, voter disenfranchisement, and police brutality are conveniently ignored.

Given Mac Donald's history of racist publications and her membership in a think tank that institutionally targets people of color, she seems a rather dubious figure of authority on the state of the humanities in American higher education. What exactly are Mac Donald's qualifications? Prior to joining the Manhattan Institute, Mac Donald studied English at Yale and Cambridge, and then received her law degree from Stanford. A profile of Mac Donald in

The New York Times notes that her shift towards a conservative political worldview came about as a backlash against the shifting currents of university English departments: "Her conversion occurred when she moved to New York in 1987 after an Environmental Protection Agency stint convinced her that she was not meant to be a practicing attorney. She intended to return to Ivy League academia. 'But the campuses had been taken over by multiculturalism and this yahoo rejection of Western culture by a bunch of students who had barely read a book,' she says."[17] Mac Donald clearly harbors a deep resentment towards anyone attempting to expand the canon, and has built her career attacking communities of color and poor people, precisely the communities which the canon excludes.

Lehman's argument that academic challenges to the Eurocentric, patriarchal nature of the canon have driven students away from the humanities is a narrative drawn straight from right-wing think tanks. In addition to quoting Mac Donald, Lehman also references the article "Humanist: Heal Thyself" written by Russell A. Berman, a Stanford professor, a senior fellow at Stanford's conservative think tank The Hoover Institute, and the author of books such as *Anti-Americanism and Europe: A Cultural Problem*, and *Freedom or Terror: Europe Faces Jihad*. In his foreword, Lehman draws a connection between the decline in humanities majors from their mid-century peak to Berman's assertion that "the marginalization of the great works of the erstwhile canon has impoverished the humanities."

Significantly, recent research has shown that this dropoff in humanities majors actually occurred almost entirely in the decade of the 1970s.[18] This shift can be attributed to women entering a broader range of career paths, as well as changes in the economy that put pressure on students of all genders to choose majors that would lead to more profitable employment. Thus, the assertion that theories of race, class, gender, and sexuality (which only became prevalent in the academy beginning in the 1980s) have caused a declining interest in the humanities is historically baseless.[19]

This panic over the supposed decline of the humanities mirrors conservative fears over the decline of our society as a whole, an anxiety that is often mapped along racial lines. Jeff Chang, in his new book *Who We Be: The Colorization of America,* writes about fears arising from the demographic shift by which, by the middle of the twenty-first century, the population of the United States will show a majority of people of color. Chang writes about Pat Buchanan's speech before the 1992 Republican National Convention that "captured the spirit of the growing backlash." In this speech, Buchanan framed the discourse of what would become known as the "Culture Wars." Chang writes:

> He decried the "across-the-board assault on our Anglo-American heritage." He said, "The combined forces of open immigration and multiculturalism constitute a mortal threat to American Civilization." To him, faith in Euro-American ideals was the basis of culture, which in turn was the very foundation upon which civilization rested. "When the faith dies, the culture dies, the civilization dies, the people die," Buchanan wrote. "That is the progression."[20]

In *Who We Be* Chang argues that, throughout the 1990s, the Culture Wars—fought on college campuses, in Congressional subcommittees, and in the news media—represented a backlash by the white establishment against an increasingly multiracial society. Chang frames the Culture Wars as embodying what scholar H. Samy Alim has termed "demographobia," or "the irrational fear of changing demographics."[21] This logic bears a remarkable resemblance to the fear expressed by Mac Donald, Lehman, and Berman. If you substitute "canon" for "civilization" in Buchanan's speech, the meaning remains almost identical. It bears asking: When the same people who are defending the Eurocentric canon are also advocating for the very policies that attack young people of color, is it any wonder that these same young people might resist reading "canonical" texts?

Lehman's foreword to *The Best American Poetry 2014* recalls the "Canon Wars," a subset of the Culture Wars that played out in the world of poetry, most infamously in Harold Bloom's essay "They Have the Numbers; We the Heights," which appeared as the foreword to *The Best of the Best American Poetry 1988-1997*. In his essay, Bloom assails writers concerned with identity for destroying the "aesthetic tradition" of Western literature, and claims that all those who desire an expansion of the canon belong to the "School of Resentment," comprised of "the multiculturalists, the hordes of camp-followers afflicted by the French diseases, the mock-feminists, the commissars, the gender-and-power freaks, the hosts of new historicists and old materialists."[22] Lehman sounds similar notes but at a muted volume, more appropriate for our "post-racial" era.

Drawing from Claudia Rankine, I ask the question: What makes Lehman think this is an okay conversation to be having? It is staggering how at odds Lehman's foreword is with the anthology that it prefaces. After his coded diss against the very same groups of people who comprise Bloom's "School of Resentment," Lehman praises Terrance Hayes, whose poems he says "reflect a deep interest in matters of masculinity, sexuality, and race," and affirms Cave Canem as "the organization that has done so much to nourish the remarkable generation of African American poets on the scene today." As in Rankine's car scene, there is a cognitive dissonance between the inclusion of writers of color and what is being said about them right to their faces.

It is striking that every single critic and scholar—other than Terrance Hayes—that David Lehman cites in his introduction is white. This is a perfect example of the need for expanding the scope of whom we read and give critical authority to. In fact, Mac Donald would very likely call many of the poems in this anthology an assault on the Western canon. To name but a few examples: Yusef Komunyakaa's "Negritude," Camille Dungy's "Conspiracy (to breathe together)," Patricia Lockwood's "Rape Joke," Kwame Dawes's "News From Harlem," Jon Sands's "Decoded," Rita Dove's "The Spring Cricket Repudiates His Parable of Negritude," and Afaa Michael Weaver's "Passing Through Indian Territory." These poems are nuanced, daring, and extraordinary. They disturb the notion that a "canon" is a fixed entity, stuck in a patriarchal, Eurocentric past. These poems have things to say to Shakespeare and Shakespeare has things to say to them. Let them be in conversation. This would truly represent the "constant, sophisticated dialogue between past and present" that Mac Donald invokes.

The canon is evolving, expanding, and changing. This is something to be celebrated, not bemoaned. In this way, there is a greater not a lesser place of importance for poetry in our public (and private) lives. While lamenting a declining interest in the humanities, Lehman paradoxically acknowledges that there is more poetry being written today than ever before.[23] This fact could point us towards a moment of opportunity rather than cynicism. Including the study of contemporary poetry that engages with issues of identity in K-12 education, undergraduate curricula, and graduate programs will not erode the critical reading and writing skills that Lehman believes are so essential to our society. In fact, studying the present landscape of poetry can give us new perspective and fervor in engaging with the poetic lineages that led us to this point (and vice versa). This is the missed opportunity of Lehman's foreword. He is stuck in a Culture Wars dichotomy of a past generation, rather than embracing the emergence of new possibilities for what poetry can become.

At all levels of the field, poets of color are writing and publishing some of the most visionary and paradigm-shifting work being written today, precisely because they are writing from an artistic perspective that acknowledges difference along lines of race, class, gender, and sexual orientation. This exploration of human identity has not weakened the writing. On the contrary, it has pushed the field forward by expanding the range of human experience that poetry can encompass. In fact—contrary to the arguments of Lehman, Mac Donald, Berman, and Bloom—a refusal to acknowledge the ways in which our identities affect our experiences is a profoundly limited, parochial view of human existence, not the other way around. Each and every one of us is circumscribed by our identities, even as we exist as multidimensional and nuanced human beings. This contradiction is worth investigating, and, as many contemporary poets have demonstrated, this kind of investigation can yield extraordinary results.

Here are but a few recent examples of the way in which contemporary poets of color are shifting the field: Terrance Hayes won the 2010 National Book Award for *Lighthead*, Nikky Finney won the 2011 National Book Award for *Head Off & Split*, Tracy K. Smith won the 2012 Pulitzer Prize for *Life on Mars*, Vijay Seshadri won the 2014 Pulitzer Prize for *3 Sections*. Natasha Trethewey, the United States Poet Laureate from 2012 to 2014, was also, in 1999, the recipient of the first annual Cave Canem Poetry Prize. While titles and prizes should not be our primary barometer for assessing artistic merit or impact, these and many other authors point to a sea change taking place today in American poetry.

Terrance Hayes addresses this very issue in his introduction to *The Best American Poetry 2014*, albeit through a tongue-in-cheek aside. His introduction is written as an interview between himself and Dr. Charles Kinbote (the fictional narrator who appears in Vladimir Nabokov's novel *Pale Fire*). At one point Dr. Kinbote lists the posthumously published poets who were included in this year's anthology: "Kurt Brown, Joseph Ceravolo, Adam Hammer, Larry Levis, Jake Adam York. Interestingly, all of them are deceased *white male poets*. Is this to suggest the white male poet is a dying breed?" Terrance Hayes responds, "[laughing]: Of course not! You really shouldn't be drinking red wine and espresso."

Obviously, white male poets (myself included) continue to participate in the field of contemporary American poetry, but we do not deserve to occupy a place of privilege above any other group of writers (and yes, as much as we may attempt to deny it, white male poets are a group of writers). In the words of Toni Morrison, referenced by Claudia Rankine during a recent conversation held at New York University: "If you can only be tall because someone else is on their knees, then you have a serious problem, and my feeling is that white people have a very, very serious problem."[24] While white male poets may not be "a dying breed," white male poets who tacitly endorse dehumanizing patterns of thought increasingly resemble what poetry most deeply strives to avoid: a cliché.

Notes

1. Claudia Rankine, *Citizen: An American Lyric* (Minneapolis: Graywolf Press, 2014), 10.
2. David Lehman, "Foreword," *The Best American Poetry 2014* (New York: Scribner, 2014), xiii.
3. Lehman, "Foreword."
4. Ibid.
5. Jaswinder Bolina. "The Writing Class." Poetry Foundation. November 12, 2014. Web.
6. Lehman, Foreword, xvi.
7. "Manhattan Institute Scholar: Heather Mac Donald." Manhattan Institute For Policy Research. Web.
8. Heather Mac Donald, "The Illegal-Alien Crime Wave," *City Journal*, Winter 2004. Web.
9. Heather Mac Donald, "The Myth of Racial Profiling," *City Journal*, Spring 2001. Web.
10. Mike Pesca, "NYC Mulls Effectiveness of Racial Profiling," National Public Radio. Web.
11. Lance Morrow, "Necessity or Atrocity?" *The New York Times,* Books, January 29, 2006.
12. Heather Mac Donald, "Is the Criminal-Justice System Racist?" *City Journal*, Spring 2008. Web.
13. Heather Mac Donald, "The Billions of Dollars That Made Things Worse." *City Journal*, Autumn 1996. Web.
14. Michelle Alexander, *The New Jim Crow: Mass Incarceration in the Age of Colorblindness* (New York: The New Press, 2010).
15. Mac Donald, "Is the Criminal-Justice System Racist?"
16. Heather Mac Donald, "Ferguson's Unasked Questions," *City Journal*, October 6, 2014. Web.
17. Robin Finn. "Excoriating the Enablers, in 12 Chapters." *The New York Times,* November 28, 2000. Web.
18. Colleen Flaherty, "Princeton Grad Student Takes on the Humanities Crisis from a Decidedly Gendered Perspective," *Inside Higher Ed,* July 11, 2013. Web.

19. Michael Bérubé, "The Humanities, Declining? Not According to the Numbers," *The Chronicle of Higher Education,* July 1, 2013. Web.

20. Jeff Chang, *Who We Be: The Colorization of America* (New York: St. Martin's Press, 2014), 119.

21. Chang, *Who We Be*, 245.

22. Harold Bloom, "They Have the Numbers; We, the Heights," *Boston Review,* April 1, 1998. Web.

23. Lehman, "Foreword," xvii.

24. "Charlie Rose with Toni Morrison." Charlie Rose, Inc. 2007. DVD. Also available on YouTube: "Toni Morrison Takes White Supremacy to Task." Web.

Chapter Reflection

Questions for Discussion

(Some of the following questions were generated by creative writing student Angela Compton.)

1   Do you relate to any of the experiences that the authors describe? Do you see yourself in any of these readings? Have you had the experience of being "pigeonholed" or of "pigeonholing" someone?

2   In creative writing, it is common to talk about "finding one's voice." Is "finding a voice" completely up to an individual author, or is "voice" a social issue—affected by audience expectations, cultural biases, inequities in the publishing industry, or other factors? How do your background, identity, heritage, and so on shape your understanding of, or regard for, your voice?

3   Think of the films you've seen and the stories you've read in the past month. Who are the protagonists in these stories? What is their gender identity? Their sexual orientation? Their race? Ethnicity? Religion? How is ability/disability portrayed in these stories? And are there characters in the story who are of different genders, sexual orientations, races, ethnicities, religions, or abilities, and do these characters exist only in service of the protagonist—as a sidekick, and so on—or are they portrayed as having agency, complexity, and plot lines of their own?

4   As you do the inventory of the plots you've encountered this month, you might notice some trends. As Joanna Russ noted in her 1972 essay "What Can a Heroine Do?", authors "do not make up their stories out of whole cloth; they are pretty much restricted to the attitudes, the beliefs, the expectations, and above all the plots that are 'in the air.'" Certain identities are regularly slotted into certain social roles, and only certain plot lines are available to those roles. What do the plots you know indicate about cultural bias?

Writing Prompt

Write a story, essay, or poem that calls into question a common idea about identity. Write something that subverts the attitudes, beliefs, expectations, and plots that are, as Russ says, "in the air."

Suggestions for Further Reading

1   Hong, Cathy Park. "Delusions of Whiteness in the Avant-Garde," *Lana Turner: A Journal of Poetry and Opinion* (2014). Web.

2   McCullough, Laura, ed. *A Sense of Regard: Essays on Poetry and Race*. University of Georgia Press, 2015.

3   McLeod, Neal, ed. *Indigenous Poetics in Canada*. Wilfrid Laurier University Press, 2014.

4   Russ, Joanna. "What Can a Heroine Do? Or Why Women Can't Write." *Images of Women in Fiction; Feminist Perspectives*. Ed. Susan Koppelman Cornillon. University of Popular Press, 1972. 3–20.

5   Verduyn, Christl, ed. *Literary Pluralities*. Broadview Press, 1998.

3

Privilege

On the Response to Junot Díaz's "MFA vs. POC"

David Mura

The following piece by David Mura references the much-discussed essay "MFA vs. POC," written by Junot Díaz and published initially as the introduction to *Dismantle: An Anthology of Writing from the VONA/ Voices Writing Workshop* and, in condensed form, in the *New Yorker* in April 2014. In the following piece, originally published on Mura's personal blog and subsequently in *Revolver*, Mura offers a snapshot of the response that Díaz's piece prompted. Mura has written widely about the field of creative writing, with essays such as "White Writing Teachers," published in the *Journal of Creative Writing Studies*, and "Ferguson, Whiteness as Default, & the Teaching of Creative Writing," published in the AWP *Writer's Chronicle*. A third-generation Japanese-American, Mura has also published two memoirs—*Turning Japanese: Memoirs of a Sansei* (Atlantic Monthly Press, 1991; reissued, Grove Press, 2006) and *Where the Body Meets Memory* (Anchor/Random, 1996)—along with several books of poems, a work of criticism, and a monograph on race, identity, and narrative.

On the *New Yorker* web page, fiction writer Junot Díaz recently published a critique of the "whiteness" of MFA programs. This is a shortened version of his intro to the VONA anthology, *Dismantle: An Anthology of Writings from the VONA/Voices Writing Workshop*.

Some of the responses to Díaz's intro in the comment section are reprehensible, and I've written this post in response to those comments:

"The number of ad hominem attacks here certainly give weight to Díaz's arguments. When the person of color brings up a critique, the response is often to critique the so-called character or personality faults of the person of color—or to critique the language in which the critique is expressed (too angry, uses too many swear words, the person doesn't have the right to make this critique because he or she is in some other way privileged, etc.). These critiques are all ways the dominant culture uses to dismiss concrete and systemic issues.

One key issue: Are the faculty in MFA programs well versed in a variety of literary traditions and thought? When I was in an English PhD program I read a handful of poems by Amiri Baraka and that was it. In my MFA program I was not taught anything about the tradition of African American letters (much less about Asian American, Native American or Latino American, much less the traditions of global writing or post-colonial theory). Many of my students at VONA and other writers of color I've encountered also express a similar absence in their MFA training and thus, in the faculty that teach in these programs.

A second issue about the 'whiteness' of MFA workshops is addressed not to individual white people, but to the literary practices and ways of thinking which are deemed standard in a white dominated society and literary world. For example, the default literary practice in American writing is that white writers do not have to identify their white characters as being white. Is this practice politically and racially neutral or is it a practice which can be examined in light of a literary and political critique? In most current MFA workshops, what would happen if such a critique were expressed? Would it be acknowledged that there are actually at least two sides—if not many more—that are addressing this practice? Or would such a critique be dismissed as too political, as 'PC' and therefore not literary? And what would the response be to the student who offered up such a critique?

One exercise of power is to keep critiques of the dominant power from ever being voiced. Ad hominem attacks are one way, ignoring the existence of the critiques are another (i.e., not knowing the literary traditions and thought of people of color), and standard practices of how workshops are run are another. The motive is to keep actual debate of the issues outside the classroom or from occurring in the literary world."

I know, as so many suggest, I shouldn't be looking at comment sections. I can certainly understand the argument that it's useless to respond to "trolls."

Still one comment about Junot's piece on the *New Yorker* blog seemed to me to voice a valid concern. Here's the comment:

"This is my perspective as a white guy in the academic world. . . . My concern is, if I try to talk about race, people's reaction is likely to be: nice try guy, but you can't understand the experiences of people of color. On the other hand, based on Junot Díaz's remarks, it seems like if I choose to keep silent about matters of race the reaction is: you're afraid to confront these issues, so you're part of the problem. I have no doubt that it's hard for people of color, especially when it seems like their concerns are widely ignored. But it's hard for me too — I honestly don't think anyone, person of color or otherwise, wants to hear my perspective on race. I've never felt encouraged to join that conversation."

Here's what I wrote back:

"I can understand how you, as 'a white guy in the academic world,' might feel you're damned if you do and damned if you don't. Many whites don't think race is a pressing issue so they don't feel the dilemma in the way you seem to. But your dilemma isn't the same as POC in the academic world who, when they do voice their critiques about institutional practices concerning race, are met with disbelief or ad hominem attacks or derision (as shown in this commentary section).

I recall talking recently with a young white male writer who said while he knew race was an important subject, he was afraid to write about it because he was afraid of being called a "racist." So I'm sure there are other whites—writers and academics—who feel like you, that perhaps they're better off not engaging, remaining silent.

Conversations are, of course, two way streets. But when individuals of different races converse, that conversation doesn't take place in a neutral, ahistorical realm. Richard Wright has indicated that white and black Americans are engaged in a struggle over the description of reality. But one key difference is that that white description has prevailed and dominated our society and culture.

As a Japanese American, I grew up thinking I wanted to be a white person and thought it a compliment when white people told me they thought of me as a white person. I went through twenty-six years of education without really being presented anything like the black description of our social reality and history (much less a Japanese American description). I only got that education after I left English grad school. On my own.

So the thing is, when you as a white person enter a conversation about race, most likely there are many things you don't know—about the cultures and histories of people of color, about the arguments and theories we have of our mutual history and how this society functions, about the lives of people of color. But people of color, if we have gone through your school systems, know we have to know how whites tell their histories to themselves, how they regard themselves and their racial identity (which is often—"whites don't have a racial identity"). We have heard the white side and view of things; we can't avoid it. We have read books about white people by white people, seen movies and television shows about white people by white people. We have listened a lot to white people. It is really hard, if not impossible, for us to be successful in this society without listening to white people—and often, listening while holding or biting our tongues.

If you are really interested in having a true conversation about race with people of color, then you should realize that historically this has been a mainly one-sided conversation. Since whites have been dominating the conversation so long, perhaps the role for you as an individual white person is, at first, simply to listen, to find out what you don't know. As Donald Rumsfeld has infamously observed, there are things we don't know we don't know. That is often the case when whites enter conversations with people of color about race. Whites don't actually know how much they do not know about the lives of people of color. The only antidote to this is to be curious and listen. Listening too is part of the art of conversation.

Unfortunately, as so many of the negative responses here to Díaz's article indicate, there's a sizable number of whites who simply cannot hear people of color describe their experiences. That simple description of one's life as a person of color so challenges white assumptions about our social reality that the white person cannot even entertain that the person of color may actually be telling the truth about his or her experience—as in sjdmccarthy's comments below.

In Baldwin's *The Devil Finds Work*, there's a great quotation about identity. In it, Baldwin pictures a stranger walking into a village. Encountering that stranger, says Baldwin, should cause one to question one's identity because the stranger looks at the world and herself and you differently than you, and your identity must now shift to include not just the stranger, but the perspective of the stranger in your consciousness of yourself. But for that to happen, you have to listen to the stranger, you have to learn from the stranger. And that requires you, said Baldwin, to change your robes, to reconstruct your identity. Listening then is dangerous, threatening. But as Baldwin implies, necessary and life affirming."

At the Stonecoast MFA program, I and Alexis Pate teach a workshop, "Writing About Race." In it, writers examine literary and other issues that arise from writing about race. The workshop is an attempt to create a safe space for white writers and writers of color to discuss race.

I also teach at the VONA Voices Writers' Workshop, a writers' conference for writers of color taught by writers of color. VONA is there for writers of color to examine and discuss their work and the issues that arise from that work. It provides a space where writers of color don't have to spend a majority of the workshop explaining their work or their lives to white writers or arguing with white writers about our right to tell our truths and lives in our own voices.

We need more of both of these spaces.

Unpacking Privilege in Creative Writing

Janelle Adsit

A version of the following was originally published in the book *Toward an Inclusive Creative Writing* (Bloomsbury, 2017).

What follows is based on Peggy McIntosh's well-known heuristic "White Privilege: Unpacking the Invisible Knapsack."[1] The list is meant to help students and teachers reflect on the biases that may be embedded in their approach to literary production and to become more self-reflexive about their positionality and assumptions as these operate in the creative writing classroom. Each sentence can prompt a discussion about how privilege may operate in creative writing.

1 I have never noticed when an anthology, literary journal, or magazine consists primarily of white or male writers.
2 I assume that the works that don't get published or canonized are always examples of bad or lesser writing.
3 I grew up admiring heroes from movies and books that shared my race or gender. It was easy to find these protagonists in the films, shows, and books available to me.
4 I can be sure that the curricular materials I receive in a creative writing class will present characters and narrators that share my racial, ethnic, gender, sexual, class, national, linguistic, or religious identity or that have bodies that look like mine.
5 To my mind, only less important or less skilled forms of literature are political or politicized.
6 I have never experienced censorship.
7 I have never received punishment for something I wrote.
8 I assume that my experiences and my writing can reach a universal or mainstream audience.
9 I believe that the people who really have something to say are the people that get large audiences.

10 I have never considered how my first or last name might be perceived by publishers, literary agents, or application review committees.

11 I believe writers are born and not made.

12 When I name the great authors of the literary tradition, most of the names that come to mind are white or male writers.

13 I rarely feel the need to examine the ways I present race, gender, sexuality, class, nationality, or religion in my writing.

14 I rarely feel the need to examine the ways I present the body or ability in my writing.

15 I feel comfortable writing about characters of political/cultural/linguistic/social/ethnic identities that I do not share, and I do not go out of my way to check my representation of these characters against perspectives other than my own.

16 I often don't name the race of my characters because I assume readers will know the characters are white, or I feel that race doesn't matter.

17 I do not consider how audiences of differing identities, backgrounds, and experiences will experience the texts I produce.

18 I feel comfortable writing in genres (e.g., haiku, slam poetry, etc.) that have cultural legacies of which I am unaware.

19 I feel comfortable portraying the speech patterns of characters from cultural backgrounds that I don't know well. I feel comfortable using a vernacular, code, or language that I do not speak or have never sought to learn.

20 I do not worry about cultural appropriation in my storytelling or poetic practices. I feel I can resource whatever I want to use in my work, and I do not need to account for my positionality when I do.

21 I've never experienced microaggressions in a creative writing workshop.

22 I can note bias in the creative writing workshop without being accused of displaying extreme emotion, being irrational, being militant, or being too self-interested.

23 I do not sympathize with requests to preface literary texts with trigger warnings or content warnings about forms of prejudice, abuse, and dismissal of lived oppressions (e.g., anti-trans views, racism, ableism).

24 When readers are offended by something they read, I believe the offense is the reader's individual problem—and not the writer's.

25 Readers do not expect me to speak for all people of my racial, ethnic, gender, sexual, class, national, linguistic, or religious group in my writing.

26 I do not worry that my peers or teachers will be disapproving of my taste in literature.

27 I do not fear being seen as a cultural outsider to creative writing.

Note

1. Peggy McIntosh, "White Privilege: Unpacking the Invisible Knapsack," Working Paper 189. *White Privilege and Male Privilege: A Personal Account of Coming to See Correspondences through Work in Women's Studies* (1988).

On Parsing

Kavita Das

In 2015, Claire Vaye Watkins gave a lecture titled "On Pandering" at a summer writers' workshop hosted by the journal *Tin House*. The lecture was subsequently posted on the journal's website. Watkins's piece prompted several writers to respond (see, for another example, Alison Stine's essay "On Poverty," published by *Kenyon Review* in 2016). Kavita Das's "On Parsing" takes on the issue of race, which is elided in Watkins's original speech. Where Watkins may seem to speak for all women, she is specifically speaking as a white woman, Das notes. "On Parsing" was originally published on the website of *VIDA Women in Literary Arts* in 2016. Das has written on culture, race, feminism, and their intersections for publications including *Kenyon Review*, *Guernica*, *Los Angeles Review of Books*, and *The Atlantic*. Her biography about Grammy-nominated Hindustani singer Lakshmi Shankar is forthcoming from Harper Collins India. (Introduction written by creative writing student Angela Compton.)

A few months ago, Claire Vaye Watkins's courageous piece, "On Pandering" was published on the website for the literary magazine *Tin House*. I watched as it blew up on my social media feed, shared by so many fellow writers, especially women writers. In fact, by the time I tried to log on to read the piece a few hours later, the site had crashed due to the volume of traffic. The overwhelming response alongside my own conflicted reaction was strangely reminiscent of what I had experienced a few months ago when I heard Watkins deliver her lecture (then subtitled *How to Write Like a Man*) while participating at the same magazine's summer writing workshop.

It was a truth-telling session tinged with a spiritual aura, in part because her talk was delivered in a campus chapel. Her piece deals with her own struggle to find and value her own voice as a white woman writer in the face of age-old and pervasive patriarchy and misogyny in literature. She not only took on the old white men, living and dead, whose works and voices have dominated the literary establishment. She took on the alleged misogynist behavior of a relatively well-known white male writer and editor towards her.

I was familiar with both the writing and reputation of the male writer in question. I had heard about his erratic behavior so I didn't doubt her account. If anything, I was impressed by her candor and courageousness, given how small and interconnected the literary world often seems. But I also knew that he had created *The Rumpus*, one of the most progressive literary websites, which had the prescience to bring on board Cheryl Strayed, as an empathetic literary advice columnist, and Roxane Gay, as a nonfiction editor and contributor, several years ago, before they both went on to become two of today's most popular and respected feminist voices. At that time, Gay was one of few women of color editors on the masthead of a literary magazine, a trend that continues today. It is also important to note that the masthead of the magazine that published Watkins isn't racially diverse.

As a woman of color writer, I sat in the pews taking it all in, her words punctuated alternately by gasps, laughter, and claps from the audience, the majority of which were white women writers. I wanted to feel the same ribald enthusiasm as they did but couldn't. And I was frustrated at myself for this. Watkins ended her talk with the fiery manifesto—"let us burn this motherfucking system to the ground and build something better"—the whole room burst into thunderous applause and hoots and hollers. I felt compelled to rise to my feet and clap even though I couldn't shake the feeling that the celebration belonged more to the other women in the room than to myself. Essentially, the woman half of me cheered the takedown of patriarchy, but the person of color half felt incidental to the celebration.

I have grown used to reading the work of white feminist writers who reference their own experiences and the experiences of other white feminists and extrapolate it to represent the entire feminist experience with no caveats for class or race. However, in her piece, Watkins referenced experiences of writers of color, including one that made her aware of her "invisible cloak of white privilege." But at my core, I sensed a certain hollowness in these references—as if these people's significance and relevance were tied solely to their identities and how they related to Watkins' identity. Watkins evoked their identity and experiences to make a point about her relative privilege as a white female writer but didn't delve any further below her cloak and even admitted, "I want to unsee it, make it invisible again, and usually I do, because it feels better. I have that privilege. Others don't."

While Watkins honesty about her discomfort at her own privilege is to be lauded, it also gets to the heart of one of the fundamental problems with the piece and many people's reaction to it: when a white woman writes about the experiences of people of color especially in relation to her own, acknowledging her privilege, she is usually heralded as courageous and compassionate. However, when a person of color writes about their experiences relative to the mainstream population, it is often viewed solely as a grievance.

Women writers have long struggled to have their writing valued, even resorting to writing under a male nom de plume, effectively sacrificing their female identity for their writer identity—the two being mutually exclusive, at the time. Watkins' piece illustrates that even today, the pervasive force of patriarchy in literature still shapes the perspectives and voices of women writers until and unless they examine the explicit and implicit patriarchical influences on their work, and decide to stop pandering to them. Do they gravitate to reading mostly male writers or do they unconsciously emulate the style of only male writers?

However, white women writers have a significant advantage over women writers of color when it comes to being published: according to a recent demographic survey of the publishing sector, the majority of people working in publishing, at every level, are white and female, making it much more likely that they relate to and value writing from fellow white women. Now that this survey has made visible this long suspected trend, will it continue to go collectively unseen and uncorrected so that the majority of the field can feel better?

On Pandering also reminded me of workshop experiences where white writers would include people of color as pivotal characters and yet they would remain nameless or devoid of physical description. In this way they were walking contradictions, critical plot devices who never quite achieved any humanity because they were merely built around identities rather than personal characteristics. Ultimately, Watkins only recognizes the burdens and marginalization that come with the identity of writers of color, but not the unique empowerment they receive when they harness those burdens, as she eventually does at the end of her piece. Their primary purpose in her piece is to illustrate her privilege and the privilege of her fellow white writers.

Meanwhile, in her takedown of the white male canon, Watkins erects in its place a white female canon, albeit a hip, updated one, filled with female punk rock stars and comedians who published memoirs last year—Patti Smith, Carrie Brownstein, Kim Gordon, Sally Mann, and Amy Poehler. But last year was also the year that punk muse, Grace Jones, and intrepid comedian, Mindy Kaling, wrote their own memoirs. This replacement of one list with another made me think that her call to burn down the canon is akin to creating a new Burning Man Festival, as undiverse as the one we have now.

It was only when I sat down to talk to other writers of color about Watkins' talk that everyone was buzzing about, that I was able to parse out my feelings. The other writers also expressed a nagging dissatisfaction with the talk, a feeling that it didn't quite speak to them. I remember saying that I thought the lecture represented progress because it referenced the experiences of people of color, even if the references were hollow. I went on to note that five years ago, it was unlikely that the lecture would have included any references to people of color.

To navigate the writing world as a woman of color writer is a complicated thing—sometimes you find conflict in the very space that you found community, you find pain in the very individual you found inspiration. Just a few weeks ago I was reading the latest issue of a literary magazine that includes work by a few writer friends. I turned the pages savoring their work and was thrilled to also discover brilliant work by writers and poets I didn't know of before. Then I turned the page and felt a jolt of recognition—it was a poem by Michael Derrick Hudson, the white male poet who assumed the pseudonym of Yi-Fen Chou because he claimed it was a surefire shortcut to publication. I forced myself to read his poem because I wanted to see and understand the poetry that came from a person whose actions I found so objectionable. I didn't like it. I wasn't impressed by its structural or thematic elements, but I will always be left with a nagging doubt about whether I gave it a truly fair read.

Two years ago, I was the only person of color in a nonfiction workshop held by the same magazine that published Watkins' piece. Although I noticed the lack of cultural diversity, I hoped it wouldn't be a barrier since I was workshopping a biography about an Indian American woman artist overlooked by history. I was told by fellow white women writers that in order for them to immerse themselves in her narrative, I needed to evoke the smell of cow dung and mangoes, which they thought were emblematic of life in India. I was also told to remove all of her quotes but to leave in a quote by James Joyce. And while I've seen and heard all manner of critiques in workshop directed at others and myself, even I was surprised by the lack of cultural sensitivity and wondered why no one else was struck by it, including the white female instructor. After the workshop I forced myself to review their critique once again. I realized that it wasn't that I needed to remove her quotes, which would only further erase her voice from history, but that I needed to do a better job of curating them. In my attempt to prioritize her voice, I was in danger of losing her story. I wasn't grateful to my fellow writers for this realization, but I did have gratitude for the experience, though offensive, that led me to this understanding.

Outside of this workshop, I was glad to see a lecture on the syllabus entitled *Beyond Sympathy; Writing Past the Cliches of Class, Race, and Subculture*. It was delivered by a white woman writer and while that, in itself, was not problematic, the lecture was. She seemed to conflate the obstacles, stigmas, and stereotypes of class, sexual identity, and racial and cultural identity with those faced by individuals who cosplay as pirates. I was deeply disappointed and couldn't help feeling like a meaningful opportunity to explore these issues had been lost, especially given what I was experiencing in my own workshop. During the question and answer period, I summoned the courage to ask a question. "How do we explore and address race and identity stereotypes, if the race and cultural identity of characters aren't developed?" I was stunned by the curt answer that came back to me. "Well, I don't believe in policing." I left the lecture stung by its unabashed inadequacy but thankful for the diverse cohort of writing friends I had made who felt the same way. The truth is that the same workshop that felt lacking in its racial diversity and cultural sensitivity is also one that introduced me to inspirational writers of color including Manuel Gonzalez, Major Jackson, Luis Alberto Urrea, and Natalie Díaz.

Just as I felt compelled to stand up and clap in the chapel last summer, I now found myself sharing Watkins' *On Pandering* on Facebook noting its importance for calling out pervasive patriarchy and misogyny in literature. And just as before, I felt a bit disingenuous. Thankfully, I stumbled upon social media responses from the likes of Porochista Khakpour, Roxane Gay, and Marlon James, some of the writers of color I most admire for their writing but also for their perspectives on being writers of color. Their responses validated my discomfort with the piece and offered insightful analysis. As an emerging forty-one year old writer, who worked for fifteen years in social change, on issues ranging from homelessness, to health disparities, to racial justice, I shouldn't need the words of fellow writers of color to validate my own understanding and experience, but I did. The next day, I erased my post and composed a new one explaining why I had removed it and my actual experience and mixed feelings about the piece.

Although I was initially embarrassed about putting up this replacement post, I soon came to feel squared away in my conscience, what Gandhi describes as when your thoughts, words, and actions are all in harmony. Within a short time, I began receiving positive affirmations from several other fellow writers of color, confessing that they had similar misgivings when they read the piece. More and more writers chimed in, thanking me for my honesty and we discussed both its positive points and where it fell short for us.

In the end, I agree partially with the lecturer about policing. The policing I most believe in is self-policing, wherein writers become aware of and engage their blind spots on race. But beyond this, I believe all writers, myself included, must engage what Junot Díaz refers to as the blind spots shaped like ourselves—the ones shaped by all the layers of our identities. And in my writing, I've been trying to live up to Watkins' important call to "use our words and our gazes to make the invisible visible. Let us tell the truth." Anything else would be pandering.

Chapter Reflection

Questions for Discussion

(Some of the following questions were generated by creative writing student Angela Compton.)

1   What privilege might you carry unknowingly in your writing? Why is it important to examine privilege? When you think about privilege, what feelings arise for you? Is it difficult or easy for you to talk about privilege—and why might this be the case? What from your background might condition your response to the idea of privilege?

2   Consider the concept of privilege in relation to the next poem, story, play, or essay that you read. What could be the role of privilege in this piece's coming-into-being, its publication history, or its content?

3   When we read in creative writing, we read with different lenses and for different purposes: We read to understand how a text works, how it was built and designed. We read to locate how a text fits in the web of other texts. We read to connect, to find ourselves in a text and to honor the vulnerability of the author who shares with us. We also read to consider the effects a text might have on the world, which prompts us to ask: To what extent does this text affirm or intervene in the attitudes, beliefs, expectations, and myths that circulate among its audiences?

4   Larry Diamond has argued in an essay titled "Fiction as Political Thought" that literature "is an active influence, reinforcing or refashioning values, beliefs, ideas, perceptions and aspirations. The teller of a story can become a powerful force in shaping the way a people think about their social and political order, and the nature, desirability and direction of change." What do you think of this idea?

Writing Prompt

Look at a piece of writing you've already drafted and that you're working to revise. Now read it with a word like "inequity" or "power" in your mind. What do you discover when you do this?

Suggestions for Further Reading

1   Nguyen, Viet Thanh. "Critic's Take: How Writers' Workshops Can Be Hostile." *New York Times* (April 2017).

2   Mura, David. *A Stranger's Journey: Race, Identity and Narrative Craft in Writing.* U of Georgia P, 2018.

3   Rankine, Claudia, Beth Loffreda, and Max King Cap, eds. *The Racial Imaginary: Writers on Race in the Life of the Mind.* Fence Books, 2015.

4   Row, Jess. "What Are White Writers For?" *New Republic* (September 2016).

For a list of responses to Díaz's "MFA vs. POC," see: Aitken, Neil. "Writers of Color Discussing Craft: An Invisible Archive." *De-Canon: A Visibility Project.* (May 2017). Web.

4

Representation

The Craft of Writing Queer

Barrie Jean Borich

Barrie Jean Borich is a creative nonfiction writer living in Chicago. Borich teaches at DePaul University, where she edits *Slag Glass City*, a digital journal of the urban essay arts. She is also a member of the MFA faculty of the Rainer Writing Workshop. Her books include *My Lesbian Husband* (Graywolf Press 2000), which received the ALA Stonewall Book Award; *Body Geographic* (American Lives/University of Nebraska Press 2013), winner of a Lambda Literary Award in Memoir and an IPPY (Independent Publisher Book Award) Gold Medal in Essay/Creative Nonfiction; and, most recently, *Apocalypse, Darling* (Machete/Ohio State University Press 2018). The following essay, which was published in the journal *Brevity* in 2012, explores the relationship between genre and gender and asks, "What if all nonfiction writers imagined a queer aesthetic at the center of our discourse?"

When I discovered creative nonfiction I'd just turned thirty, was self-schooled in queer and activist literatures, newly in love with the woman who is still my spouse, newly sober, even newly tattooed, and recently returned to university. I'd dropped out of pre-journalism school in the late 1970s, in part because no line of study fit me and no course syllabus included the books I was reading. More than one professor told me feminist and lesbian content was not literary and I didn't even know I could major in creative writing, so I left college to work as a community organizer, a waitress, a feminist theater publicist and a temp secretary—and to write.

When I returned to school, in the 1980s heyday of radical theory, the academic mood had changed. I knew I was a writer by then, and I was no longer the only one intent on studying writing in ways that put the desires of the body before convention. I began work on a self-designed BA that merged creative writing, poetics, film studies, a bit of feminist theory—trying to make a place for myself—but I also knew that places shift and lived narrative is never linear. Discovering, in a writing workshop, creative nonfiction was like finding my lost city.

What I've loved, from the start, about CNF has been the ways this genre is creatively weird, much like myself—both misunderstood and claimed by more than one constituency, attentive to form but difficult to classify, with quirky yet intentionally designed exteriors, slippery rules, a mutating understanding of identity, a commitment to getting past the bullshit and making unexpected connections, and a grounding in an unmasked, yet lyric, voice.

Half-a-dozen years later, at the Outwrite LGBT writers' conference, in one of those grand, flocked-wallpaper, old-city hotels, I convened a panel called *Creative Nonfiction: A Queer Genre?* I was interested by then in the ways the fluidity of gender in the queer community echoed the shifting genre parameters of this new-but-old literary category. I'd just published my first book, a memoir I described—to myself at least—as montage-prose, in the same way I described myself, on that panel, as a boho-femme-lesbian-creative-nonfiction-writer. In both cases I felt pulled to pin down the meaning of formal and corporeal experimentation. What were the concerns and possibilities of queer bodies and female autobiographical texts? I was still exploring my newly found genre city; my urge to define my non-story/non-poems was bound to a desire to name myself.

I know now, near to a quarter century into this work, that even the most familiar homes are partly invisible to their inhabitants, but I'm still interested in the act of naming who and where I am. So as much as I enjoy contemporary skirmishes over truthiness, appropriation, found fragment, and the efficacy of genre categories, I'm frustrated by the endlessly reproducing conference panels and web threads where a few men declare genre definitions passé, creating personality-centric controversies that dominate the conversation and avoid the messy intersections of actuality and text that drew me to nonfiction in the first place.

Why isn't the work of women, especially that of queer women, even the most successful and prolific among us—say Alison Bechdel, Mary Cappello, Michelle Tea—leading us into the central debates of our genre times? Why aren't we arguing about our concerns: the image and sense base (as in Bechdel's graphic memoirs) of body-centered narrative, or the merging of intellectual and narrative discourse (as in Cappello's books), or explicit depiction of women as sexual agents (as in the nonfiction/fiction-blurs of Michelle Tea), or whether (possibly the central question of our writing times) linear narrative is a form of mainstream captivity or an activist embrace of the social possibilities of storytelling.

It's fine to build a literary persona around eschewing category, rejecting definition, and refusing to self-describe. Fine, for some straight, white males who seem to have more categories than they need. As in all forms of privilege, it's the ones who can best afford to purge who create an ethos of absence, rather like the trust fund rebel who decides to give up his weekend Harley for the good of the environment. Those of us who've spent decades attempting to be seen—in literature, in families and communities, in workplaces and academic departments, in American law—might be less inclined to give up the names it took us so long to claim, or to spend our intellectual lives arguing about why we won't.

I do find the current controversies compelling and do read and teach (along with under-recognized books by queers, women, and writers of color) all the works nonfiction writers are fighting about. Yet these debates spin far from what the women in my communities need and want to write and read. I ask us to notice that once again women, especially queer women, are not setting the terms of the discussion.

There is no one queer nonfictional issue to replace the current conversation, and a feminist community revision would require that no one debate is central. Still, what I want most to talk about instead are ways our unconventional genre might claim a tradition of queerness and invite the production of work we haven't seen enough of yet. What if all nonfiction writers imagined a queer aesthetic at the center of our discourse?

By queer aesthetic I mean not just the work of queer authors but all voices and forms that are equally open to pleasure and injury, that are not afraid of the body, that are both sex-positive and self-critical, that are as interested in intersections and critique as they are in the personal politics of memory. Work that does not hold to sentimental definitions of love, marriage, monogamy, childrearing, family, and friendship; work that is as explicit and confessional as it needs to be, withholding only for reasons of flow, impact, and design rather than to uphold community, intellectual, or art-world standards; work that breaks rather than maintains codes, doesn't keep secrets to retain power, is eager to pay debts and reveal the means and archives of its own production.

This work I dream of is Cherríe-Moraga-meets-Eileen-Myles-meets-Audre Lorde meets Rebecca-Brown—meets-Dorothy-Allison-meets-Lois-Weaver-and-Peggy-Shaw-meets-Virgina-Woolf-meets-Maxine-Hong-Kingston-meets-drag-king-cabaret-meets-some-young-voice-we-haven't-heard-yet-meets-Shakespeare's-Sister, and is formed, aural, innovative, gorgeous, gender-aware art—according to both received and self-made models.

This is the work that as a journal editor I don't see enough of, from women or men, trans, queer or straight—I fear because such essays are not often enough written, or perhaps not frequently enough rewarded with publication, kudos, tenure. What I do see is queerish content with too little attention to form, and queerish form with too little attention to content. As an editor I seek out the work that is a synthesis of both—what I taught myself to write first in the damp basement apartments of my youth, making up both body and form, within the tensions of my still-barely-visible city, from the scraps that came to me from bed to mouth to page.

Writing Trans Characters

Alex DiFrancesco

Alex DiFrancesco is a fiction writer and essayist. Among their books is an essay collection called *Psychopomps* from Civil Coping Mechanisms Press (2019) and a novel called *All City* from Seven Stories Press (2019). Their fiction has appeared in the *Carolina Quarterly*, *New Ohio Review*, and *Monkeybicycle*. Nonfiction has appeared in the *Washington Post*, *Tin House*, and *Crixeo*. Their storytelling has been featured at The Fringe Festival, Life of the Law, The Queens Lit Festival, and The Heart podcast. The following essay appeared as a craft essay in *Brevity* in 2015.

When I was in my early twenties in the early part of the aughts, I gravitated towards anything with a transgender character. Hubert Selby's *Last Exit to Brooklyn*, John Cameron Mitchell's *Hedwig and the Angry Inch*, the bizarre zombie flick and Guitar Wolf vehicle *Wild Zero*, The Kink's "Lola," Lou Reed's "Walk on the Wild Side." Because these books and films and songs were largely written by cis (non-trans) people, there was never anything about the day to day of these characters included. They were tragic, or glamorous, or both, but they were certainly not real to me. It's no wonder that, though I devoured these depictions, it wasn't until I was in my thirties that I realized I was trans myself. I didn't know of any trans-masculine characters at all.

I began a few years ago to discover the fiction of trans authors. Imogen Binnie's *Nevada* is almost queer canon, and in it I was delighted to find a main character who was funny, smart, a jerk, and dealt with issues like working in retail and getting lied to by her girlfriend. And though Maria, the main character of *Nevada*, does her share of heroin, she's a far cry from Selby's overdosing Georgette. In the Brit Mandelo edited collection of speculative fiction *Beyond Binary*, I found characters who moved between genders and sexualities fluidly and, despite their far-flung and often fantastical worlds, spoke to my own identity as a genderqueer person. In Casey Plett's collection of stories, *A Safe Girl to Love*, the characters face the broad violence that trans people encounter—from over-aggressive sex with a trusted friend's roommate to being chased down the street by transphobes—but they are never defined by it. They are characters who take each other in, sleep with each other, lie to each other, befriend each other, work together, know one another's parents—in short, they are characters bound by their transness, but it is not the entirety of who they are.

The project of many trans writers who write trans characters seems to be to bring these characters to trans readers—a demographic who rarely see themselves portrayed accurately in literature. But why do cis writers choose to write trans characters? Too often the answer is to present a symbol for the quest for self, because trans is the word of the moment, to sensationalize, or to present the trans character as a foil for the cis characters in the story. If a cis writer is to view trans characters beyond these ends, to write them as fleshed out humans with aspirations, who have overcome obstacles, who exist three-dimensionally, a great deal of work needs to be done beyond what currently exists in literature.

So how does one write a trans character? The big secret is that there is no such thing as "the trans experience." Trans characters may have some things in common: some of them may have come out at some point in their lives, which can go a variety of ways, or happen at a variety of ages—others may be every bit as trans and never admit it to anyone; many have lost the love and support of their families, but others have not; some trans people experience dysphoria, the sensation of being at odds with the gender they were assigned at birth and elements of their physical body, while others do not; trans people may or may not choose to transition in any number of ways including socially (e.g. gender presentation, changed name or pronouns), hormonally, or surgically; trans people statistically experience high rates of homelessness, intimate partner violence, rape, and murder while other trans people live in mansions with people who love and support them. These are all important things to consider if you are writing a trans character, but, unless you are writing a story about their transition (which far too many trans narratives by cis writers seem focused on), a lot of these questions will just be deep character background. Furthermore, while trans characters will inevitably have common points to their stories, there are many things about them that need to surprise and delight the reader—they'll need hobbies like knitting or strong political affiliations or literary heroes or undying dedications to brands of sneakers. It seems to be easier for trans writers to keep this in mind and not try to make trans characters symbols like Hedwig or wrecks like Georgette.

I recently wrote a short sci-fi story. In it, there are characters who change gender. Two of these characters are most comfortable in an agender presentation, but that is where their similarities end. One comes from an open-minded region with people who, even if they didn't understand them, accepted them. This character is quiet, reserved, level-headed, always planning the best way of doing things, self-confident. The other is from a wild-west like outpost, experienced "corrective" rape as a child, and is constantly in fight-or-flight mode, looking for the best way to mold any situation to their benefit. Though their non-conforming gender identities mirror each other, their radically different backgrounds make them complete opposites.

I tell these stories because, in many ways, they are my stories. When these two characters find each other, they feel like they are the only people like them who ever existed—as my partner and I did after coming out to each other, and before finding the support of the LGBTQIA community. I feel a propriety over stories like these, and though I would never tell a writer they could not write a character who is unlike them, I would tell a writer that they must understand these stories deeply if they are ever to tell them with conviction.

Today, with trans books by trans authors to read, I don't need Lola and I don't need Georgette. I can't change the writing about trans characters that I grew up with, and I can't change the effect they had on me as a person. But I and the rest of the trans community can insist that we be portrayed accurately, even if that means we're the main ones doing it.

White Flights

American Fiction's Racial Landscape

Jess Row

Jess Row is the author of two collections of short stories, *The Train to Lo Wu* and *Nobody Ever Gets Lost*, and a novel, *Your Face in Mine*. His stories have appeared three times in *The Best American Short Stories*, and have won two Pushcart Prizes and a PEN/O. Henry Award. His nonfiction appears often in *The New York Times Book Review, Bookforum, The New Republic*, and other venues. "White Flights," which reviews tendencies in American fiction's representation of race, originally appeared in Boston Review in 2013, and is the basis for his first collection of essays, *White Flights: Race, Fiction, and the American Imagination* (2019).

There's a moment toward the end of Marilynne Robinson's *Housekeeping* when Ruth, the young narrator whose mother has recently committed suicide, finds herself utterly alone. She is exploring an abandoned homestead at the edge of a lake while her eccentric and unreliable aunt Sylvie has wandered off, perhaps never to be seen again. Ruth imagines the homesteaders who once lived there and the ghosts of children who died there, until gradually she begins to feel herself among them, more ghostly than real.

"Loneliness is an absolute discovery," she says,

> When one looks from inside at a lighted window, or looks from above at the lake, one sees the image of oneself in a lighted room, the image of oneself among trees and sky—the deception is obvious, but flattering all the same. When one looks from the darkness into the light, however, one sees all the difference between here and there, this and that. Perhaps all unsheltered people are angry in their hearts, and would like to break the roof, spine, and ribs, and smash the windows and flood the floor and spindle the curtains and bloat the couch.

A few moments later she gives in to this feeling of abandonment and lies down on the grass: "Sylvie is nowhere, and sometime it will be dark. I thought, Let them come unhouse me of this flesh, and pry this house apart."

While the kind of total isolation Robinson describes is quite unusual in late twentieth century America, the feeling Ruth experiences for a moment—what we can only call social guilt, the knowledge that out there, on any given night, are others raging against the cold and the indifference of a world that refuses to house them decently—is not. One could almost call this an allusion to the looming problem of homelessness (*Housekeeping* was published in 1980) if the novel didn't immediately send Ruth into a spiral of self-pity and despair that excludes everything outside herself. Loneliness, after all, is an "absolute" discovery—a state, that is, of exquisite and bottomless self-absorption. In making such claims for uniqueness, isolation, and solitude, *Housekeeping* is, in a fundamental way, antisocial.

In a 2012 essay about the origins of *Housekeeping*, "When I Was A Child I Read Books," Robinson reflects on European history and classical literature, the most important companions of her childhood in a remote Idaho town. "Relevance was precisely not an issue for me," she says,

> But I think it was in fact particularly Western to feel no tie of particularity to any single past or history, to experience that much underrated thing called deracination, the meditative, free appreciation of whatever comes under one's eye.

"Deracination" is a fascinating word. The *Oxford English Dictionary* sources it in the French *deraciné, racine* meaning "root," and gives it the meaning "to pluck or tear up by the roots, eradicate, exterminate," with the secondary meaning of "uprooted from one's national or social environment." In a British context, it means "rootless" in the pejorative sense: a pretender, an *arriviste*, a fraud. But—not entirely surprisingly—in the hands of Marilynne Robinson, a firm believer in American uniqueness, it turns into an ideal: an Englishman's self-eradication is an Idahoan's starting point. In American language, we can't help but acknowledge that the word defines itself, *OED* or no: it means not to strip the roots but to strip away race, to de-race oneself.

Language, as any philosopher or critical theorist will tell you, is its own kind of real estate, a field, whose ownership is hotly contested, and so it's no surprise that Robinson stakes her claim to the American present by a reclamation, a reordering of words: race, identity, community, individual, democracy. At the same time, Calvinist that she is, she stresses that the struggle to undo race and achieve individuality is already lost. In modern culture, loneliness is seen as a pathology: "By some sad evolution . . . now people who are less shaped and constrained by society are assumed to be disabled and dangerous." In another instance, but on the same theme, she lingers on how the word "identity" has changed from Whitman's time to our own: "Rather than acknowledging the miraculous privilege of existence as a conscious being," she writes, "identity seems now to imply membership in a group, through ethnicity or affinity or religion or otherwise . . . and this is taken to be a good thing."

Robinson's work derives much of its distinctive power from the way it brings an old and mostly forgotten severity of language and spirit back, just barely, into American English. But deracination is a long-lived and nearly universal trope in white American literature, and it remains an ideal and a covert fantasy in a country which today is about as far from racially homogeneous as has been possible in the history of humankind. In the most superficial moral sense, deracination invokes the old dream of colorblindness, the chimera of "the content of our character." Subconsciously deracination probably has more to do with a desire not to have one's visual field constantly invaded by inconveniently different faces—relationships that are fraught, unfixed, capable of producing equal measures of helplessness and guilt. But there is also, perhaps almost too easy to ignore, the question of scale—the scale our lives are measured against, the fundamental American desire to stand out on the horizon, alone with our thoughts, to be a figure against the visual field around us.

For many white writers since the 1960s, the fantasy of deracination has become uncoupled from the wilderness as such. Wilderness is now more and more remote, as a concept or a destination, and has migrated onto the experience of landscape more generally—absorption in a landscape, confinement within a landscape, quest for a landscape, loneliness or alienation within a landscape. These landscapes, where inner and outer experience fuses in interesting ways, are nearly always empty of people of color. Of course, the absence of the original inhabitants is a defining, if usually unacknowledged, trope of American nature writing, but here I'm talking about a broader and more willful kind of elimination—a turn toward regions, spatial and psychic, where whiteness is once again normative, invisible, unquestioned, and unthreatened, and where repressed social guilt becomes a vague subjective state of discomfort and anomie, if it does not evaporate altogether.

* * *

In *Crabgrass Frontier* (1987), his definitive study of the rise of American suburbia after World War II, historian Kenneth Jackson lays out the facts very simply: compared to every other industrialized country, "the United States has thus far been unique in four important respects . . . : affluent and middle-class Americans live in suburban areas that are far from their work places, in homes that they own, and in the center of yards that by urban standards elsewhere are enormous."

What Jackson doesn't say—at least in part because it's implicitly obvious—is that each of these four characteristics (population density, home ownership, residential status, commuting distance) is tinged, if not altogether saturated, with the racial history of the postwar era.

Speaking very loosely, we can divide this history into two periods: that of active, explicit racism, from the 1940s to the 1970s, in which most of our present-day suburbs were established, and that of implicit racism, elective segregation, and racism-by-proxy, beginning with forced busing and still operating robustly today. This second period transformed the suburbs and gave birth to "exurbs." In these formerly rural areas, far from urban centers, development occurs very quickly, town centers spring up mostly on an ad-hoc basis (if at all), and workers commute long distances to cities or to the suburbs themselves.

During the first period, the suburbs played a leading role in one subset of American fiction—most obviously the works of Richard Yates and John Cheever. In those days the suburbs were new, but a generation later they became a theme and a subject in themselves. By the 1980s, when the center of gravity in American fiction had shifted back toward conventional, descriptive, narrative realism in the 1980s—it was the heyday of Raymond Carver, Richard Bausch, Tobias Wolff, Ann Beattie, Anne Tyler, Mary Gordon, Joyce Carol Oates, and Alice Adams—and the suburbs were a *fait accompli*. So too was the assumed failure of the great project of integration and racial reconciliation that occupied Baby Boomers in their youth.

Probably the most astute chronicler of this second postwar period is Charles Baxter, whose early stories traverse the suburbs and exurbs of Detroit, industrial America's imploded icon. In "Fenstad's Mother," a white, thirty-something, childless, divorced computer programmer and composition teacher, whose great joy in life is ice skating—"to express grief on skates seemed almost impossible"—visits his mother, who was once a minor luminary in the civil rights movement and now is in the early stages of dementia:

> The apartment smelled of soap and Lysol, the signs of an old woman who wouldn't tolerate nonsense. Out on her coffee table, as usual, were the letters

she was writing to her congressman and to political dictators. . . . Martin
Luther King's eyes locked into his from the framed picture on the wall
opposite him. In the picture King was shaking hands with Fenstad's mother,
the two of them surrounded by smiling faces.

Deracination, in Baxter's stories, is largely an unintended, unwanted side effect
of geography: the collapse of the public sphere by the disappearance of the
public square, what we might call the atomizing effects of the Reagan era,
when the late Margaret Thatcher told us that there is "no such thing as society."
Deracination here is a profound sense of helplessness that extends from
questions of historical purpose and racial justice down into the earth itself.

Describing the landscape of southeast Michigan in his story "Westland,"
Baxter writes:

> This land has been beaten up. The industrial brass knuckles have been applied
> to wipe out the trees, and the corporate blackjack has stunned the soil, and
> what grows there—the grasses and brush and scrub pine—grows tentatively.
> The plant life looks scared and defeated, but all the other earthly powers are
> busily at work.

A more typical writer of this era, Ann Beattie, elides race simply by
narrowing the aperture of her lens to one rigidly demarcated social milieu—
northeastern, white, liberal semi-bohemians, most of whom originate in New
York City and then flee to Westchester, Connecticut, Vermont, Maine, Utah,
Key West. (Not for nothing is her selected stories entitled *Park City.*) Beattie's
characters, like so many people of their generation and demographic, see
certain landscapes, certain visual and spatial markers, as a comprehensive
balm for all that ails them: to choose one example among a thousand, Tom,
a bereft divorced father in "Greenwich Time,"

> makes the night-light pulse like a buoy bobbing in the water and tries to
> imagine that his bed is a boat, and that he is setting sail, as he and Amanda
> did years before, in Maine, where Perkins Cove widens into the choppy, ink-
> blue ocean.

Often, as one might expect, these fantasies turn out badly—the vacation
houses are sold, or abandoned; the supposedly quaint town is vulgar and
overpriced; the neighbors disappoint; the new friendship goes sour—but
Beattie's faith in the enterprise remains largely unchanged, if to judge only
by the fact that her stories have followed the same trajectory for nearly four
decades. And Beattie is a relatively mild and agnostic example: more fervent
adherents of the cult of Elsewhere—Annie Proulx, Kent Haruf, Rick Bass,
Jim Harrison, Robinson herself—have tailored their whole careers around

remote, awe-inducing landscapes peopled by quirky, salt-of-the-earth, hard-living folks, nearly all of whom happen to be white.

* * *

If we come to see ownership and flight as the two interdependent forces, in yin-yang fashion, shaping white American experience in the late twentieth and early twenty-first centuries, we couldn't ask for a better literary icon than Richard Ford, whose novels and stories have ridden both of these trajectories more or less simultaneously, moving back and forth from the New Jersey suburbs of his celebrated Pulitzer-winning Frank Bascombe trilogy to the mountain-and-plains West of such books as *Rock Springs* (1987), *Wildlife* (1990), and *Canada* (2012). Ford also represents a third notable chapter of this same story: that of a child of the Jim Crow South. Ford left Jackson, Mississippi for Michigan State as a teenager, determined—as he suggested in a 1996 *Paris Review* interview—to leave his Southern identity behind:

> I simply didn't understand some very fundamental things in Mississippi in the early sixties and fifties: why it was we went to separate schools, why all this violence. . . . I couldn't piece it out, couldn't make racism make sense. . . . I was not brave enough or committed enough or selfless enough to stay in Mississippi during the civil-rights movement. . . . I wasn't enlightened. I was nothing, that's what I was. But I knew I was a little nothing—which helped.

The defining feature of Ford's work could be summed up in the word "rootlessness," both in the subjective sense—refusal to be defined by one's family of origin, hometown, region—and in the broader, if not quite objective sense: a resistance to the claims of any kind of history or consciousness of the past. It's this second rootlessness—what Robinson calls "the meditative, free appreciation of whatever comes under one's eye"—that characterizes Frank Bascombe, who in other ways is very much a stick-in-the-mud, a transplanted Southerner who settles in New Jersey as a young family man and stays through three careers and two marriages into prostate-ridden old age. In a characteristic early passage in *The Sportswriter* (1986), Bascombe puts it this way:

> My own history I think of as a postcard with changing scenes on one side but no particular or memorable messages on the back. You can get detached from your beginnings, as we all know, and not by any malevolent designs, just by life itself, fate, the tug of the ever-present. The stamp of our parents on us and the past in general is, to my mind, overworked, since at some point we are whole and by ourselves upon the earth, and there is nothing that can change that for better or worse, and so we might as well think about something more promising.

Or, to put it even more baldly, a little earlier in the novel: "There are no transcendent themes in life. In all cases things are here and they're over, and that has to be enough. The other view is a lie of literature and the liberal arts."

Make that an emphasis on the word "liberal." What Bascombe articulates here, and what Ford has made clear in his personal essays, could be called a kind of homespun existentialism, or pragmatic, bedrock American common sense, or post-Protestant agnosticism, but in its most basic formulation it's what the philosopher J.M. Bernstein has called the ideology of the "sovereign individual," the belief shared by virtually every American conservative:

> We presume the government is answerable to us, governs only with our consent, our dependence on it a matter of detached, reflective endorsement; and further, that we intrinsically possess a battery of moral rights that say we can be bound to no institution unless we possess the rights of 'voice and exit.' . . . All these institutions and practices should be seen as together *manufacturing*, and even inventing, the idea of a sovereign individual who becomes, through them and by virtue of them, the ultimate source of authority . . . suppressing to the point of disappearance the manifold ways that individuality is beholden to a complex and uniquely modern form of life.

What makes Ford's work so appealing, I think, even to people who don't accept (or don't pay attention to) the political implications of his logic, is that he invests this sovereign individuality with great pathos. He makes it seem, as few others have, the necessary, natural, unavoidable order of things. Take, for example, the story "Optimists," from *Rock Springs*, in which a middle-aged man recounts in great detail the night when, at fourteen, he witnessed his father murder another man by punching him in the heart. After that night, the boy lived with his mother for two more years while his father was in prison. Then he joined the Army, leaving the wreckage of his unhappy family behind. "I was apart from all of it," he says. "And when you are the age I was then, and loose on the world and alone, you can get along better than at almost any other time, because it's a novelty, and you can act for what you want, and you can think that being alone will not last forever." But being alone, apparently, *does* last forever. At the end of the story, the man meets his mother in a supermarket; they have not seen each other in fifteen years, and he is all but incapable of accounting for himself:

> 'I've been down in Rock Springs, on the coal boom,' I said. 'I'll probably go back down there.'
> 'And I guess you're married, too.'
> 'I was,' I said. 'But not right now.'
> 'Do you ever see your dad?'

'No,' I said. 'I never do.'

'I wish we knew each other better, Frank,' my mother said to me. She looked down, and I think she may have blushed. 'We have our deep feelings, though, don't we? Both of us.'

'Yes,' I said. 'We do.'

'So. I'm going out now,' my mother said. 'Frank.' She squeezed my wrist and walked away through the checkout and into the parking lot.

The Irish writer Frank O'Connor, in his book *The Lonely Voice* (1963), called these kinds of characters a "submerged population," that is, a marginalized, isolated group capable of evoking great pity. But in truth Ford's characters are never really played for our sympathy: their reticence, their hard-won self-sufficiency and disinterest in family ties, are not antiheroic in the existential sense but *actually* heroic. The wisdom granted by their sometimes-tragic circumstances doesn't just assuage their pain; it allows them to affirm their authentic selves.

What unites Ford with other writers of the same persuasion (including Beattie, Raymond Carver, Tobias Wolff, Bobbie Ann Mason, and Joy Williams) is a belief that individuals are best exposed (or only exposed) against a largely erased background, a deliberately subtracted and elided social and cultural context. Strangely, though this approach is highly stylized and deliberately artificial, critics have always described these writers as realists: Joyce Carol Oates praised *Rock Springs* as "the very poetry of realism." This kind of wishful thinking explains a great deal about the spatial imagination of the '80s, in which the minimalist aesthetic embraced "a concept of 'free' space, unrelated to intention," to quote Jay Parini's essay as the critic Jay Parini once wrote about Beattie. But, as any real estate developer knows, there is no such thing as free space. To put it more plainly, the non-assertion of privilege, even the rejection of privilege, doesn't mean that the privilege disappears. It only becomes more difficult to dislodge.

* * *

The problem with reading Ford sympathetically—as an anguished Southern exile who has tried to develop a broader frame of reference, a kind of humanistic, individuated outlook impossible in the land of his birth—is that he has a habit of crossing over the lines of normative, polite, post—Civil Rights era behavior. In all of his books, including last year's *Canada*, his present-day narrators—white men who live well outside the South—refer to black people, repeatedly if not consistently, as "Negroes." In the first paragraph of *Independence Day*, set in 1988, Ford sensuously evokes the town of Haddam, New Jersey in midsummer: "Summer floats over tree-softened streets like a sweet lotion balm from a careless, languorous god." And

> In the Negro trace, men sit on stoops, pants legs rolled above their sock tops, sipping coffee in the growing, easeful heat.

"Negro trace" draws on a common Southern expression for a neighborhood or quarter, but it is completely out of character in a novel about New Jersey in the '80s. No one in Haddam—or Princeton, its real analogue—would have any idea what Frank Bascombe meant if he used the phrase in conversation. A few pages later he renames it the "darktown section." Moreover, the description of men "sitting on stoops, pants legs rolled above their sock tops," brings to mind pictures of sharecropper's shacks in the South, an image more appropriate of *To Kill a Mockingbird*.

It would be unfair and inaccurate to say that Ford's relationship with black characters remains at this level of stereotype and objectification, just as it would be unfair to say, as many people assume, that as an ex-Southerner he has tried to erase or evade the presence of black people in his fictional America. Race, he says, is a subject that he would rather avoid, but in point of fact he can't resist bringing it up in idiosyncratic, sometimes troubling, sometimes moving ways. *Independence Day*, which strikes all the notes of the major chord called America—July 4, the Baseball Hall of Fame, *Self Reliance*, The Declaration of Independence—is also, when viewed as a very loose but still-consistent plot, a parable of racial reconciliation. Though the novel's focus is Bascombe's disastrous attempt to heal his troubled teenage son Paul by taking him to Cooperstown, that quest is framed by Bascombe's agonizing efforts to sell a home to a highly annoying pair of clients, the Markhams. The Markhams are, for complicated reasons, leaving an idyllic pottery-making life in Vermont for what Bascombe calls, over and over, "the real world." The Markhams can't even begin to afford the kind of house they want, and Bascombe would like nothing more than to rent them one of two houses he happens to own in the Negro trace. Not that Bascombe is a slumlord—at least not by his own admission. He invested in this property, he says, partly to "stash money where it'd be hard to get at," but mostly for "the satisfaction of reinvesting in my community":

> I would, I felt, be the perfect modern landlord: a man of superior sympathies and sound investments, with something to donate from years of accumulated life led thoughtfully if not always at complete peace. Everybody on the street

would be happy to see my car come cruising by, because they'd know I was probably stopping in to install a new faucet. . . . What I thought I had to offer was a deep appreciation for the sense of belonging and permanence the citizens of these streets might totally lack in Haddam (through no fault of their own), yet might long for the way the rest of us long for paradise. . . . The residents of Haddam's black neighborhood, I concluded, had possibly never felt at home where they were either, even though they and their relatives might've been here a hundred years. . . . And so what I thought I could do was at least help make two families feel at home and let the rest of the neighbors observe it.

It's an astonishing dramatization of what we might call postmodern white paternalism: "superior sympathies and sound investments." The Markhams, however, aren't buying it. Joe, the plug-ugly, snarling ex-potter, is an unreconstructed racist (odd, in a person from his time and place), and not until a dismaying series of reversals and the near-end of his marriage, plus the calamities Bascombe suffers in the meantime, does Joe finally, inevitably suffer a change of heart, four hundred-odd pages later. Whereupon Bascombe exults in the triumph of his ideals: "Alive but unrecognized in their pleased but dizzied heads," he says of the Markhams,

> is at least now the *possibility* of calling on [the neighbors] with a hot huckleberry pie . . . of letting little dark-skinned kids sleep over; of nurturing what they both always knew they owned in their hearts but never exactly found an occasion to act on in the monochrome Green Mountains: that magical sixth-sense understanding of the other races.

"That magical sixth-sense understanding of the other races" isn't how anyone would describe Ford's own writing on race, in *Independence Day* or elsewhere. To use another Southern colloquialism, it's a hot mess, a mangling of excellent though questionable intentions, resentful subterfuge, orotund sentence architecture, and, more than all the rest, an unspeakable certitude that the speaker is free to declaim and an authority on whatever his eye rests upon. Ford's is a prose of ownership, of confidence in its own ontological condition. It reflects an unquestionable self-assurance that in our culture and era only white males can have.

And what happens, we might wonder, when this roving eye comes to rest on the subject of race itself? Ford's writing and interviews are full of asides on the subject, but the closest he's ever come to a full-on reckoning is a 1999 *New York Times Magazine* essay, "In the Same Boat." Ford's assignment—which in retrospect is so absurd it seems to have come out of a comic novel—was to travel down the Mississippi from Hannibal, Missouri, in a riverboat. He would be joined by Stanley Crouch, whom he had never met. Due to inclement weather, the riverboat trip barely happened. But Crouch and Ford, like any writers would, made the most of the opportunity to collect their checks. After beginning with obligatory remarks about *Huck Finn* and how Crouch was a very affable and pleasant man to spend a few hours with, Ford presents the good news and the bad news together:

> Most of what I currently think about race involves just the usual rotating miscellany of racial attitudes and reactions that are on most white people's minds—whites, that is, who aren't bigots. These include a self-conscious awareness that I wouldn't knowingly bar anybody from anything because of his race; that I don't get nervous when I see that my 747 pilot is black. . . . The usual liberal agenda. On the less ecumenical side. . . . "White" and "black" are not really races to me, and I have no wish to make them be, or to make being white a consideration in knowing me. And so I don't completely understand why black politics, black culture, black literature, black identity are still so widely sanctified and haven't become passé in the view of most intelligent people. [. . .]

This, in Ford's view, is how race appears as a subject to "most white people— who aren't bigots." There's perhaps no more honest expression of default white attitudes toward race in the age of white flight and re-segregation: for white people living in low-density suburbs or exurbs, which is to say most white Americans, to think about race is a choice, and not a very serious or meaningful one.

* * *

Why do well-intentioned, intelligent, thoughtful people so often fail to grasp the extent of their own privilege, and respond so belligerently to any suggestion that corrective action might be justified as compensation? One answer, developed over decades in academic circles, and now slowly filtering into the wider cultural conversation, is the concept of "invisible capital": the enormous interlocking network, or feedback loop, of social, cultural, and economic advantages that white people have historically possessed and passed down, often unconsciously, to their children. In *The Possessive Investment in Whiteness* (1998), the sociologist George Lipsitz argues that probably the least visible—and most significant—node in this network is control over real estate:

> Blacks are not likely to number themselves among the forty-six million Americans today who can trace the origins of their family wealth to the

Homestead Act of 1863, because almost all that land was allocated to whites. . . . 98 percent of Federal Housing Authority loans [between 1932 and 1962] went to whites. . . . The living legacy of past discrimination combines with the impact of contemporary discriminatory practices in mortgage lending, real estate sales, automobile credit financing, and employment to impose artificial impediments against asset accumulation . . . . Because they face an artificially restricted housing market, the current generation of blacks has lost $82 billion collectively; the next generation is likely to lose $93 billion.

It's not hard to imagine that the spatial deracination we've seen in white fiction of the last three decades arises out of a profound discomfort with the persistence of profound and worsening structural discrimination; deficits in education, resources, and health; and economic segregation even after the enormous changes of the Civil Rights era. Of course, there are any number of white writers of Ford's generation who have taken the opposite tack and written brave and wonderful novels that interweave characters of different races: Russell Banks, Madison Smartt Bell, Rosellen Brown, Susan Straight, Susan Richards Shreve, and Richard Price, just to name a few.

But those are lonely voices; those are the exceptions. The dominant strain of fiction by white writers in this era represents what we might cynically call a massive reinvestment in white identity through the demarcation of new terrain (the exurbs) or through the reinvention of old (wilderness, urban gentrification). A more generous interpretation would be to see this fiction as a kind of willed amnesia, underscored by the reluctance of many creative writing teachers to confront issues of race and identity directly in the classroom and by the disinclination of most prominent book critics—an overwhelmingly white group—to bring race into play when writing about white authors.

Deracination, as a fantasy, even as a whole category of thinking, isn't going anywhere. It's part of the American bedrock, like peanut butter, Paul Revere, and the personal Jesus. (It's present, in a different mode, in African American fiction too, from *Invisible Man* to Baldwin's "Stranger in the Village.") But among these writers of the last thirty or so years, it reflects not so much an interest in dispassionate empathy as an impulse toward erasure and avoidance. Deracination invokes a fear of the present, which boxes writers into smaller and smaller spaces.

Moreover it elides and whitewashes what Leslie Fiedler, in his seminal essay "Come Back Ag'in to the Raft, Huck Honey," called "that moral discrepancy before which we are helpless, having no resources for dealing with a conflict of principle and practice." In the most concrete sense, deracination underwrites the fantasies of escape that drive so many of our movements and impulses today: the desire to "get away from it all," to find our own piece of paradise, a gated, filtered, curated realm of experience in which the ordinary world is kept at bay.

If we think back to Ruth's moment of awakening to the plight of "all unhoused people" in *Housekeeping*, we can see how fragile, and how potent, the experience of radical empathy can be. Empathy, and a subsequent understanding of justice, can't be sustained in a vacuum. Yet, in so much contemporary American fiction, a vacuum is exactly what we have: a systematically, if not intentionally, denuded, sanitized landscape, at least when it comes to matters of race. An optimist might say that this trend can't possibly continue, but if we look at the popularity of the HBO series *Girls*—a fantasy of a virtually all-white, bohemian, twenty-something Brooklyn that critics hail as the "voice of a generation"—we might say that, to the contrary, spatial deracination has begun to metastasize. Nature may abhor a vacuum, but in our current situation, many American readers, even well-meaning ones, haven't learned to live outside one.

Which Subjects Are Underrepresented in Contemporary Fiction?

Ayana Mathis

Ayana Mathis is a novelist and faculty member at the Iowa Writers' Workshop. Mathis's first novel, *The Twelve Tribes of Hattie*, was a *New York Times* Bestseller, a *New York Times* Notable Book of the Year, one of NPR's Best Books of 2013 and was chosen by Oprah Winfrey as the second selection for Oprah's Book Club 2.0. The following response to the question of what is underrepresented in contemporary fiction was published in 2013 in *The New York Times* Bookends section with Siddhartha Deb.

Writers are a bit flummoxed by joy. With few exceptions, we (I am no less guilty than anyone else) seem to have decided that despair, alienation and bleakness are the most meaningful, and interesting, descriptors of the human condition. In our ennui and end-of-days malaise, we have elevated suffering to the highest of virtues. We are a postmodern band of medieval monks, self-flagellating and deprived, suspicious of the joy and fullness of life.

In our insistence on despair as the most authentic iteration of experience, we risk writing fiction that is hamstrung in its ability to represent our humanity with the necessary breadth and nuance. The despairing self, characterized by alienation and misery, is limited and incomplete, and not a particularly accurate representation of the lushness of life as it is lived, mingled thing that it is. In our fixation on bleakness, we echo a deleterious conception of our humanity already rampant in the culture. We court a literature that veers toward categories of discourse we mean to write against: the flattened depiction of the human being used in advertisements and political speeches.

In his "Summa Theologica," Thomas Aquinas wrote, "Joy and sorrow proceed from love, but in contrary ways." His conception is religious, of course, but we can consider it through a secular lens—joy and pain as reactions to the same stimulus, that is, the enormous complexity of being alive. Real joy is rare and transcendent. Think of the scene in Dostoyevsky's "The Brothers Karamazov" in which Dmitri hosts a frenzied fete, complete with dancing girls in bear costumes, in the village to which he escapes just before being arrested for his father's murder. Or the bucolic rapture William Wallace and company feel while dredging the river bottom for his pregnant wife's body in Eudora Welty's "The Wide Net." In both examples joy asserts itself unexpectedly in onerous circumstances, and its effect on the narrative is transformative.

Joy, it must be remembered, is nothing like happiness, its milquetoast cousin. It is instead a vivid and extreme state of being, often arrived at in the aftermath of great pain. I was reminded of this recently, during a class I teach on hip-hop music as a narrative form. Each week, my students and I listen to a few songs and think about what sorts of narrative devices they use; then we consider a piece of fiction that might have similar strategies and preoccupations. A few weeks ago we listened to Grandmaster Flash and the Furious Five's 1982 classic, "The Message." It describes a terrifying and dysfunctional reality, in which the people of the South Bronx of the '70s and early '80s were abandoned to slumlords, drugs, rampant arson and a reduction in desperately needed municipal and government services. After listening, one of my students described hip-hop music as a byproduct of a terrible situation, the sometimes gruesome expression of rage and woe of a people living in gruesome conditions. Another questioned the dissonance between the lyrics—"Got a bum education, double-digit inflation./Can't take the train to the job, there's a strike at the station"—and the lighthearted, up-tempo beat. The student found these elements contradictory and distracting. I suggest another interpretation: "The Message," like much of hip-hop, is a series of complicated gestures toward the exuberance the music elicits, which exists side by side with the pain sometimes described in the lyrics.

Hip-hop is more than lament, more than protest. It's a modern-day blues, which Albert Murray characterized as a vessel containing the whole of experience: sorrow and defeat and misery and also ecstasy, triumph and maintaining one's cool under near unbearable pressure. Hip-hop certainly includes its fair share of despair, but it also urges its listeners, and composers, toward a kind of revelry and transcendence in spite of it all — or perhaps because of it all. The joy in hip-hop is paradoxical and complicated, which is, of course, the stuff of fiction.

Chapter Reflection

Questions for Discussion

1   Toni Morrison has defined "master narrative" as "whatever ideological script that is being imposed by the people in authority on everybody else." The master narrative governs what is designated "true" or "right" or "real," and stands to denigrate or silence any experience that falls outside of its designation. How is the idea of a "master narrative" related to the question of what does and doesn't get represented in contemporary literature? ("Representation" can be defined as the way we write about our subjects—the way we construct, describe, and develop our subjects, what we choose to include, what we choose to leave out.)

2   Speaking of hip-hop specifically but in a way that applies also to other literary and cultural forms, Mathis's essay identifies how "the exuberance the music elicits . . . exists side by side with the pain." Think of a text that allows exuberance and pain to exist side-by-side. How does the text achieve this?

3   Imagine you were asked to write a short craft essay titled "The Craft of Writing _____" or "Writing _____ Characters," in the mode of Borich's and DiFrancesco's essays. What would you write about? How would you help fellow writers think about your topic in more nuanced, complex, and respectful ways?

4   Imagine you were asked to write a review essay about a particular tendency in a genre of your choice. Following the model of Row's essay, what observations would you offer about the common representations you see in your chosen genre?

Writing Prompt

Choose a piece you've drafted, and select a character that is referenced in it. Read your piece through this character's eyes. How do you imagine this person feels to read your representation of them? Do they see themselves in your representation, feel you truly know and understand them in all their dimensions and history? What words would they use to describe your portrayal: well-researched, complex, insightful, intimate, empathetic, respectful, fair? Or presumptuous, stereotypical, caricatured, offensive?

Suggestions for Further Reading

1 Adichie, Chimamanda Ngozi. "The Danger of a Single Story." TED Talks (July 2009). Web.
2 Bartlett, Jennifer, Sheila Black, and Michael Northen, eds. *Beauty Is a Verb: The New Poetry of Disability.* Cinco Puntos, 2011.
3 Morrison, Toni. *Playing in the Dark: Whiteness and the Literary Imagination.* Vintage, 1993.
4 Shawl, Nisi, and Cynthia Ward. *Writing the Other: A Practical Approach.* Aqueduct Press, 2005.
5 Also see the articles published in the October/November 2016 issue of the AWP *Writer's Chronicle.*

5

Language

Language and Literature from a Pueblo Indian Perspective

Leslie Marmon Silko

Leslie Marmon Silko is an essayist, poet, and fiction writer. She has described herself in this way: "I am of mixed-breed ancestry, but what I know is Laguna" (from an interview with Alan Velie). Her essay "Language and Literature from a Pueblo Indian Perspective" began as an oral presentation and was later adapted into text, appearing in *English Literature: Opening Up the Canon* (Johns Hopkins, 1981). In the oral presentation, Silko purposefully did not read from a prepared paper, enabling her audience to experience the characteristics of oral tradition that the essay below portrays—the message is in the means. In what follows, one learns how language is story, connection, and identity. Each word is its own story and as the words are built upon, one-by-one, a web is created. Silko is well-known for her books *Ceremony* (1977), *Storyteller* (1981), and *Almanac of the Dead* (1991); short stories such as "Lullaby," "Yellow Woman," and "Tony's Story"; and poetry collections *Laguna Woman* (1974) and *Rain* (1996). (Introduction written by creative writing student Jan Calderon.)

Where I come from, the words most highly valued are those spoken from the heart, unpremeditated and unrehearsed. Among the Pueblo people, a written speech or statement is highly suspect because the true feelings of the speaker remain hidden as she reads words that are detached from the occasion and the audience. I have intentionally not written a formal paper because I want you to *hear* and to experience English in a structure that follows patterns from the oral tradition. For those of you accustomed to being taken from point A to point B to point C, this presentation may be somewhat difficult to follow. Pueblo expression resembles something like a spider's web—with many little threads radiating from the center, crisscrossing one another. As with the web, the structure emerges as it is made, and you must simply listen and trust, as the Pueblo people do, that meaning will be made.

My task is a formidable one: I ask you to set aside a number of basic approaches that you have been using and probably will continue to use, and, instead, to approach language from the Pueblo perspective, one that embraces the whole of creation and the whole of history and time.

What changes would Pueblo writers make to English as a language for literature? I have some examples of stories in English that I will use to address this question. At the same time, I would like to explain the importance of storytelling and how it relates to a Pueblo theory of language.

So I will begin, appropriately enough, with the Pueblo Creation story, an all-inclusive story of how life began. In this story, Tse'itsi'nako, Thought Woman, by thinking of her sisters, and together with her sisters, thought of everything that is. In this way, the world was created. Everything in this world was a part of the original Creation; the people at home understood that far away there were other human beings, also a part of this world. The Creation story even includes a prophecy that describes the origin of European and African peoples and also refers to Asians.

This story, I think, suggests something about why the Pueblo people are more concerned with story and communication and less concerned with a particular language. There are at least six, possibly seven, distinct languages among the twenty pueblos of the southwestern United States, for example, Zuñi and Hopi. And from mesa to mesa there are subtle differences in language. But the particular language being spoken isn't as important as what a speaker is trying to say, and this emphasis on the story itself stems, I believe, from a view of narrative particular to the Pueblo and other Native American peoples—that is, that language *is* story.

I will try to clarify this statement. At Laguna Pueblo, for example, many individual words have their own stories. So when one is telling a story and one is using words to tell the story, each word that one is speaking has a story of its own, too. Often the speakers, or tellers, will go into these word stories, creating an elaborate structure of stories within stories. This structure, which becomes very apparent in the actual telling of a story, informs contemporary Pueblo writing and storytelling as well as the traditional narratives. This perspective on narrative—of story within story, the idea that one story is only the beginning of many stories and the sense that stories never truly end—represents an important contribution of Native American cultures to the English language.

Many people think of storytelling as something that is done at bedtime, that it is something done for small children. But when I use the term *storytelling,* I'm talking about something much bigger than that. I'm talking about something that comes out of an experience and an understanding of that original view of Creation—that we are all part of a whole; we do not differentiate or fragment stories and experiences. In the beginning, Tse'itsi'nako, Thought Woman, thought of all things, and all of these things are held together as one holds many things together in a single thought.

So in the telling (and you will hear a few of the dimensions of this telling), first of all, as mentioned earlier, the storytelling always includes the audience, the listeners. In fact, a great deal of the story is believed to be inside the listener; the storyteller's role is to draw the story out of the listeners. The storytelling continues from generation to generation.

Basically, the origin story constructs our identity—with this story, we know who we are. We are the Lagunas. This is where we come from. We came this way. We came by this place. And so from the time we are very young, we hear these stories, so that when we go out into the world, when one asks who we are or where we are from, we immediately know: we are the people who came from the north. We are the people of these stories.

In the Creation story, Antelope says that he will help knock a hole in the Earth so that the people can come up, out into the next world. Antelope tries and tries; he uses his hooves but is unable to break through. It is then that Badger says, "Let me help you." And Badger very patiently uses his claws and digs a way through, bringing the people into the world. When the Badger clan people think of themselves, or when the Antelope people think of themselves, it is as people who are of *this* story, and this is *our* place, and we fit into the very beginning when the people first came, before we began our journey south.

Within the clans there are stories that identify the clan. One moves, then, from the idea of one's identity as a tribal person into clan identity, then to one's identity as a member of an extended family. And it is the notion of extended family that has produced a kind of story that some distinguish from other Pueblo stories, though Pueblo people do not. Anthropologists and ethnologists have, for a long time, differentiated the types of stories the Pueblos tell. They tended to elevate the old, sacred, and traditional stories and to brush aside family stories, the family's account of itself. But in Pueblo culture, these family stories are given equal recognition. There is no definite, preset pattern for the way one will hear the stories of one's own family, but it is a very critical part of one's childhood, and the storytelling continues throughout one's life. One will hear stories of importance to the family— sometimes wonderful stories—stories about the time a maternal uncle got the biggest deer that was ever seen and brought it back from the mountains. And so an individual's identity will extend from the identity constructed around the family—"I am from the family of my uncle who brought in this wonderful deer, and it was a wonderful hunt."

Family accounts include negative stories, too; perhaps an uncle did something unacceptable. It is very important that one keep track of all these stories—both positive and not so positive—about one's own family and other families. Because even when there is no way around it—old Uncle Pete *did* do a terrible thing—by knowing the stories that originate in other families, one is able to deal with terrible sorts of things that might happen within one's own family. If a member of the family does something that cannot be excused, one always knows stories about similarly inexcusable things done by a member of another family. But this knowledge is not communicated for malicious reasons. It is very important to understand this. Keeping track of all the stories within the community gives us all a certain distance, a useful perspective, that brings incidents down to a level we can deal with. If others have done it before, it cannot be so terrible. If others have endured, so can we.

The stories are always bringing us together, keeping this whole together, keeping this family together, keeping this clan together. "Don't go away, don't isolate yourself, but come here, because we have all had these kinds of experiences." And so there is this constant pulling together to resist the tendency to run or hide or separate oneself during a traumatic emotional experience. This separation not only endangers the group but the individual as well—one does not recover by oneself.

Because storytelling lies at the heart of Pueblo culture, it is absurd to attempt to fix the stories in time. "When did they tell the stories?" or "What time of day does the storytelling take place?"—these questions are nonsensical from a Pueblo perspective, because our storytelling goes on constantly: as some old grandmother puts on the shoes of a child and tells her the story of a little girl who didn't wear her shoes, for instance, or someone comes into the house for coffee to talk with a teenage boy who has just been in a lot of trouble, to reassure him that someone else's son has been in that kind of trouble, too. Storytelling is an ongoing process, working on many different levels.

Here's one story that is often told at a time of individual crisis (and I want to remind you that we make no distinctions between types of story— historical, sacred, plain gossip—because these distinctions are not useful when discussing the Pueblo *experience* of language). There was a young man who, when he came back from the war in Vietnam, had saved up his army pay and bought a beautiful red Volkswagen. He was very proud of it.

One night he drove up to a place called the King's Bar, right across the reservation line. The bar is notorious for many reasons, particularly for the deep arroyo located behind it. The young man ran in to pick up a cold six-pack, but he forgot to put on his emergency brake. And his little red Volkswagen rolled back into the arroyo and was all smashed up. He felt very bad about it, but within a few days everybody had come to him with stories about other people who had lost cars and family members to that arroyo, for instance, George Day's station wagon, with his mother-in-law and kids inside. So everybody was saying, "Well, at least your mother-in-law and kids weren't in the car when it rolled in," and one can't argue with that kind of story. The story of the young man and his smashed-up Volkswagen was now joined with all the other stories of cars that fell into that arroyo.

Now I want to tell you a very beautiful little story. It is a very old story that is sometimes told to people who suffer great family or personal loss. This story was told by my Aunt Susie. She is one of the first generation of people at Laguna who began experimenting with English—who began working to make English speak for us, that is, to speak from the heart. (I come from a family intent on getting the stories told.) As you read the story, I think you will hear that. And here and there, I think, you will also hear the influence of the Indian school at Carlisle, Pennsylvania, where my Aunt Susie was sent (like being sent to prison) for six years.

This scene is set partly in Acoma, partly in Laguna. Waithea was a little girl living in Acoma and one day she said, "Mother I would like to have some *yashtoah* to eat." *Yashtoah* is the hardened crust of corn mush that curls up. *Yashtoah* literally means "curled up." She said, "I would like to have some *yashtoah*," and her mother said, "My dear little girl, I can't make you any *yashtoah* because we haven't any wood, but if you will go down off the mesa, down below, and pick up some pieces of wood and bring them home, I will make you some *yashtoah*." So Waithea was glad and ran down the precipitous cliff of Acoma mesa. Down below, just as her mother had told her, there were pieces of wood, some curled, some crooked in shape, that she was to pick up and take home. She found just such wood as these.

She brought them home in a little wicker basket. First she called to her mother as she got home, "*Nayah, deeni!* Mother, upstairs!" The Pueblo people always called "upstairs" because long ago their homes were two, three stories, and they entered from the top. She said, "*Deeni! Upstairs!*" and her mother came. The little girl said, "I have brought the wood you wanted me to bring." And she opened her little wicker basket to lay out the pieces of wood, but here they were snakes. They were snakes instead of the crooked sticks of wood. And her mother said, "Oh my dear child, you have brought snakes instead!" She said, "Go take them back and put them back just where you got them." And the little girl ran down the mesa again, down below to the flats. And she put those snakes back just where she got them. They were snakes instead, and she was very hurt about this, and so she said, "I'm not going home. I'm going to Kawaik, the beautiful lake place Kawaik, and drown myself in that lake, byn'yah'nah [the 'west lake']. I will go there and drown myself."

So she started off, and as she passed by the Enchanted Mesa near Acoma, she met an old man, very aged, and he saw her running, and he said, "My dear child, where are you going?" "I'm going to Kawaik and jump into the lake there."

"Why?" "Well, because," she said, "my mother didn't want to make any *yashtoah* for me." The old man said, "Oh, no! You must not go, my child. Come with me and I will take you home." He tried to catch her, but she was very light and skipped along. And every time he would try to grab her she would skip faster away from him.

The old man was coming home with some wood strapped to his back and tied with yucca. He just let that strap go and let the wood drop. He went as fast as he could up the cliff to the little girl's home. When he got to the place where she lived, he called to her mother. *"Deeni!"* "Come on up!" And he said, "I can't. I just came to bring you a message. Your little daughter is running away. She is going to Kawaik to drown herself in the lake there." "Oh my dear little girl!" the mother said. So she busied herself with making the *yashtoah* her little girl liked so much. Corn mush curled at the top. (She must have found enough wood to boil the corn meal and make the *yashtoah*.)

While the mush was cooling off, she got the little girl's clothing, her *manta* dress and buckskin moccasins and all her other garments, and put them in a bundle—probably a yucca bag. And she started down as fast as she could on the east side of Acoma. (There used to be a trail there, you know. It's gone now, but it was accessible in those days.) She saw her daughter way at a distance and she kept calling: "Stsamaku! My daughter! Come back! I've got your *yashtoah* for you." But the little girl would not turn. She kept on ahead and she cried: "My mother, my mother, she didn't want me to have any *yashtoah*. So now I'm going to Kawaik and drown myself." Her mother heard her cry and said, "My little daughter, come back here!" "No," and she kept a distance away from her. And they came nearer and nearer to the lake. And she could see her daughter now, very plain. "Come back, my daughter! I have your *yashtoah*." But no, she kept on, and finally she reached the lake and she stood on the edge.

She had tied a little feather in her hair, which is traditional (in death they tie this feather on the head). She carried a feather, the little girl did, and she tied it in her hair with a piece of string; right on top of her head she put the feather. Just as her mother was about to reach her, she jumped into the lake. The little feather was whirling around and around in the depths below. Of course the mother was very sad. She went, grieved, back to Acoma and climbed her mesa home. She stood on the edge of the mesa and scattered her daughter's clothing, the little moccasins, the *yashtoah*. She scattered them to the east, to the west, to the north, to the south. And the pieces of clothing and the moccasins and *yashtoah* all turned into butterflies. And today they say that Acoma has more beautiful butterflies: red ones, white ones, blue ones, yellow ones. They came from this little girl's clothing.

The version I have given you is just as Aunt Susie tells it. You can occasionally hear some English she picked up at Carlisle—words like *precipitous*. You will also notice that there is a great deal of repetition, and a little reminder about *yashtoah* and how it is made. There is a remark about the cliff trail at Acoma—that it was once there but is there no longer. This story may be told at a time of sadness or loss, but within this story many other elements are brought together. Things are not separated out and categorized; all things are brought together, so that the reminder about the *yashtoah* is valuable information that is repeated—a recipe, if you will. The information about the old trail at Acoma reveals that stories are, in a sense, maps, since even to this day there is little information or material about trails that is passed around with writing. In the structure of this story the repetitions are, of course, designed to help you remember. It is repeated again and again, and then it moves on.

There are a great many parallels between Pueblo experiences and those of African and Caribbean peoples—one is that we have all had the conqueror's language imposed on us. But our experience with English has been somewhat different in that the Bureau of Indian Affairs schools were not interested in teaching us the canon of Western classics. For instance, we never heard of Shakespeare. We were given Dick and Jane, and I can remember reading that the robins were heading south for the winter. It took me a long time to figure out what was going on. I worried for quite awhile about our robins in Laguna because they didn't leave in the winter, until I finally realized that all the big textbook companies are up in Boston and *their* robins do go south in the winter. But in a way, this dreadful formal education freed us by encouraging us to maintain our narratives. Whatever literature we were exposed to at school (which was damn little), at home the storytelling, the special regard for telling and bringing together through the telling, was going on constantly.

And as the old people say, "If you can remember the stories, you will be all right. Just remember the stories." When I returned to Laguna Pueblo after attending college, I wondered how the storytelling was continuing (anthropologists say that Laguna Pueblo is one of the more acculturated pueblos), so I visited an English class at Laguna-Acoma High School. I knew the students had cassette tape recorders in their lockers and stereos at home, and that they listened to Kiss and Led Zeppelin and were well informed about culture in general. I had with me an anthology of short stories by Native American writers, *The Man to Send Rain Clouds*. One story in the book is about the killing of a state policeman in New Mexico by three Acoma Pueblo men in the early 1950s. I asked the students how many had heard this story and steeled myself for the possibility that the anthropologists were right, that the old traditions were indeed dying out and the students would be ignorant of the story. But instead, all but one or two raised their hands— they had heard the story, just as I had heard it when I was young, some in English, some in Laguna.

One of the other advantages that we Pueblos have enjoyed is that we have always been able to stay with the land. Our stories cannot be separated from their geographical locations, from actual physical places on the land. We were not relocated like so many Native American groups who were torn away from their ancestral land. And our stories are so much a part of these places that it is almost impossible for future generations to lose them—there is a story connected with every place, every object in the landscape.

Dennis Brutus has talked about the "yet unborn" as well as "those from the past," and how we are still *all* in *this* place, and language—the storytelling—is our way of passing through or being with them, of being together again. When Aunt Susie told her stories, she would tell a younger child to go open the door so that our esteemed predecessors might bring their gifts to us. "They are out there," Aunt Susie would say. "Let them come in. They're here, they're here with us *within* the stories."

A few years ago, when Aunt Susie was 106, I paid her a visit, and while I was there she said, "Well, I'll be leaving here soon. I think I'll be leaving here next week, and I will be going over to the Cliff House." She said, "It's going to be real good to get back over there." I was listening, and I was thinking that she must be talking about her house at Paguate village, just north of Laguna. And she went on, "Well, my mother's sister [and she gave her Indian name] will be there. She has been living there. She will be there and we will be over there, and I will get a chance to write down these stories I've been telling you." Now you must understand, of course, that Aunt Susie's mother's sister, a great storyteller herself, has long since passed over into the land of the dead. But then I realized, too, that Aunt Susie wasn't talking about death the way most of us do. She was talking about "going over" as a journey, a journey that perhaps we can only begin to understand through an appreciation for the boundless capacity of language that, through storytelling, brings us together, despite great distances between cultures, despite great distances in time.

How to Tame a Wild Tongue

Gloria Anzaldúa

Gloria Evangelina Anzaldúa (September 26, 1942–May 15, 2004) was a writer, scholar, and cultural theorist. Born to farm workers and raised on a ranch in South Texas, her writing explores the cultures found within the Mexico/Texas border and in Mexican and Indigenous histories. Her writing engages feminism, queer theory, and spirituality, intertwining matters of language, culture, sex, and identity. In the following essay, "How to Tame a Wild Tongue," from her book *Borderlands/La Frontera: The New Mestiza* (Aunt Lute, 1987), Anzaldúa blends poetry, prose, and different codes to trace how language can shape one's identity, and how language is tied to power. (Introduction written by creative writing student Jan Calderon.)

"We're going to have to control your tongue," the dentist says, pulling out all the metal from my mouth. Silver bits plop and tinkle into the basin. My mouth is a motherlode.

The dentist is cleaning out my roots. I get a whiff of the stench when I gasp. "I can't cap that tooth yet, you're still draining," he says.

"We're going to have to do something about your tongue," I hear the anger rising in his voice. My tongue keeps pushing out the wads of cotton, pushing back the drills, the long thin needles. "I've never seen anything as strong or as stubborn," he says. And I think, how do you tame a wild tongue, train it to be quiet, how do you bridle and saddle it? How do you make it lie down?

Who is to say that robbing a people of
its language is less violent than war?

—Ray Gwyn Smith[1]

I remember being caught speaking Spanish at recess—that was good for three licks on the knuckles with a sharp ruler. I remember being sent to the corner of the classroom for "talking back" to the Anglo teacher when all I was trying to do was tell her how to pronounce my name. "If you want to be American, speak 'American.' If you don't like it, go back to Mexico where you belong."

"I want you to speak English. *Pa' hallar buen trabajo tienes que saber hablar el inglés bien. Qué vale toda tu educación si todavía hablas inglés con un* 'accent,'" my mother would say, mortified that I spoke English like a Mexican. At Pan American University, I, and all Chicano students were required to take two speech classes. Their purpose: to get rid of our accents.

Attacks on one's form of expression with the intent to censor are a violation of the First Amendment. *El Anglo con cara de inocente nos arrancó la lengua.* Wild tongues can't be tamed, they can only be cut out.

Overcoming the Tradition of Silence

Ahogadas, escupimos el oscuro.
Peleando con nuestra propia sombra
el silencio nos sepulta.

En boca cerrada no entran moscas. "Flies don't enter a closed mouth" is a saying I kept hearing when I was a child. *Ser habladora* was to be a gossip and a liar, to talk too much. *Muchachitas bien criadas*, well-bred girls don't answer back. *Es una falta de respeto* to talk back to one's mother or father. I remember one of the sins I'd recite to the priest in the confession box the few times I went to confession: talking back to my mother, *hablar pa' 'trás, repelar. Hocicona, repelona, chismosa*, having a big mouth, questioning, carrying tales are all signs of being *mal criada*. In my culture they are all words that are derogatory if applied to women—I've never heard them applied to men.

The first time I heard two women, a Puerto Rican and a Cuban, say the word "*nosotras*," I was shocked. I had not known the word existed. Chicanas use *nosotros* whether we're male or female. We are robbed of our female being by the masculine plural. Language is a male discourse.

> And our tongues have become
> dry   the wilderness has
> dried out our tongues   and
> we have forgotten speech.
>
> —Irena Klepfisz[2]

Even our own people, other Spanish speakers *nos quieren poner candados en la boca.* They would hold us back with their bag of *reglas de academia.*

Oyé como ladra: el lenguaje de la frontera

Quien tiene boca se equivoca.

—Mexican saying

"*Pocho*, cultural traitor, you're speaking the oppressor's language by speaking English, you're ruining the Spanish language," I have been accused by various Latinos and Latinas. Chicano Spanish is considered by the purist and by most Latinos deficient, a mutilation of Spanish.

But Chicano Spanish is a border tongue which developed naturally. Change, *evolución, enriquecimiento de palabras nuevas por invención o adopción* have created variants of Chicano Spanish, *un nuevo lenguaje. Un lenguaje que corresponde a un modo de vivir*. Chicano Spanish is not incorrect, it is a living language.

For a people who are neither Spanish nor live in a country in which Spanish is the first language; for a people who live in a country in which English is the reigning tongue but who are not Anglo; for a people who cannot entirely identify with either standard (formal, Castilian) Spanish nor standard English, what recourse is left to them but to create their own language? A language which they can connect their identity to, one capable of communicating the realities and values true to themselves—a language with terms that are neither *español ni inglés*, but both. We speak a patois, a forked tongue, a variation of two languages.

Chicano Spanish sprang out of the Chicanos' need to identify ourselves as a distinct people. We needed a language with which we could communicate with ourselves, a secret language. For some of us, language is a homeland closer than the Southwest—for many Chicanos today live in the Midwest and the East. And because we are a complex, heterogeneous people, we speak many languages. Some of the languages we speak are:

1 Standard English
2 Working class and slang English
3 Standard Spanish
4 Standard Mexican Spanish
5 North Mexican Spanish dialect
6 Chicano Spanish (Texas, New Mexico, Arizona and California have regional variations)
7 Tex-Mex
8 Pachuco (called caló)

My "home" tongues are the languages I speak with my sister and brothers, with my friends. They are the last five listed, with 6 and 7 being closest to my heart. From school, the media and job situations, I've picked up standard and working class English. From Mamagrande Locha and from reading Spanish and Mexican literature, I've picked up Standard Spanish and

Standard Mexican Spanish. From *los recién llegados*, Mexican immigrants, and *braceros*, I learned the North Mexican dialect. With Mexicans I'll try to speak either Standard Mexican Spanish or the North Mexican dialect. From my parents and Chicanos living in the Valley, I picked up Chicano Texas Spanish, and I speak it with my mom, younger brother (who married a Mexican and who rarely mixes Spanish with English), aunts and older relatives.

With Chicanas from *Nuevo México* or *Arizona* I will speak Chicano Spanish a little, but often they don't understand what I'm saying. With most California Chicanas I speak entirely in English (unless I forget). When I first moved to San Francisco, I'd rattle off something in Spanish, unintentionally embarrassing them. Often it is only with another Chicana *tejana* that I can talk freely.

Words distorted by English are known as anglicisms or *pochismos*. The *pocho* is an anglicized Mexican or American of Mexican origin who speaks Spanish with an accent characteristic of North Americans and who distorts and reconstructs the language according to the influence of English.[3] Tex-Mex, or Spanglish, comes most naturally to me. I may switch back and forth from English to Spanish in the same sentence or in the same word. With my sister and my brother Nune and with Chicano *tejano* contemporaries I speak in Tex-Mex.

From kids and people my own age I picked up *Pachuco*. Pachuco (the language of the zoot suiters) is a language of rebellion, both against Standard Spanish and Standard English. It is a secret language. Adults of the culture and outsiders cannot understand it. It is made up of slang words from both English and Spanish. *Ruca* means girl or woman, *vato* means guy or dude, *chale* means no, *simón* means yes, *churo* is sure, talk is *periquiar*, *pigionear* means petting, *que gacho* means how nerdy, *ponte águila* means watch out, death is called *la pelona*. Through lack of practice and not having others who can speak it, I've lost most of the *Pachuco* tongue.

Chicano Spanish

Chicanos, after 250 years of Spanish/Anglo colonization have developed significant differences in the Spanish we speak. We collapse two adjacent vowels into a single syllable and sometimes shift the stress in certain words such as *maíz/maiz, cohete/cuete*. We leave out certain consonants when they appear between vowels: *lado/lao, mojado/mojao*. Chicanos from South Texas pronounce *f* as *j* as in *jue* (*fue*). Chicanos use "archaisms," words that are no longer in the Spanish language, words that have been evolved out. We say *semos, truje, haiga, ansina,* and *naiden.* We retain the "archaic" *j,* as in *jalar,* that derives from an earlier *h,* (the French *halar* or the Germanic *halon* which was lost to standard Spanish in the 16th century), but which is still found in several regional dialects such as the one spoken in South Texas. (Due to geography, Chicanos from the Valley of South Texas were cut off linguistically from other Spanish speakers. We tend to use words that the Spaniards brought over from Medieval Spain. The majority of the Spanish colonizers in Mexico and the Southwest came from Extremadura—Hernán *Cortés* was one of them—and Andalucía. Andalucians pronounce *ll* like a *y,* and their *d*'s tend to be absorbed by adjacent vowels: *tirado* becomes *tirao.* They brought *el lenguaje popular, dialectos y regionalismos.*[4])

Chicanos and other Spanish speakers also shift *ll* to *y* and *z* to *s.*[5] We leave out initial syllables, saying *tar* for *estar, toy* for *estoy, hora* for *ahora (cubanos* and *puertorriqueños* also leave out initial letters of some words). We also leave out the final syllable such as *pa* for *para.* The intervocalic *y,* the *ll* as in *tortilla, ella, botella,* gets replaced by *tortia* or *tortiya, ea, botea.* We add an additional syllable at the beginning of certain words: *atocar* for *tocar, agastar* for *gastar.* Sometimes we'll say *lavaste las vacijas,* other times *lavates* (substituting the *ates* verb endings for the *aste*).

We use anglicisms, words borrowed from English: *bola* from ball, *carpeta* from carpet, *máchina de lavar* (instead of *lavadora*) from washing machine. Tex-Mex argot, created by adding a Spanish sound at the beginning or end of an English word such as *cookiar* for cook, *watchar* for watch, *parkiar* for park, and *rapiar* for rape, is the result of the pressures on Spanish speakers to adapt to English.

We don't use the word *vosotros/as* or its accompanying verb form. We don't say *claro* (to mean yes), *imagínate,* or *me emociona,* unless we picked up Spanish from Latinas, out of a book, or in a classroom. Other Spanish-speaking groups are going through the same, or similar, development in their Spanish.

Linguistic Terrorism

Deslenguadas. Somos los del español deficiente. We are your linguistic nightmare, your linguistic aberration, your linguistic *mestizaje,* the subject of your *burla.* Because we speak with tongues of fire we are culturally crucified. Racially, culturally and linguistically *somos huérfanos*—we speak an orphan tongue.

Chicanas who grew up speaking Chicano Spanish have internalized the belief that we speak poor Spanish. It is illegitimate, a bastard language. And because we internalize how our language has been used against us by the dominant culture, we use our language differences against each other.

Chicana feminists often skirt around each other with suspicion and hesitation. For the longest time I couldn't figure it out. Then it dawned on me. To be close to another Chicana is like looking into the mirror. We are afraid of what we'll see there. *Pena.* Shame. Low estimation of self. In childhood we are told that our language is wrong. Repeated attacks on our native tongue diminish our sense of self. The attacks continue throughout our lives.

Chicanas feel uncomfortable talking in Spanish to Latinas, afraid of their censure. Their language was not outlawed in their countries. They had a whole lifetime of being immersed in their native tongue; generations, centuries in which Spanish was a first language, taught in school, heard on radio and TV, and read in the newspaper.

If a person, Chicana or Latina, has a low estimation of my native tongue, she also has a low estimation of me. Often with *mexicanas y latinas* we'll speak English as a neutral language. Even among Chicanas we tend to speak English at parties or conferences. Yet, at the same time, we're afraid the other will think we're *agringadas* because we don't speak Chicano Spanish. We oppress each other trying to out-Chicano each other, vying to be the "real" Chicanas, to speak like Chicanos. There is no one Chicano language just as there is no one Chicano experience. A monolingual Chicana whose first language is English or Spanish is just as much a Chicana as one who speaks several variants of Spanish. A Chicana from Michigan or Chicago or Detroit is just as much a Chicana as one from the Southwest. Chicano Spanish is as diverse linguistically as it is regionally.

By the end of this century, Spanish speakers will comprise the biggest minority group in the U.S., a country where students in high schools and colleges are encouraged to take French classes because French is considered more "cultured." But for a language to remain alive it must be used.[6] By the end of this century English, and not Spanish, will be the mother tongue of most Chicanos and Latinos.

So, if you want to really hurt me, talk badly about my language. Ethnic identity is twin skin to linguistic identity—I am my language. Until I can take pride in my language, I cannot take pride in myself. Until I can accept as legitimate Chicano Texas Spanish, Tex-Mex and all the other languages I speak, I cannot accept the legitimacy of myself. Until I am free to write bilingually and to switch codes without having always to translate, while I still have to speak English or Spanish when I would rather speak Spanglish, and as long as I have to accommodate the English speakers rather than having them accommodate me, my tongue will be illegitimate.

I will no longer be made to feel ashamed of existing. I will have my voice: Indian, Spanish, white. I will have my serpent's tongue—my woman's voice, my sexual voice, my poet's voice. I will overcome the tradition of silence.

> My fingers
> Move sly against your palm
> Like women everywhere, we speak in code. . . .
> —Melanie Kaye/Kantrowitz[7]

"Vistas," corridos, y comida: My Native Tongue

In the 1960's, I read my first Chicano novel. It was *City of Night* by John Rechy, a gay Texan, son of a Scottish father and a Mexican mother. For days I walked around in stunned amazement that a Chicano could write and could get published. When I read *I Am Joaquín*[8] I was surprised to see a bilingual book by a Chicano in print. When I saw poetry written in Tex-Mex for the first time, a feeling of pure joy flashed through me. I felt like we really existed as a people. In 1971, when I started teaching High School English to Chicano students, I tried to supplement the required texts with works by Chicanos, only to be reprimanded and forbidden to do so by the principal. He claimed that I was supposed to teach "American" and English literature. At the risk of being fired, I swore my students to secrecy and slipped in Chicano short stories, poems, a play. In graduate school, while working toward a PhD, I had to "argue" with one advisor after the other, semester after semester, before I was allowed to make Chicano literature an area of focus.

Even before I read books by Chicanos or Mexicans, it was the Mexican movies I saw at the drive-in—the Thursday night special of $1.00 a carload—that gave me a sense of belonging. "*Vámonos a las vistas*," my mother would call out and we'd all—grandmother, brothers, sister and cousins—squeeze into the car. We'd wolf down cheese and bologna white bread sandwiches while watching Pedro Infante in melodramatic tear-jerkers like *Nosotros los pobres*, the first "real" Mexican movie (that was not an imitation of European movies). I remember seeing *Cuando los hijos se van* and surmising that all Mexican movies played up the love a mother has for her children and what ungrateful sons and daughters suffer when they are not devoted to their mothers. I remember the singing-type "westerns" of Jorge Negrete and

Miguel Aceves Mejía. When watching Mexican movies, I felt a sense of homecoming as well as alienation. People who were to amount to something didn't go to Mexican movies, or *bailes* or tune their radios to *bolero, rancherita, and corrido* music.

The whole time I was growing up, there was *norteño* music sometimes called North Mexican border music, or Tex-Mex music, or Chicano music, or *cantina* (bar) music. I grew up listening to *conjuntos*, three-or four-piece bands made up of folk musicians, playing guitar, *bajo sexto,* drums and button accordion, which Chicanos had borrowed from the German immigrants who had come to Central Texas and Mexico to farm and build breweries. In the Rio Grande Valley, Steve Jordan and Little Joe Hernández were popular, and Flaco Jiménez was the accordion king. The rhythms of Tex-Mex music are those of the polka, also adapted from the Germans, who in turn had borrowed the polka from the Czechs and Bohemians.

I remember the hot, sultry evenings when *corridos*—songs of love and death on the Texas-Mexican borderlands—reverberated out of cheap amplifiers from the local *cantinas* and wafted in through my bedroom window.

Corridos first became widely used along the South Texas/Mexican border during the early conflict between Chicanos and Anglos. The *corridos* are usually about Mexican heroes who do valiant deeds against the Anglo oppressors. Pancho Villa's song, *"La cucaracha,"* is the most famous one. *Corridos* of John F. Kennedy and his death are still very popular in the Valley. Older Chicanos remember Lydia Mendoza, one of the great border *corrido* singers who was called *la Gloria de Tejas.* Her *"El tango negro,"* sung during the Great Depression, made her a singer of the people. The everpresent *corridos* narrated one hundred years of border history, bringing news of events as well as entertaining. These folk musicians and folk songs are our chief cultural mythmakers, and they made our hard lives seem bearable.

I grew up feeling ambivalent about our music. Country-western and rock-and-roll had more status. In the 50s and 60s, for the slightly educated and *agringado* Chicanos, there existed a sense of shame at being caught listening to our music. Yet I couldn't stop my feet from thumping to the music, could not stop humming the words, nor hide from myself the exhilaration I felt when I heard it.

There are more subtle ways that we internalize identification, especially in the forms of images and emotions. For me food and certain smells are tied to my identity, to my homeland. Woodsmoke curling up to an immense blue sky; woodsmoke perfuming my grandmother's clothes, her skin. The stench of cow manure and the yellow patches on the ground; the crack of a .22 rifle and the reek of cordite. Homemade white cheese sizzling in a pan, melting inside a folded *tortilla*. My sister Hilda's hot, spicy *menudo, chile colorado* making it deep red, pieces of *panza* and hominy floating on top. My brother Carito barbecuing *fajitas* in the backyard. Even now and 3,000 miles away, I can see my mother spicing the ground beef, pork and venison with *chile*. My mouth salivates at the thought of the hot steaming *tamales* I would be eating if I were home.

Si le preguntas a mi mamá, "¿Qué eres?"

Identity is the essential core of who
we are as individuals, the conscious
experience of the self inside.

—Kaufman[9]

Nosotros los Chicanos straddle the borderlands. On one side of us, we are constantly exposed to the Spanish of the Mexicans, on the other side we hear the Anglos' incessant clamoring so that we forget our language. Among ourselves we don't say *nosotros los americanos, o nosotros los españoles, o nosotros los hispanos.* We say *nosotros los mexicanos* (by *mexicanos* we do not mean citizens of Mexico; we do not mean a national identity, but a racial one). We distinguish between *mexicanos del otro lado* and *mexicanos de este lado.* Deep in our hearts we believe that being Mexican has nothing to do with which country one lives in. Being Mexican is a state of soul—not one of mind, not one of citizenship. Neither eagle nor serpent, but both. And like the ocean, neither animal respects borders.

Dime con quien andas y te diré quien eres.

(Tell me who your friends are and I'll tell you who you are.)

—Mexican saying

Si le preguntas a mi mamá, "¿Qué eres?" te dirá, "Soy mexicana." My brothers and sister say the same. I sometimes will answer *"soy mexicana"* and at others will say *"soy Chicana" o "soy tejana."* But I identified as *"Raza"* before I ever identified as *"mexicana"* or "Chicana."

As a culture, we call ourselves Spanish when referring to ourselves as a linguistic group and when copping out. It is then that we forget our predominant Indian genes. We are 70 to 80% Indian.[10] We call ourselves Hispanic[11] or Spanish-American or Latin American or Latin when linking ourselves to other Spanish-speaking peoples of the Western hemisphere and when copping out. We call ourselves Mexican-American[12] to signify we are neither Mexican nor American, but more the noun "American" than the adjective "Mexican" (and when copping out).

Chicanos and other people of color suffer economically for not acculturating. This voluntary (yet forced) alienation makes for psychological conflict, a kind of dual identity-we don't identify with the Anglo-American cultural values and we don't totally identify with the Mexican cultural values. We are a synergy of two cultures with various degrees of Mexicanness or Angloness. I have so internalized the borderland conflict that sometimes I feel like one cancels out the other and we are zero, nothing, no one. *A veces no soy nada ni nadie. Pero hasta cuando no lo soy, lo soy.*

When not copping out, when we know we are more than nothing, we call ourselves Mexican, referring to race and ancestry; *mestizo* when affirming both our Indian and Spanish (but we hardly ever own our Black ancestry); Chicano when referring to a politically aware people born and/or raised in the U.S; *Raza* when referring to Chicanos; *tejanos* when we are Chicanos from Texas.

Chicanos did not know we were a people until 1965 when Cesar Chavez and the farmworkers united and *I Am Joaquín* was published and *la Raza Unida* party was formed in Texas. With that recognition, we became a distinct people. Something momentous happened to the Chicano soul—we became aware of our reality and acquired a name and a language (Chicano Spanish) that reflected that reality. Now that we had a name, some of the fragmented pieces began to fall together—who we were, what we were, how we had evolved. We began to get glimpses of what we might eventually become.

Yet the struggle of identities continues, the struggle of borders is our reality still. One day the inner struggle will cease and a true integration take place. In the meantime, *tenemos que hacerla lucha. ¿Quién está protegiendo los ranchos de mi gente? ¿Quién está tratando de cerrar la fisura entre la india y el blanco en nuestra sangre? El Chicano, sí, el Chicano que anda como un ladrón en su propia casa.*

Los Chicanos, how patient we seem, how very patient. There is the quiet of the Indian about us.[13] We know how to survive. When other races have given up their tongue, we've kept ours. We know what it is to live under the hammer blow of the dominant *norteamericano* culture. But more than we count the blows, we count the days the weeks the years the centuries the eons until the white laws and commerce and customs will rot in the deserts they've created, lie bleached. *Humildes* yet proud, *quietos* yet wild, *nosotros los mexicanos*-Chicanos will walk by the crumbling ashes as we go about our business. Stubborn, persevering, impenetrable as stone, yet possessing a malleability that renders us unbreakable, we, the *mestizas and mestizos,* will remain.

Notes

1. Ray Gwyn Smith, *Moorland Is Cold Country,* unpublished book.
2. Irena Klepfisz, "*Di rayze aheym*/The Journey Home," in *The Tribe of Dina: A Jewish Women's Anthology,* eds. Melanie Kaye/Kantrowitz and Irena Klepfisz, (Montpelielier, VT: Sinister Wisdom Books, 1986), 49.
3. R. C. Ortega, *Dialectología Del Bamo,* trans. Horlencia S. Alwan (Los Angeles, CA: R. C. Ortega Publisher & Bookseller, 1977), 132.
4. Eduardo Hernandéz-Chávez, Andrew D. Cohen, and Anthony F. Beltramo, *El Lenguaje de los Chicanos*: *Regional and Social Characteristics of Language Used by Mexican Americans* (Arlington, VA: Center for Applied Linguistics, 1975), 39.
5. Hernandéz-Chávez, *El Lenguaje de los Chicanos,* xvii.
6. Irena Klepfisz, "Secular Jewish Identity: Yidishkayt in America," in *The Tribe of Dina: A Jewish Women's Anthology,* eds. Melanie Kaye/Kantrowitz and Irena Klepfisz, (Montpelielier, VT: Sinister Wisdom Books, 1986), 43.
7. Melanie Kaye/Kantrowitz, "Sign," in *We Speak in Code: Poems and Other Writings* (Pittsburgh, PA: Motheroot, 1980), 85.
8. Rodolfo Gonzales, *I Am Joaquín/Yo Soy Joaquín* (New York, NY: Bantam Books, 1972). It was first published in 1967.
9. Gershen Kaufman, *Shame: The Power of Caring* (Cambridge, MA: Schenkman Books, Inc., 1980), 68.
10. John R. Chávez, *The Lost Land: The Chicago Images of the Southwest* (Albuquerque, NM: University of New Mexico Press, 1984), 88–90.
11. "Hispanic" is derived from *Hispanis* (Espñla, a name given to the Iberian Peninsula in ancient times when it was a part of the Roman Empire) and is a term designated by the U.S. government to make it easier to handle us on paper.
12. The Treaty of Guadalupe Hidalgo created the Mexican-American in 1848.
13. Anglos, in order to alleviate their guilt for dispossessing the Chicano, stressed the Spanish part of us and perpetrated the myth of the Spanish Southwest. We have accepted the fiction that we are Hispanic, that is Spanish, in order to accommodate ourselves to the dominant culture and its abhorrence of Indians. Chávez, *The Lost Land,* 88–91.

Writing Deaf: Textualizing Deaf Literature

Kristen Harmon

Kristen Harmon is a writer and professor of English at Gallaudet University in Washington, D.C. In the essay that follows, Harmon reveals the workings of language—how language shapes thought, interaction, and ways of being. The standards of written English are in many ways incompatible with Deaf meaning-making; this essay explores the implications of this for all creative writers. This essay was published in the academic journal *Sign Language Studies* in 2007. Harmon has co-edited two anthologies of *Deaf American Prose*, published in the Gallaudet Deaf Literature Series in 2012 and 2013. She has written scholarly articles that focus on literature, culture, ethnography, and education. In addition to academic work, she has published short stories in collections put out by the Tactile Mind Quarterly Press, HandType Press, Cinco Puntos Press, and the *Disability Studies Quarterly*. In 2017, Harmon appeared in the PBS documentary *Through Deaf Eyes*.

I begin with a question: What does it mean to transliterate American Sign Language (ASL) and the visual realities of a Deaf life into creative texts written in English? The question is larger than the necessities of transliteration and conventions of print. If fiction writers or poets happen to be Deaf—meaning that they consider themselves to be members of the Deaf community and use ASL as their primary language—then they must also consider how writing in English (or other print languages) displaces a cultural identity grounded in a visual-spatial language, one that has historically been denigrated, suppressed, and erased from sight.

Indeed, it seems that even on the sentence level, written English resists the unsettling presence of transliteration across modalities; turn-taking in sign language cannot easily be slotted into conversation tags (e.g., he said, she said). A sign cannot be "said." In English, dialogue without quotation marks is, in effect, speechless. Without the conventionalized use of quotation marks, dialogue shifts inward and inhabits an internal territory, for without quotations, what separates thought from conversation on the page?

If one uses the conventions of written English, then the results are awkward and imply a one-to-one correlation between signs and English words (e.g., "What's up?" Dave signed). Tonal dialogue tags reveal problems with trying to sequence information on the page that, for a signer, would be perceived in a simultaneous, not linear, fashion (e.g., "You should have gone to the meeting," she signed, disappointed). So, in effect, if one uses the conventions of printed English, then the story or poem embodies the hearing, not the Deaf, world.

To evoke a resistant perspective, some Deaf writers and Deaf poets make use of code mixing, untranslated ASL gloss, and other hybrid forms that show the postcolonial possibilities for textualizing Deaf lives and sign language. It is important to remember that many Deaf people who are creative writers and who are innovative in their use of ASL simply do not bother with writing literary forms of English. Why should they? ASL has a long tradition of visual poetics and a rich traditional linguistic history with many genres—ASL poetry, narratives, jokes, and rap, to name just a few. With the advent of visual recording devices, ASL has its own form of "print" in that DVDs and videotapes can be watched repeatedly and disseminated to a larger audience.

So, for the purposes of writing Deaf, why bother with English? It is, after all, the dreaded and always fragmented, incomplete language of speech therapy: words forced, unwieldy and thick, from mouths. There is also the uneven and sometimes humiliating experience of learning to read and write English, with its idiosyncratic orthography based, in many cases, upon phonetics. So much of English has to be heard in order to be understood and then used. As is the case with other diglossic subcultural groups, the use of written English, for many Deaf people, has been largely seen as utilitarian, a necessary tool for participation in U.S. social institutions. English is, after all, the language of government and business.

More to the point, literary English and the attendant displays of hearing cultural norms do not reflect the lived, embodied realities of a Deaf person's life or sign language. Like Singer in Carson McCuller's *The Heart Is a Lonely Hunter,* the few deaf characters in literary English are most often written as metaphors for the human (i.e., hearing) condition.

Historically, Deaf bodies have been pathologized, and their ears, as one specific site of conflict, have been colonized through attempts to "fix" deafness. The deafened ear, the silenced body, and endangered soul have all been mapped out by centuries of medical and religious literature. In the long campaign against sign language, Deaf people have been told to sit on their hands and speak up, have been ordered not to marry each other, and, to this day, continue to suffer the effects of an imperialist and audist directive to conform, to speak, and to not unsettle or disrupt the ongoing narratives of the hearing world. In direct contrast, Deaf people are a people of the eye, so it is easy to see why so many have not bothered with aesthetic or literary forms of written English. Note that here I am referring to the use of English for the sole purpose of creative, "literary" writing; I am not addressing the use of written English for educational, professional, or personal reasons.

Yet some deafened people and some Deaf people choose to use written English as one possible medium for creative expression. Let me make a distinction here: Some writers not published in anthologies such as *No Walls of Stone* and *The Deaf Way II Anthology* are hard of hearing or deafened and are not fluent in American Sign Language; these writers are not the focus of this article. Writers who are culturally Deaf, who are fluent in American Sign Language, and who also choose to write and publish in English are my interest; what are their literary and connotative strategies for writing ASL in English? Is there a subaltern sensibility emerging in the texts generated by Deaf writers?

Let me give you a specific context for my query; in the fall of 2000, I taught a creative writing class in fiction at Gallaudet University, in Washington, D.C. At some point during the third week of classes, I realized that the students were writing prose that was virtually indistinguishable from the clunky, cliché-ridden first efforts of hearing undergraduate students. My students at Gallaudet used tonal dialogue tags, wrote mysteries with plots that turned upon overheard information, and everywhere were characters with voices quavering with emotion. Their characters were chatterboxes!

Interestingly, all of my students considered themselves to be culturally entrenched in the Deaf world. They used ASL with pride and awareness, they loved being young and Deaf at a Deaf university, they saw themselves as members of an emancipated post-Deaf President Now generation of young Deaf adults, and yet their writing represented a mimesis of hearing phenomenology. There's the old adage, "write what you know." Well, they were writing what they knew—in English. Without any sense of irony, they wrote themselves and other characters as hearing. They had become accustomed to the idea that ASL and Deaf lives were separate and lived in different realities. So, in print, the people of the eye did not exist.

On one September day I showed them photographs from *"Deaf Maggie Lee Sayre"*: *Photographs of a River Life*.[1] Maggie Lee Sayre, a Deaf woman from the Depression-era South, did not write any of the book's text; these are her photographs, snapshots that reveal her sensibility, her world, and her eye for significant, revealing details. I then asked my students to imagine writing her snapshots in sensory, visual, tactile ways that revealed what they knew and experienced in their lives and could imagine in Maggie Lee Sayre's life. I asked them to write as Deaf writers. After a few stunned, glassy-eyed moments, this is what they wrote:

1. Just Bolts of ideas. Not in forms yet. Vision of Reality.[2]

2. Look at my snapshot.
   Look at how we do things
   I want to show you
   Look at the catfish-
   —isn't it big?—
   —hanging on evergreen—my father reeled it in.
   Look at my house. It's on the river.
   That's my home.[3]

3. House
   No stay
   Constantly
   Moving.
   Adrift.[4]

4. Maggie Lee was a hard worker all her life: her life is[5]

Due to the time limits of that writing exercise, none of these first, surprised efforts were developed at length, but I wanted to show you some of the pauses, the gaps, and yet, some of the textual, linguistic, syntactic, and rhetorical strategies that they glimpsed as possibilities for writing Deaf lives.

With the exception of the abrogating presence of the near-ASL gloss in L. Mann's writing, few of these writers evince textual strategies of postcolonial writers as they recognize their own erasure from English; two such strategies are abrogation (i.e., the denial of privilege to English, a refusal of the categories of imperialism) and appropriation, or the "process by which the language is taken and made to 'bear the burden' of one's own cultural experience."[6] The writing from J. Temby approaches something like the textual strategy of appropriation (which can include the use of glosses, untranslated words, interlanguage, syntactic fusion, code switching and vernacular transcription) as he makes over English to represent a visual sensibility, a Deaf eye.[7] Even so, in his writing there is still the presence of a presumably hearing viewer/reader, as seen in the imperative "look" and in the declarative "I want to show you." However, Temby's direct address to a reader is inherently postcolonial in its suggestion that, in this case, Deaf phenomenology, identity, and language are inseparable: This is home.

The conversation did not stop with that exercise. Several of the same creative writing students took my British literature survey class the following spring, and again we discussed the concept of the canon and why there was no parallel body of work in English, written by Deaf people. One young man raised a point that is reflective of the experiences of linguistically oppressed cultures; he noted that, because we have fought so hard to gain fluency in English, we should not risk alienating our hearing audience—and thereby any chances for publishing—by trying anything innovative on the page, anything that would make a hearing reader struggle for comprehension. He also noted that, to date, the overriding challenge has been to prove that we are human beings, not just deaf ears, silenced bodies. This struggle, he argued, mandates that we universalize our experiences, even if it means we fragment ourselves in the process.

Another writer, from a Deaf family, described the difficulties of dragging along what Ashcroft, Griffiths, and Tiffin call the machinery of explanation: "If we were to write [all of the necessary explanations of visual-spatial meaning in ASL], it would get into the way of the meaning of the sentence. . . . However, it's too bad that hearing people are not able to understand our culture, how we function daily, the little things, and so on. Those things would go a long way in allowing them to understand our culture, instead of thinking that we're those people who can't hear—'they're helpless'—'those dumb people.'"[8] This writer, like the other students in class, saw the primary motivation for writing in English as using the dominant language in order to be fully understood—articulated—so to speak, for a hearing audience.

In this sense, the students are concerned with authenticity and the recognition, verification, and transmission of cultural information across seemingly impermeable boundaries. They recognize their inherent alterity in relation to English but do not yet have a sense of themselves as a subaltern, subversive presence in written English. They are all too aware of what it means to assume a culture through the use of a language.

Despite an awareness of what Frantz Fanon calls the "weight of a civilization," there are Deaf writers who assume that it is possible to restructure the written world.[9] Most of the published creative work by Deaf writers is fairly standard in its use of English, but some of it rejects the imperialist directives for norming, and these are the closest to a resistant, subaltern presence that we have in written English. These writers use ASL gloss, italics, fingerspelling, traces of interlanguage, and other typographic and syntactic devices to make English strange or foreign to a hearing reader.

This is an excerpt from a story about a gay couple just before one partner leaves the other. The narrator has just met a gay man at an art gallery and is planning to go to New York City with him:

> "Money where?"
> "G-a-l-l-e-r-y-o-w-n-e-r money have."
> "O-h. You-like money? Himself gay?"
> "Gay, not-matter, want-want help me important."
> "Slept-with-him finish?"
> "Me-don't-like-that. Me-thought you trust me?"[10]

Here is a selection from a poem written from the perspective of a young deaf child:

> Me little, almost high wash-wash machine
> Down basement, me have blue car
> Drive drive round round
> Basement[11]

In a transcription of one of his ASL poems, Peter Cook describes a young Deaf boy playing with another young boy, who then gets Peter's attention by tapping, tapping on his shoulder. When Peter turns to look, this boy flips his tongue back and forth like he is a snake. Peter turns to see some garter snakes in the grass of his backyard:

> A mind-editing image flashed in my head;
> A teacher holding a picture card of a green snake
> Next to her mouth.
> She did what Ron did to me:
> SSS NAA EE K
> She pointed at the picture.
> She did again what Ron did to me:
> SSS NAA EE K
> She did repeat with the picture until I become her
> Dog: I nodded my head.
> All I know is that snakes have tiny tongues
> But what it got have do with ss naaee k?[12]

These writers use interlanguage, ASL gloss, fingerspelling, and typographic features to set language apart, to mark it as a sign of difference and to locate the writers and characters within that difference. These examples are just a few of the many textual strategies that can be used to abrogate, and in the process appropriate or hijack English and create nonstandard, hybrid forms that do not clearly belong to anyone, forms that exist in the interstices, the overlap and resultant displacement of domains of cultural and linguistic differences between Deaf and hearing, between English and ASL.

By pointing out the slipperiness of meaning, by breaking English, by making over English into hybrid forms, and by demanding that the reader *look*, Deaf writers are slowly raising a resistant, disruptive, subaltern presence with a gathering collective locus of agency. By commandeering written English and insisting upon our status as a bilingual, bicultural people living in a diglossic subculture, Deaf writers theorize a relationship with a dominating language. It does not valorize or covet agency made available in that language but instead begins to break it apart on the page, begins to see even the word, the layout on the page, as a mode of resistance.

Notes

1. Maggie Lee Sayre, "Deaf Maggie Lee Sayre," in *Photographs of a River Life*, ed. T. Rankin (Jackson: University Press of Mississippi, 1995).
2. A. Sittner, September 20, 2001. In-class writing, English 392.
3. J. Temby, September 20, 2001. In-class writing, English 392.
4. L. Mann, September 20, 2001. In-class writing, English 392.
5. K. Jannson, September 20, 2001. In-class writing, English 392.
6. Bill Ashcroft, Gareth Griffiths, and Helen Tiffen, *The Empire Writes Back: Theory and Practice in Post-Colonial Literatures* (New York: Routledge, 1989), 38–39.
7. Temby, In-class writing, 59–77.
8. S. Nowak, April 6, 2001. Assignment, English 404.
9. Frantz Fanon, *Black Skin, White Masks*, translated by Charles Lam Markmann (New York: Grove, 1967), 18.
10. Raymond Luczak, "The Finer Things," *No Walls of Stone: An Anthology of Literature by Deaf and Hard of Hearing Writers*, ed. Jill Christine Jepson (Washington, DC: Gallaudet University Press, 1992), 105.
11. Conley, Willy. "Salt in the Basement: An American Sign Language Reverie in English," in *The Deaf Way II Anthology*, edited by Tonya M. Stremlau (Washington, DC: Gallaudet University Press, 2002), 184.
12. Peter Cook, "Ringoes," in *No Walls of Stone: An Anthology of Literature by Deaf and Hard of Hearing Writers*, edited by Jill Christine Jepson (Washington, DC: Gallaudet University Press, 1992), 212–13.

The Filipino Author as Producer

Conchitina Cruz

Conchitina Cruz was born in Manila. She teaches creative writing and literature at the University of the Philippines in Diliman. The essay that follows is part one of a three-part essay. It tells a story that has many dimensions: colonialism, stacked hierarchies in global literature, the complexities of privilege. In conversation with Walter Benjamin's "The Author as Producer" as indicated by its title, Cruz's essay probes what it means to write in English in the context of complex political realities. A recipient of Fulbright and Rockefeller Foundation grants, her books of poetry include *Dark Hours*, winner of the National Book Award for Poetry in the Philippines; *elsewhere held and lingered*; and *There Is No Emergency*. She is part of the Manila-based small presses High Chair and the Youth & Beauty Brigade. She also helps run the small press/DIY expo Better Living Through Xeroxography (BLTX). She currently lives in Quezon City.

Ten days after the strongest typhoon to hit the planet in recorded history made landfall in the Philippines, I flew from Albany, New York to Hong Kong for a poetry festival. Months earlier, as I coordinated my trip with the organizers, who were all strangers to me, I thought it absurd that they would want to bring an obscure Filipino writer attending graduate school in the United States to Hong Kong to do a reading of her poetry. I was, however, happy to overlook the strangeness of their invitation in exchange for a free plane ticket to a country in the same time zone as the Philippines. Filipinos could enter Hong Kong without a visa, and it was close enough to Manila, where my partner was living, which meant he could afford to travel to the festival and we could spend a week together.

When Typhoon Yolanda, known internationally as Haiyan, hit the Visayas, it pulled ships from the sea and sent them pummeling into coastal neighborhoods. It destroyed roads and farms, cut off communication lines, and wiped out entire villages. Those in evacuation centers found no refuge as the centers succumbed to the force of the typhoon. In the aftermath of the storm, survivors searched for loved ones in the ruins and among the many corpses that littered the streets. At the UN Climate Change Convention in

Warsaw, the Philippines' chief negotiator, whose hometown was in the path of the typhoon and who had yet to confirm the safety of his own family, went on hunger strike to demand specific policy changes and resource allocations to address the climate crisis. Rejecting the term "natural disaster," he insisted that Haiyan and the like be understood as outcomes of social and economic inequity on a global scale, with the poorest of the world enduring the repercussions of unchecked progress and consumption.[1] The death toll from Haiyan would eventually reach 6,300. The typhoon, which affected close to a fifth of the Philippine population, destroyed over a million houses and displaced 4.1 million people.[2]

As the Philippine government's response to the calamity shifted from silent to painfully slow, and as survivors, who were literally living among the dead, struggled with hunger and disease, I embarked on a series of flights two hours short of taking me home. On one of the flights, the attendants handed out envelopes to passengers for donations to the Filipino victims of the typhoon. I saw my partner "in real life" again at the Hong Kong airport. It seemed absurd to be alive and intact, even happy. We shared a car to the hotel with an American poet, an editor for New Directions, who was also a guest at the festival. Our small talk during the drive was sporadic. It was evening in Hong Kong, and two of us had just emerged from long-haul flights. The American poet asked after our families back home. At some point during the ride, I mentioned to him that a Filipino poet, José Garcia Villa, was an editor for New Directions in the late 1940s. I was surprised by his interest in this bit of information. Apparently, he was quite familiar with the history of the publishing house yet he had never heard of Villa. He asked me to repeat the Filipino poet's name. The American poet promised to look him up.

* * *

Hong Kong has the fifth highest concentration of Overseas Filipino Workers (OFWs) in the world. Of the 331,989 domestic helpers working in the country, 173,726 are Filipinos.[3] Months before I attended the poetry festival, the Hong Kong Court of Final Appeal ruled that foreign domestic helpers, unlike all other foreigners employed in Hong Kong, could not obtain permanent residency after working in the country for seven consecutive years. Two Filipino domestic helpers had taken the fight for permanent residency to court, and the legal battle, which spanned a couple of years, culminated in the landmark decision. The Hong Kong court maintained that foreign domestic workers should not be regarded as "ordinarily resident" in the country.[4] Its tautological logic invoked the precarity of the domestic worker's labor as justification to keep her vulnerable, subject to deportation upon unemployment, and permanently ineligible to move her own family to the country where she works. At the festival, when people learned where I was from, the conversation often turned to Haiyan, which continued to figure prominently in the news. Occasionally, and noticeably when in the company of Americans living in Hong Kong, I was asked about the "situation" of Filipino domestic workers, a matter more contentious where we were and therefore less palatable as material for small talk than the catastrophic typhoon. That Filipinos were "the help" in Hong Kong was a reality one would be hard pressed to ignore, observed the Americans, who were mostly working in the country as translators, university professors, or teachers of English. Maids were an ordinary part of Hong Kong households. Some of the Americans, in fact, employed Filipino helpers at home. More than one of them said to me that I was the first Filipino they had met in the country who was not a domestic worker. They were unanimous in their recognition of the gulf between their position as "expatriates" and those regarded as "migrant workers." They were equally incredulous over the Court of Final Appeal decision.

The first Filipino I met at the festival was a woman with whom I locked eyes as I stood among the crowd outside the performance hall after a poetry reading. When I returned her smile, she approached and greeted me warmly in English, saying I must be the Filipino participant at the festival. Oo, I said. She said she had been on the lookout for me. Buti andito ka, I responded, referring to her attendance of the reading. Ako ang yaya niya, she said, pointing to a child in the crowd, the son of the Chinese poet who was the director of the festival. Ah, sikat yang boss mo, I chuckled, which prompted Auntie L—to tell me about her employer, whom she described as a kind and generous amo. He was easy to talk to. He had a house full of books that she was welcome to read. He hosted writers from all over the world in his home; she was in charge of their meals, but she often also got to meet them. Auntie L—first learned about the festival when her amo was planning it, and she told him she hoped he would invite a Filipino poet. She was unfamiliar with Filipino poets herself, but surely they were out there. He seemed to think this was a good idea, because after a few days he mentioned the name of a male Filipino poet to her as a possible guest. It would be nice if you chose a woman instead, she suggested. Later, he told her about a female poet, a Filipino-American living in the US. She said he could consider inviting a poet who actually grew up and still lives in the Philippines. Now the festival was happening at last, and Auntie L— couldn't be happier that a Filipina was chosen to represent our country. She said her boss even invited a Filipino band based in Hong Kong to perform in the same program as my reading. He insisted that she invite her friends to the event. She hoped they would go; there would be no reason for them to miss it since it falls on a Sunday, their day off from work.

I had been wondering to whom I should credit my invitation to the festival, which had reached me via what seemed a convoluted route (a message sent via academia.edu, a platform I rarely use) that bore no distinct link to my department in the University of the Philippines, where I was employed, or to any of the writers I knew back home. As I laughed and listened to Auntie L—, who was quite the energetic storyteller, it became clear to me that I owed my presence in the poetry festival to her, a Filipino domestic helper, whose intervention occurred as she went about her household duties while chatting with her employer, a famous poet in Hong Kong.

* * *

Only two of Auntie L—'s friends joined her at my reading, two equally maternal aunties who were lavish in their praise of my performance, my ease as I read my work onstage, my excellent command of the English language. I myself wouldn't want to spend my day off at a poetry reading, I (half)-joked to appease Auntie L—, who was unhappy that the rest of her friends didn't show up. We were sitting at one of the tables outside the performance hall for post-reading refreshments. Over snacks, the aunties told me where I should go to get good shopping deals in Hong Kong. They also talked about their amo, and once again I heard how lucky Auntie L— was, this time according to her friends, whose working conditions were far less ideal and whose employers were not particularly kind to them. The conversation drifted to longed-for trips back home, the never-ending work hours of domestic helpers, God, Yolanda, the annoying children they were helping to raise, the adorable children they were helping to raise, the children they left back home to be raised by relatives, the extended families they needed to support. Periodically, one of them would look in the direction of the festival crowd and say to me, Kaya mabuting andito ka, para makita nilang hindi tulad namin lahat ng Pilipino.

Between Auntie L—'s broad-strokes description to her employer of what she thought a Filipino poet should be (similar to her, a woman born and raised in the Philippines) and why the aunties approved of my presence at the festival (I was a Filipina who was *not* like them) lies a thicket of political and economic realities that intensify my lack of conviction in the capacity of poetry (or art) to represent national identity and serve as an agent of social transformation. When I am asked to produce one, then two, then three identification cards in a Tokyo bank so that I can have my money changed, I know that I am being sized up and subjected to bureaucratic tediousness because I am presumed to be an entertainer, which my documents and a brief conversation about the university where I am an exchange student eventually dispute. When I hold up an immigration line in the Amsterdam airport because I'm asked to explain what a writer's residency is, and then show the letters to prove that I am indeed on my way to one, I know I'm being made to dispel the suspicion that I am actually a domestic helper with fake travel documents. When my travel companion and I are taken to the "inner room" at the airport in Detroit because his tone in responding to an immigration officer's question is deemed insufficiently subservient, I know that we are being trained, through the threat of deportation, to combine our unquestionably legal travel papers with the appropriate demeanor of Filipinos seeking entry into the United States. When we are presented to the deporting officer, I do the speaking for both of us, because a petite Filipino woman seems more likely to communicate deference effectively than a burly Filipino man.

In all instances, I experience the treatment endured by and reproduce the submissiveness expected of the aunties, my newfound friends in Hong Kong, on a daily basis as Filipino women who are overseas domestic workers. In all instances, our sameness is short-lived, and it is in my interest for our sameness to be disproven. The sooner it is determined that I am not an "unskilled worker," let alone an undocumented immigrant, the less likely it becomes that I would be at risk of deportation, or detention, or harassment, or plain old rudeness, which domestic workers must contend with on top of the low wages, long hours, lack of security and benefits, and susceptibility to abuse and violence that are part and parcel of the work that they do. In a letter sent by José Garcia Villa in 1950 to his employer at the American publishing firm New Directions, the Filipino poet rages against what he believes to be unjust treatment from his boss by declaring, in no uncertain terms, the types of blue-collar work he has been forced to but *should not* be made to do. To retrieve his dignity, Villa insists that certain forms of labor are beneath him; in effect, the Filipino expatriate poet asserts difference from the Filipino migrant worker, distancing himself from his contemporaries who take on undesirable, low-wage jobs in the United States, and from the aunties of the globalized world.[5]

My profile in the professionalized world of poetry is not unusual: schooled in academic institutions of creative writing, both in the Philippines and the US, published by university presses and literary journals based in universities, employed in an English Department as a teacher of literature and creative writing courses. It is unsurprising to see these details recur in the brief biographies of eighteen poets from eighteen countries in attendance at a poetry festival. In a country where "Filipino" is regarded as synonymous to "maid," I go onstage, buttressed by my academic degrees and the grants that granted me time to write, and read my poems in English to an international audience. Behind me, translations into Chinese of my lines, as I read them, are flashed on a big screen. The space I am given to present my work is made possible with the help of a domestic helper, who reminded her employer to consider including a Filipino in the festival lineup. My poems betray preoccupations removed from the realities of the three Filipino aunties in the audience, who have, perhaps unwisely, decided to dedicate a portion of their day off to showing their support for a Filipino poet. The poems are what they are in part because I believe that what's worse than a Filipino poet in English who does not in her poetry speak on behalf of fellow Filipinos is a Filipino poet in English who does.

On the international stage of professionalized poetry, I belong to the minority by virtue of nationality and ethnicity, and my presence both signals and advocates inclusivity in the world of letters, whose achievement continues to define the struggle of writers from the margins. My presence, however, is also indicative of multiple privileges that set me apart from the minority that I appear to represent. I am the Filipino at the festival precisely because I do not come from the margins of Philippine society. I neither live below the poverty line, like most Filipinos, nor am I forced to migrate to other countries in search of better (minimum) wages, like Auntie L— and many others. My privilege is encoded in the very language that I use to write. A Filipino poet who writes in the language of the educated and the elite cannot easily claim to represent the oppressed in her work. A Filipino poet can hardly claim to address or express solidarity with the marginalized, if she writes in the language that excludes them.

The need to reckon with the privileges inscribed in Philippine literary production in English is obscured, I think, by the minority position of Philippine literature in the "world republic of letters," combined with the likelihood that Philippine literature in English, rather than in other

Philippine languages, would gain access to this minority position, since it can be read by a global audience without the aid of translation.[6] What dominates the hierarchy of literatures in the Philippines becomes a stand-in for Filipino national identity in the global literary arena, where it is an extremely minor player and must struggle for visibility. I think this struggle, or even just the idea of it, at times emboldens Filipino writers in English to testify to the global audience about the lives of Filipinos, and to occupy or represent, in art, subject-positions of the marginal from which they are estranged in their immediate environment. Such moves can predictably generate essentialist or exoticized renditions of "the Filipino experience" by these authors, whose deployment of otherness to pander to the market is arguably compensated for by the space they strive to carve out for Philippine literature (in English) on the world literary map. More complex and nuanced imaginings of national identity, while contributing more meaningfully to the struggle for representation, are nevertheless still embedded in the *business* of representation. This inevitably commodifies the struggle and converts it to cultural and economic capital, whose immediate beneficiary, for good or ill, is the writer herself. It is simply more likely that efforts at literary representation would translate to accolades, or sales, or promotion points, or plain old recognition or credibility among the smallest of audiences, or an additional line in the writer's curriculum vitae, than to a world where the exportation as cheap human labor of Filipinos (who live in the margins that frame the writer's speech) becomes obsolete.

The invisibility of Philippine literature globally, when generalized to a degree that downplays the hierarchy of literatures locally, also reinforces the valorization of writing as a struggle in itself and thus in itself an explicitly politicized action. That the page is the arena in which the writer labors has yielded a routine exercise in the local world of letters that presents itself as a form of activism. In a country prone to disaster and rife with atrocity, the Filipino poet, myself included, responds to disaster or atrocity by writing poetry about it. In some instances, the magnitude of the death toll, or the extent of the violence, can drive a poet to mobilize other poets to write more poems, to post the poems on social media to reach a wider audience, perhaps put together an anthology, perhaps donate the sales from the anthology to the victims. Such gestures seem to restate even as they conceal the division between aesthetics and politics. There is something amiss in collective action when all that comes out of it is more poetry.

I don't think I have ever felt the uselessness of being a Filipino poet more acutely as I did when the aunties in Hong Kong regarded me with pride because I was not like them. That I did not represent them made me fit to represent them at the festival. My privilege is indeed my loss.[7] It is hardly consolation that the gulf between us would remain unaltered, even if I had written poems on domestic helpers for the occasion.

Notes

1. Yeb Saño's exact words were: "Disasters are never natural. They are the intersection of factors other than physical. They are the accumulation of the constant breach of economic, social, and environmental thresholds. Most of the time disasters is a result of inequity and the poorest people of the world are at greatest risk because of their vulnerability and decades of maldevelopment, which I must assert is connected to the kind of pursuit of economic growth that dominates the world; the same kind of pursuit of so-called economic growth and unsustainable consumption that has altered the climate system." See "'It's time to stop this madness'—Philippines plea at UN climate talks" in *Climate Home*, November 13, 2013.
2. Two years later, less than ten percent of the 16,331 houses pledged by the government and non-government organizations for typhoon victims have been built. Thousands of families remain in makeshift housing. See USAID Philippines' Typhoon Yolanda/Haiyan Fact Sheet #22, 21 Apr. 2014; Jazmin Bonifacio, "Less than 10% of target homes built for displaced Tacloban families" in *Rappler*, November 5, 2015.
3. The top destinations for exported Filipino laborers, in order, are as follows: Saudi Arabia, United Arab Emirates, Singapore, Kuwait and Qatar, and Hong Kong. Approximately a third of the 2.32 million OFWs are laborers and unskilled workers. Remittances from OFWs total P173.19 billion. Statistics on Hong Kong's domestic workers are as of February 2015. See Jaymar G. Uy, "OFWs increase to 2.32M amid growth in lower-paid workers" in *Business World Online*, April 29, 2015; Daisy CL Mandap, "Number of Filipino domestic workers in HK at all-time high" in *Rappler*, April 17, 2015.
4. In the court's language, "The foreign domestic helper is obliged to return to the country of origin at the end of the contract and is told from the outset that admission is not for the purposes of settlement." See "Hong Kong's foreign maids lose legal battle for residency" in *Reuters*, March 25, 2013.
5. Among the facts commonly cited in biographical sketches of Villa is his stint as an associate editor of New Directions, a publisher affiliated with experimental and avant-garde writing, from 1949 to 1951. New Directions published *Volume Two* (1949), Villa's second book of poetry published in

the United States. *Volume Two* was not as well received as *Have Come, Am Here* (1942), Villa's first book of poetry released in the U.S. The lukewarm reception, writes Timothy Yu, can be attributed to the book's incompatibility with the modernist orientalism discreetly employed to celebrate his arrival in the American literary scene six years earlier (in "'The Hand of a Chinese Master': José Garcia Villa and Modernist Orientalism," *MELUS* 29, no. 1 (2004): 41–59). Villa, it seemed, had become too universal and not ethnic enough in his second book of poetry. This angry letter by Villa, which is included in the poet's archive at the Houghton Library, Harvard Library (letter to James Laughlin, N.d., TS, Box 6, José Garcia Villa papers, ca. 1920–97. 2008M-14), suggests that a falling-out with his employer, who was also his publisher, could have significantly contributed to the eventual invisibility of his work in his adopted country.

6. Pascale Casanova, *The World Republic of Letters* (2004).
7. Gayatri Chakravorty Spivak, "Can the Subaltern Speak?" (1983).

Chapter Reflection

Questions for Discussion

(Some of the following questions were generated by creative writing student Jan Calderon.)

1   To what extent does Silko's essay represent the weblike narrative of Laguna Pueblo storytelling in its form? How does the idea of storytelling as a web compare to other models of plotting/story structure that you've learned in creative writing classes (such as the Aristotelian arc)? Why is it important to know about multiple, comparative models of storytelling?

2   Make a list of all the languages Anzaldúa mentions. Can you make a similar list of your own? What languages and codes do you know? What considerations do you weigh when you are deciding which languages/codes you want to use in your work?

3   How do the essays in this chapter help you to consider the historical, social, and political implications of the language choices authors make? Think about the texts you encounter in your personal reading and in the texts assigned in your classes: What languages and codes are used in these texts? Do you read work in translation? What can you say about the choices writers and translators make as they pay close attention to language?

4   In your previous creative writing classes, how much time have you spent practicing and discussing oral storytelling or oral modes like spoken word? Have you encountered code mixing or untranslated ASL gloss? What do you notice about the modes that creative writing, as a field, prioritizes?

Writing Prompts

Create a character or narrator who holds language to be an important factor in shaping their identity. Explore how language links this character or narrator to community, heritage, history, and different ways of knowing or perceiving the world.

Suggestions for Further Reading

1   Hoang, Lily, and Joshua Marie Wilkinson, eds. *The Force of What's Possible: Writers on Accessibility and the Avant-Garde*. Nightboat, 2015.

2   Jin, Ha. "Deciding to Write in English," *The Art of the Short Story: 52 Great Authors, Their Best Short Fiction, and Their Insights on Writing*. Eds. Dana Gioia and R. S. Gwynn. Pearson Longman, 2006.

3   Lim, Shirley Geok-lin. "Lore, Practice, and Social Identity in Creative Writing Pedagogy: Speaking with a Yellow Voice?" *Pedagogy* (Winter 2010).

4   Philip, M. NourbeSe. "Who's Listening? Artists, Audiences and Language," in *New Contexts of Canadian Criticism*. Eds. Ajay Heble, Donna Palmateer Pennee, and J. R. (Tim) Struthers. Broadview Press, 1997.

5   Teleky, Richard. "'Entering the Silence': Voice, Ethnicity, and the Pedagogy of Creative Writing." *MELUS* (Spring 2001).

6

Appropriation

Chapter Outline

Inappropriate Appropriation

Rick Moody, Chimamanda Ngozi Adichie, Patrick Roth, Tsitsi Dangarembga, Minae Mizumura, Katja Lange-Muller, and Yoko Tawada

The following is a transcript from a panel conversation that was part of the inaugural PEN World Voices Festival, held in 2005. The World Voices Festival, organized and sponsored by PEN American, is an event that is still held annually in New York City during the month of April. This panel session from April 20, 2005 was sponsored by *The Believer* magazine and was titled "Inappropriate Appropriation." The event brought together the authors Chimamanda Ngozi Adichie, Patrick Roth, Tsitsi Dangarembga, Minae Mizumura, Katja Lange-Muller, and Yoko Tawada. Rick Moody served as moderator. The transcript was later reprinted in issue 7 of the literary journal *PEN America: A Journal for Writers and Readers*.

RICK MOODY: I think the pressing question of the PEN World Voices Festival is "Why, exactly, are we bothering?" The United States of America has become a culture that exports and no longer imports. If I were to project up here a graph of literature in translation published in the United States, you would see, over the last twenty-five years, a steep decline in the number of titles published in this country in translation. It's now hovering near the 5 percent mark of the twenty thousand—odd books published annually in this country, and that includes engineering manuals and the like. So in terms of literature, the art of what we do in language, an infinitesimal number of books are being published in English. Personally, I think that's political. I think it has a lot to do with a general trend in the culture away from intellectual investigation and toward a kind of recoiling from the rest of the world.

That's part of what the PEN World Voices Festival is trying to address, and it's what I'm going to try to address with these panelists tonight. *The Believer* came up with a great topic for the discussion: the rules of cross-cultural appropriation. The late '70s and early '80s, when I was first writing, was a period when identity politics was as forceful as it ever got. And there was a real unwritten law that certain kinds of cultural appropriation were not to be done. In other words, a man writing first person from a woman's point of view was considered faintly distasteful and inadvisable; a white writer trying to write from a black point of view was considered inadvisable; a first-world writer writing about the third world—same kind of thing. That has loosened up a bit, I think, these days. Imagination is given a slightly freer rein, but in a cultural context, literature is taken less seriously and translation barely happens in this country at all.

Chimamanda, do you think that there are rules of cross-cultural appropriation or rules for composition in fiction at all? Your novel Purple Hibiscus was written in English and seems, even though it's about post-colonial Nigeria, influenced in some ways by Western novel writing, and I'm curious if you thought about that while you were writing it.

CHIMAMANDA NGOZI ADICHIE: First of all, I'm ambivalent about the idea of rules when it comes to literature because I think that fiction, and literature in general, should be magical and you should let yourself be free. But going back to your examples of cross-cultural appropriation—men writing from the point of view of women and white people writing from the point of view of black people not being seen as good—I think it's important to keep things in context. I come from a place that for a long time has been grossly misrepresented by people who have written about it. When I read a book about Africa by a non-African, I'm very careful and oftentimes resentful because I think that people go into Africa and bend the reality of Africa to fit their preconceived notions. I think the same could be said for writing about women when you're a man, writing about blackness when you're white, and while I think such writing should be done, it requires sensitivity. It's easy to say that we should do whatever we want because we're writing fiction, but it's also important to remember context and to be circumspect.

MOODY: Chimamanda, can you give us examples of works where you feel the representation issue is particularly troubling?

ADICHIE: The Shadow of the Sun by Ryszard Kapuœciñski has a little blurb on the cover that describes it as the greatest intelligence to bear on Africa since Conrad. And I really was insulted by that, because it isn't the greatest intelligence to bear on Africa, and I didn't think, by the way, that Conrad was particularly writing Africa as Africa was. What's troubling is that this claim sets the norm for how we see Africa: If you're going to walk in Africa, you're told to read that book to understand Africa. But this is really not what

Africa is, at least not from the point of view of Africans in Africa, which I think is an important point of view. These books distort reality—there are many examples. Maybe I shouldn't name names because it's less about the specific people and more about the larger phenomenon of writing without an open mind.

MOODY: So there are some rules in some cases, or at least sensitivities that we have to think about in these moments when we try to write about other cultures.

PATRICK ROTH: I feel we have to judge case by case. I mean, there is a novel, Amerika, by Franz Kafka, and you're not going to tell me that he wasn't allowed to write about America. A couple of years ago, I read about a German writer who supposedly wrote a novel that took place in the former East German Republic and I thought that was wonderful. When I read it, I thought, That's a great idea, because we all had fantasies about the East German Republic at the time. Why wouldn't it be legit for us to broach that subject? Why not write a novel from the point of view of a woman, using the female part in yourself as a man—I mean, why not? Who would want to put a limit on that? It would be literary suicide to limit yourself in that case.

MOODY: Isn't it true that Kafka had never been to America when he wrote Amerika?

ROTH: That's the whole point. Exactly.

MOODY: So it's all about imagination.

TSITSI DANGAREMBGA: I'm not sure whether it's all about imagination because imagination is informed. How is general imagination about Africa informed in this part of the world? I agree with Chimamanda that there must be some limits. A young lady in my part of the world, in South Africa, wrote a short story about a maid on her Sunday off. This young lady was a white South African. She went to one of the best schools, which meant she must have been one of the 10 percent in terms of earning power—upper class—and she chooses to have, as her character, a lower-class African maid. What could she possibly know about this person? The writer was so young, she obviously hadn't had the chance to think about the implications of what she was doing, but it seemed to her like the kind of story that would win her acclaim, which it did: She got a prize in a short-story competition. But the way she represented this character was so completely false.

I had the same experience some years ago when a writer from this country wrote about a girl in my part of the world. She named this girl Nhamo, a word that means negative things in many contexts, but especially in the sense of grief. The title of this book about Nhamo was A Girl Named Disaster. Now, grief and trouble: There are similarities, but the essence—the nuances—are quite different.

Interestingly enough, this book was translated into German and the German translators had some qualms, so they asked me to read the book and write a foreword, which I did. I gave my opinion that actually the translation of this word that was the girl's name, Nhamo, was not adequate in the title. Of course they had to go back to the writer to ask her to endorse my foreword and she refused. As a Zimbabwean who understands what the German people were trying to do, and the English, I had said, "Well, let's put a preface to this that would give it a different context," and the writer refused. I think that kind of cross-cultural appropriation is really illegitimate, but there is no way to stop it. There are no rules to cross-cultural appropriation.

ADICHIE: I want to respond to Patrick. I'm not at all advocating limiting anybody or anything—not at all. As I said, I really don't believe in rules. A writer like John Gregory Dunne, who is somebody I really admire, has written a book from the point of view of a woman, which I believed as a woman. But at the same time, I do think that it's too easy to simply say, "Why not? Why not use the imagination? Why not let the imagination run free?" I think there is something to be said for authenticity, that if you're going to write about a particular experience in specifics, then the least you can do is to learn about it.

MINAE MIZUMURA: Can I just shift the topic? Right now, people are using the word "appropriation" and supposing that the people who appropriate are the dominant people—white people appropriating black discourse or African discourse or men appropriating women's discourse, et cetera. The verb "appropriate" has a force that makes you believe it's the dominant subject who is doing it. Yet if you look at the history of humanity from two or three thousand years back, it's the dominated cultures that do the appropriating. I'm thinking of Japanese literature: Twenty years after major restorations, we appropriated Western literature and that became our literature and we transformed ourselves through the literature. That sort of asymmetrical process still continues and, one hundred years later, we continue to appropriate American culture.

Now, when a Japanese writer is writing in Japanese, she might use a certain alphabet for Japanese characters that was once used only for Western names, because it sounds more modern, more American, more global, more international. The ironic fact is that this literature that appropriates American literature but doesn't really speak truth about Japan is what gets reappropriated into America, because it's the easiest to translate. What I think is the best of Japanese literature hardly ever gets translated. It's the easiest and the already appropriated Japanese literature that gets reappropriated.

DANGAREMBGA: I would argue also that in the term "appropriation," there is a notion of force. If a person is assimilating a literature—for example, Francophone Africans were assimilated into the French culture—can we then say that they have appropriated the culture? I think being assimilated and having your culture appropriated are two different things. In Zimbabwe now we have two opposed parties: one very nationalist and one more, according to Western norms, liberal. I was talking to some younger people in this liberal party and I said to them, "Do you know what you're taking on? We are veterans; we've been through the whole colonial rigmarole. Do you know what we are taking on?" And I quoted to them this limerick: "There was a young lady of Niger/ Who rode on the back of a tiger/ They came back from the ride with the lady inside/ And a smile on the face of the tiger." They said, "Yes, Tsitsi, we know the West is a tiger, but we think we're strong enough— we can tame the tiger." This is in the same sense of not understanding the difference between appropriation and assimilation. Perhaps we think we are appropriating, but we are actually being assimilated. This is problematic— we need to know where we stand so that we can have authentic voices. It's a kind of alienation if you think you're appropriating and actually you're being assimilated; your voice cannot be authentic.

KATJA LANGE-MÜLLER: I can understand this only indirectly. The question seems backward. The question for me as a writer is not "May I do this?" but "Can I do this?" Whether I manage to portray a man is not my decision. This is what the reader decides. If I practice a self-censorship, which says, "May I do this at all?" I might as well stop writing.

DANGAREMBGA: I agree entirely. The audience decides. But between you, the creator, and the audience, there is a third party. This third party is the people who have the power: They have the money, the distribution resources—they physically get your work out there. If you present your work to these people and they say, "This is no good," simply because they feel that a woman should not be writing it, how are you going to get your work out there? Look at nineteenth-century British writers like George Eliot. They did not even dare to appear physically in front of their publishers because they knew they wouldn't get published. Maybe in Germany, the situation is better, but for those people in the world who are still being appropriated, that situation still pertains. For example, a Zimbabwean writer like Chenjerai Hove, who made his name with a novel called *Bones* about a woman spirit medium, was only celebrated because people said, "Wow! He's writing in a woman's voice!" at a time when there were not so many women writers. But how many women writers like that novel, or even women readers? Very few. We have to understand the interval between creative work and the fact of that creative work getting out there. Many cultural and economic decisions prevent voices from being heard.

MOODY: I agree with that. That's how we find ourselves in this country with a paucity of translated literature.

LANGE-MÜLLER: I started writing in a country where what was published and what was not published was really a political decision because it was the GDR. Writers who were suspect wondered while writing whether they would be published or not. One can say that one does compromise because one does think about the readers, but in reality, those compromises were not convincing as literature.

MOODY: I want to move to a hidden subtext in this. Globalization and the economic climate in which we find ourselves suppress local culture in favor of a strange corporate über-culture. I want to address myself to Yoko, who is Japanese and has lived in Japan and yet writes in Germany, and has written in German as well. I'm interested in your own experience of cross-cultural thinking and if you function now in a global context or if you still think of yourself as a local writer.

YOKO TAWADA: I don't think that at this point it is possible to even talk about Japanese literature or culture because that culture has already absorbed so many others, like the Chinese or Western cultures. The same is true for American culture, which has absorbed other cultures from all over the world.

All cultures at this point are pluralist and we who live in these cultures don't belong to just one culture but to many. This does not mean that everything is the same; there are many differences. But you cannot pin them down nationally. One can only take the differences between, say, German culture and American culture as a way to differentiate between these literatures. Kafka could write the book Amerika because America itself is a fiction.

MIZUMURA: I still think that's idealistic. I understand exactly what Yoko means: Every culture is an amalgam of other cultures. But, for example, I have a grandmother who was a geisha. Now, this is a very good topic for a writer to exploit. She eloped with someone who was twenty-five years younger because she couldn't stand her life. I have this topic and still haven't done anything with it, but I want to write about it. I have a choice between whether to write it realistically and interestingly for myself, using all the historical context and proper names that people outside Japan would never understand and all the contours of the Japanese society, which only Japanese readers would understand, or whether to come up with something like Memoirs of a Geisha, which became a bestseller a few years ago. If you want your book to be translated, which I think a lot of authors do, you face these concrete problems: whether you make it more accessible to the global audience, or you don't care, you just want it to be your own thing.

DANGAREMBGA: If I could say something to Minae personally: People who care would like the version that you care about. At the end of the day, it's a question of money: Do you want your money now or do you want a legacy that remains for years?

I want to come back to the idea of appropriation and Kafka daring to write a novel called Amerika—there you are. But let's say I decided to write a novel called Amerika—who would publish it? I'm not just talking off the top of my head here because I've had this experience. Nervous Conditions is now recognized as a good novel, but what did it take to get it published? All Zimbabwean publishing houses, which were run by men at that time, turned me down, and it took a women's organization with a South African woman at the head to pick up that novel.

Between the time of writing the novel and continuing with my life, I did other things, and now I find I'm in the same situation with filmmaking. I turned to filmmaking because I thought writing wasn't working, not knowing that actually it was working, and I have the same problem with film. I've just made a film and people turned it down—Sundance eventually picked it up, but the National Arts Merits Awards in Zimbabwe said it was confused and substandard. We use certain criteria when it comes to judging on a public scale, which really do not always have to do with the merit of the work.

ROTH: This is a way of looking at things that's foreign to me. You write your stuff; you're alone with your psyche, which does not give a damn about whether your book is going to get published, does not give a damn about whether it's going to make money. If you get caught in these questions, you're not going to be able to write—or your writing is not going to be worth anything. It's not a question of whether I should, whether I may, whether I can, artistically speaking, it's whether I must, whether I'm actually compelled to. The writing process, as far as I'm concerned, is about pushing myself to the point where I can only do this one thing, and I absolutely have to do this one thing—otherwise life would not proceed for me. I could not care less at that point about who's going to publish it, is anyone going to like it, is so-and-so going to understand this or that. That is of absolutely no concern to me. I think it is pure poison.

ADICHIE: I find it particularly curious that here in the United States, there's such a thing as a black section of the bookstore—that it's really about what you look like. If I wrote a book about Poland, for example, I would still end up in the black section of the bookstores. There are still categories.

When I was trying to get an agent for *Purple Hibiscus*, I got a really nice response from a woman who said she liked the book very much but she didn't know how to sell me. She said, "You're black, but you're not African American, so I can't sell you as African American, and I can't sell you as ethnic, because right now in the United States, ethnic is Indian." So I considered becoming Indian for a short while.

MOODY: One of the effects of globalization is massive vertical integration of American publishing companies. Twenty years ago, there were two or three times as many publishers as there are now.

In line with this vertical integration comes unwillingness to take risks in terms of what gets published, and this is concurrent with a refining and dumbing down of the critical vocabulary in the country. Globalization selects for a certain kind of aesthetic. In American fiction, we're generally selecting for naturalism against an experimental impulse. We're left with a narrow bandwidth. Is there a similar process happening globally?

DANGAREMBGA: I think it's definitely happening globally. If you come to Zimbabwe, the culture that travels is the culture that people here know, and that culture is not being subsidized by Zimbabweans. The Zimbabwean government hasn't got that much money, so it subsidizes culture that's locally consumed. The culture that travels is generally subsidized by bodies from outside the country that very definitely have an agenda. We see that narrowing process.

As Americans, you don't have to think you're the baddest people in the world. I know that Germans used to think they were, but now maybe Americans think they take that position. But no. Just the fact that there's a gathering like this means that there are still sensitivities out there that we can put to good use. We just need to keep linking up in this kind of forum.

MIZUMURA: You're constantly reminded of the fact that just because what you're writing is different, so remote from what the global market wants, it's not going to be translated. My first book is a continuation of a Japanese classic and I knew from the start that it would never be translated. To have the feeling and write it is sad, because I read in English all the time and I love reading in English. I love Jane Austen, for example, and the people who enjoy Jane Austen would, I'm sure, enjoy my work if they could read in Japanese, but it's not going to get translated.

DANGAREMBGA: But then isn't the problem, "Who are you writing for?" I've had that problem in the reverse in that I have been so pressed to write things that I know European audiences would like, and I'm very capable at that. I kept on having to say, "No, I'm not going to write it until my authentic voice comes back."

MIZUMURA: I think our problem is a little different because you're writing in English.

ROTH: These are just opinions, like a filmmaker talking about his camera when he would really like to show you the film.

DANGAREMBGA: I disagree. I'm having a wonderful time here, and for me, these are issues of life and death.

I've taken to you, Patrick, so I didn't want to say this when you began to speak, but the very fact that you have the luxury to say "I'm not going to write anything unless I write my authentic voice" is something that most people in my country cannot afford to do. We have the British coming in, saying "Write this, write that, go on television, say this, say that, tell people how you've been tortured." People do it because they are hungry. Why are they hungry? It is not because the land has been taken over. It is because in the aftermath of the land being taken over, all aid was frozen. There was an embargo. That's why people are hungry. If we had fertilizer, if we had money for seed, people would not be hungry. We haven't got the luxury of that, we really have not got it. We have to fiddle to the master's tune and some of us are trying not to do that, and we take advantage of audiences like this to harangue people and say, "Please, think differently."

On Not Repeating *Gone with the Wind:* Iteration and Copyright

Jacob Edmond

Jacob Edmond is a faculty member at the University of Otago in Dunedin, New Zealand. Edmond writes on poetry in English, Chinese, and Russian and is author of *A Common Strangeness: Contemporary Poetry, Cross-Cultural Encounter, Comparative Literature* (Fordham University Press, 2012), and of a recently completed book on the poetics of iteration (forthcoming from Columbia University Press in 2019). The piece below originally appeared in a series of brief commentaries that Edmond published under the collective title "Iterations" in the online literary journal *Jacket2*. Of his research on iteration as poetic practice (including repetition, sampling, performance, versioning, plagiarism, copying, translation, and reiterations across multiple media), Edmond writes, "I'm interested in exploring how iterative poetries emerge out of and respond to the challenges to individuality, agency, authority, cultural identity, and difference posed by new technologies of reproducibility and by globalization." Edmond points to the need to acknowledge positionality (i.e., it matters who is performing a poetic project) and the social, political, legal, and cultural contexts in which a poetic project is enacted. Without examining these factors, a project like that which Edmond writes about may end up enacting the racially motivated violence to which it draws attention.

Iterative poetics can serve as a mode of questioning political authority while remaining conscious of the danger that one might be merely repeating what one seeks to overthrow. But some contemporary modes of iteration seem more concerned with contesting other forms of authority. These forms of authority include, as we have seen with Dmitri Prigov's *49th Alphabet*, the cultural authority of classic writers, as well as the economic authority of copyright and intellectual property. These two forms of authority are sometimes, as in the examples I turn to today, intimately linked.

Take appropriation artist Richard Prince's 2011 work *The Catcher in the Rye*, in which Prince seemingly demanded to be sued by publishing under his own name a copyrighted classic that had sold millions. Iterative strategies have also been used to challenge the copyright of another fiercely protected US classic: *Gone with the Wind*. Iteration here becomes a way to respond to a more pernicious form of cultural copying: stereotyping.

In 2001, the estate of Margaret Mitchell took the publisher Houghton Mifflin to court to prevent the imminent publication of Alice Randall's *The Wind Done Gone*. In *The Wind Done Gone*, Randall rewrote *Gone with the Wind* from the perspective of an imagined "mulatto" (as the publisher's blurb uncomfortably puts it) half-sister to the original book's white protagonist, Scarlett O'Hara. Randall's book appropriated some lines from *Gone with the Wind* as part of a story that attacked—and sought to overcome by rewriting—the racial stereotyping of the original. The Mitchell estate took Randall to court, and the district court judge found in favor of the estate, condemning the rewrite as "unabated piracy."

In *The Wind Done Gone* case, the Mitchell estate sought to use the protection of copyright to silence a work that was critical of *Gone with the Wind*, illustrating the dangerous line between protecting copyright and limiting free speech. The appeals court recognized this problem, overturning the decision on the grounds that one of the tests for fair use is whether there is sufficient creative contribution from the appropriator—such as parody—and finding in favor of the defendant in this case.

The Wind Done Gone case not only highlighted how copyright law can threaten free speech; it also underscored the broader stakes of copying as a social practice. If *Gone with the Wind* has become emblematic of nostalgia for the antebellum South, then the book has achieved this status through its mimetic claim to conjure up or to describe that historical moment: to present a copy of historical reality. In making this claim, *Gone with the Wind* also repeats—and so arguably legitimizes—the racial stereotyping of African Americans within US society. Copying *Gone with the Wind*, then, becomes a highly charged question of history and racial politics.

We can see the stakes of copying even more clearly in the writer Vanessa Place's more recent appropriations of *Gone with the Wind*. Place has produced a number of works based on *Gone with the Wind*. Place's "Miss Scarlett" has been discussed by Brian Reed and by me elsewhere. And in 2015, Place provoked controversy and outrage for her broadcasting of *Gone with the Wind* tweet by tweet through her Twitter feed. Here, I want to note yet another iteration: Place's "white out" performance of the text.

Apart from signaling that she is rewriting *Gone with the Wind* by reading aloud the novel's famous final line, Place's performance is a non-reading, erasure, or what she terms a "white out" of the entire novel, in which she stands silently in front of her increasingly uncomfortable audience for two minutes. Of course, "white out" might also refer to the original text's racist, white supremacist ideology and its silencing of other voices. The silence, then, is ambiguous: it could mark Place's attack by deletion on *Gone with the Wind*'s racist ideology, or it could be a performance of that racist ideology's stifling of other voices. Or the silence could refer to the copyright case over *The Wind Done Gone*. Just as the Mitchell estate sought an injunction to stop Randall's rewriting being published, Place performs the violence of this muzzling as a non-reading, as silence. Through the indeterminate meaning of these two minutes of silence, Place highlights ethical questions about copying *Gone with the Wind*, indeed about reading it at all.

On Settler Conceptualism

Michael Nardone

Michael Nardone is managing editor of *Amodern* and developer of PHONOTEXT.CA, an open-access sound recording initiative that organizes and provides metadata on sound recordings related to Canadian poetry and poetics and links to recordings that are digitally available. A postdoctoral fellow at the University of Montreal and affiliated faculty at Concordia University's Centre for Expanded Poetics, he writes on poetics, media, and sound. He was the Fall 2015 PennSound visiting fellow at the University of Pennsylvania. In the following essay, Nardone describes his process of interrogating settler identity and ways of thinking through transcriptive poetics— or what may or may not be considered conceptualism. Nardone emphasizes the political potential of these poetic projects and the responsibilities of those who undertake them.

My initial engagement with and understanding of the expanded practices of Conceptual writing is situated within a particular geography—Denendeh, or the Northwest Territories of Canada—during the proposed Mackenzie Valley Gas Project hearings held throughout the territory. The purpose of the proposed pipeline was to pump natural gas from Arctic Ocean reserves south across the entire territory to Alberta, where it would fuel the production of tar sands oil. Many considered the project to be "basin-opening," meaning that it would serve as a main artery for dozens, if not hundreds, of smaller pipelines that would tap into it, accelerating the infectious spread of Alberta's boom-and-bust petro-economics throughout the North.

The pipeline hearings and media depicting the hearings—testimonies; court transcripts; environmental impact assessments; informative publications such as pamphlets and websites produced by groups with competing interests, i.e. the National Energy Board, Indigenous governments, the pipeline proponents, and environmental organizations; radio and newspaper coverage—were a complex milieu of language. Eleven different languages were used throughout the proceedings: Chipewyan, Cree, Dogrib, English, French, Gwich'in, Inuinnaqtun, Inuktitut, Inuvialuktun, North Slavey, and South Slavey. Often, specific terms and phrases made translation—into other languages, into other epistemological frameworks—exceptionally difficult: for example, words regarding land and livelihood in the various Indigenous languages, or the scientific terms and practices of biologists and ecologists, or the industrial specificities and corporate-speak of the pipeline proponents. Additionally, these languages and their vocabularies were staged within the settler-colonial process of the hearings, which had their own procedures and jargon that were alienating to many while benefitting the corporations and governmental departments that have historically catalyzed social violence and environmental devastation in the North.

I remember attending the hearings and listening to the proponents' lawyers speak variations of the word "mitigation" over and over. The proponents would employ "mitigation measures" to offset any adverse impact the pipeline and its construction would have on the land, its animals, and inhabitants. The effects that increased resource exploration and excavation would have on the Beaufort Sea, the Arctic tundra, and Mackenzie-Valley corridor would be "mitigated." The impact the pipeline would have on the bird sanctuary where the natural gas fields were located would be "mitigated." The fact that herds of caribou would not be able to cross into their calving grounds during construction would be "mitigated." Changes to the permafrost around the pipeline would be "mitigated." The social repercussions of hundreds of temporary workers—mostly men from the south—moving into small, remote Indigenous communities would be "mitigated." Again and again, they said it. "Mitigation" became a concept that, in their mouths, had no meaning whatsoever. Yet its function was clear: "Mitigation" was a word that could satisfy the juridical demands of the process, ward off further scrutiny from environmental groups, while obfuscating and deterring others from challenging the proposal.

I remember listening to an afternoon Dogrib radio broadcast in which the pipeline was discussed at length. I wrote a list of every English word spoken during that hour:

environmental impact assessment
Norman Wells
pipeline
National Energy Board
joint review panel
Northwest Territories
Exxon-Mobil
Premier Floyd Roland
Aboriginal Pipeline Group

access agreement
Alberta-based developer
Imperial Oil
Indian and Northern Affairs Canada
community consultation

These were the words—proper nouns and phrases particular to settler-colonial governance in the North—that could not be translated, the only ones that retained their Anglo-composition in the Dogrib broadcast. If one wanted to pinpoint exact instances in which a settler-colonial epistemology infiltrates another language, one might begin with these terms and the contexts of their use.

I remember reading the National Energy Board's published final decision that approved the construction of the pipeline. It is titled: "Respecting All Voices: Our Journey to a Decision." In it, many of the Indigenous and environmental critiques of the pipeline and the hearings process are ventriloquized and recontextualized, while dissent is edited or erased. A Dene Elder's testimony about honoring the land, its peoples and animals, and her continued efforts fighting against the pipeline appears in the report, with a notable difference. Her comments about honoring the land are there—in large font beside a picture of Deh Cho (or the Mackenzie River)—but the remark about her opposition is absent. One finds instances like this again and again throughout the report. The outright protest against the pipeline is transformed into a gentle suggestion; certain Indigenous perspectives appear in the overall package to highlight the National Energy Board's "consultations"; violences past and future are acknowledged, yet done in a manner so as to be immediately eschewed.

What these examples highlight is how language enacts power, how language enforces power, how language becomes a record of that power. These figurings of settler colonialism is what initially drew me toward the expanded practices of Conceptual writing. At the time of the Mackenzie Gas Project hearings, I sought a poetic practice that engaged the ways language functioned in these milieus, not simply at the level of the word or phrase but as an overall process and structure. I wanted a poetry that confronted the various collective assemblages of enunciation that address particular structures of power. I sought a poetics that documented the institutional violences of settler-colonial empire—its texts, processes, and performances.

I looked for precedents [. . .] works [that] have in common a transcriptive poetics and a repositorial logic, two compositional features that can effectively portray the nexus of power and language. By *transcriptive poetics,*

I mean that the language of the poems is sourced from various "information genres," as John Guillory phrases it—transcripts of testimonies, broadcasts, manuals, newspapers, legal texts—and is rewritten, reframed, or reformatted within a poetic text; by *repositorial logic*, I mean that the authors are working with specific collections of archival materials from which they intentionally select, edit, and construct their poetic text.

I understand that these works arguably are or are not "Conceptual writing." I am less dedicated to a taxonomical title, and more concerned with the compositional tactics they share. They are tactics that on their own do not determine whether or not a work is an example of Conceptual writing, yet they are tactics scrutinized primarily within the milieus in which Conceptual writing has been discussed and debated. They are tactics that continue to be tested and transformed in recent works framed within the milieus of Conceptual writing: in Carlos Soto-Román's *Chile Project: Re-Classified*, a work that documents an attempted blackout of neoliberal terror; in Rachel Zolf's *Janey's Arcadia*, which dredges up and disrupts narratives of colonizing what is presently known as the Canadian prairies; and in Jordan Abel's *Un/Inhabited*, an attempt to dismantle the entire pulp-fiction genre of settler-colonial romance.

"I want a literature that is not made from literature." I read this line from Bhanu Kapil's *Ban en Banlieue* as I complete this writing, and it expresses exactly what was and continues to be for me the primary intrigue of Conceptual writing. I want a literature that is composed of an array of inscriptive practices: their systems, devices, logics. I want a literature that engages the language that forms power relations—modes of supremacy and domination—in the world. Within the milieus of contemporary poetry and poetics, Conceptual writing's ability to take up an array of inscriptive modes and to portray specific enactments of power through language is to my mind its most poignant and provocative contribution. What remains to be thoroughly examined are the differences, responsibilities, and effectivity of these textual transfigurations.

Chapter Reflection

Questions for Discussion

1   On the PEN World Voices Festival panel that is transcribed in this chapter, Chimamanda Ngozi Adichie said the following about cross-cultural appropriation: "I think that people go into Africa and bend the reality of Africa to fit their preconceived notions. I think the same could be said for writing about women when you're a man, writing about blackness when you're white, and while I think such writing should be done, it requires sensitivity." Adichie expands upon this point in the well-known TED Talk "The Danger of a Single Story." Think of a story written by someone whose identity or positionality is in some way different from their characters. Do some research, read interviews with the author, and then read the story again closely: What evidence can you find of the author's sensitivity toward issues of representation and appropriation?

2   A creative writer might be called a cultural producer. The texts we produce have the potential to shape culture. At the same time, our texts are always shaped by culture. In short, we, as writers, at once *shape* and are shaped *by* culture. What comes to mind when you think of yourself as a creative writer who is a "cultural producer"?

3   Do some reading and research on Conceptualism, as a way of thinking about a range of art-making practices. You might look at the anthology *Against Expression: An Anthology of Conceptual Writing* (edited by Craig Dworkin and Kenneth Goldsmith) for one set of examples. Based on your findings and the readings in this chapter, what is your assessment of the *risks* of Conceptual projects? What are the *possibilities* of these projects?

4   In his essay in this chapter, Nardone writes, "Within the milieus of contemporary poetry and poetics, Conceptual writing's ability . . . to portray specific enactments of power through language is to my mind its most poignant and provocative contribution." How is power enacted through language? What can make an artistic project successful in laying bare the workings of power?

Writing Prompt

Design a project that you consider to be appropriative. Your writing may include some of the transcriptive techniques that you read about in this chapter. Then consider: What does it mean that you are the one to do this project—that you are the author of this project? How do you think about your background, identity, and positionality in relation to your project? And what possible effects might this project have in the world? Does it have the potential to offend, cover over, misrepresent, denigrate, or harm? Does it have the potential to amplify, elevate, or reveal? How do you negotiate this potential? What messages might be received from the work, and are these messages what you intend?

Suggestions for Further Reading

1 Chen, Ken. "Authenticity Obsession, or Conceptualism as Minstrel Show." *Asian American Writers Workshop: The Margins* (June 2015). Web.

2 Hong, Cathy Park. "There's a New Movement in American Poetry and It's Not Kenneth Goldsmith: Writers of Color Are Not Bit Players in this Man's Drama." *New Republic* (October 2015).

3 Keene, John. "On Vanessa Place, *Gone With the Wind*, and the Limit Point of Certain Conceptual Aesthetics." *J's Theater Blog* (May 2015). Web.

4 King, Andrew David. "The Weight of What's Left [Out]: Six Contemporary Erasurists on their Craft." *Kenyon Review Online* (November 2012). Web.

5 Lethem, Jonathan. "The Ecstasy of Influence: A Plagiarism" from *The Ecstasy of Influence: Nonfictions, Etc.*, Vintage, Reprint Edition, 2012. Originally printed in *Harper's Magazine*, February 2007.

6 Ziff, Bruce, and Pratima V. Rao. *Borrowed Power: Essays on Cultural Appropriation*. Rutgers University Press, 1997.

Also see: Articles on race appropriation written in response to the Michael Derrick Hudson / "Yi-Fen Chou" *Best American Poetry* 2015 scandal are listed in the following bibliography, available online: Aitken, Neil. "Writers of Color Discussing Craft: An Invisible Archive." *De-Canon: A Visibility Project* (May 2017). Web.

7

Evaluation

Chapter Outline

The Literary/Genre Fiction Continuum

Michael Kardos

> The following piece by Michael Kardos is one of several published responses to Arthur Krystal's "Easy Writers." This piece, "Easy Writers," was published in the May 28, 2012, issue of the *New Yorker* and recounts the history of the "genre novel." Krystal's essay received a number of responses: see, for example, Lev Grossman's article "Literary Revolution in the Supermarket Aisle: Genre Fiction Is Disruptive Technology," published in *TIME* magazine online, which argues that the situation is more complex than Krystal makes it out to be. In what follows, Michael Kardos references both Krystal's and Grossman's essays. Kardos provides a continuum for mapping genre fiction and literary fiction. Michael Kardos is the author of *Before He Finds Her* (Grove Atlantic, 2015) and *The Three-Day Affair* (Grove Atlantic, 2012), along with other novels. (Introduction written by creative writing student Angela Compton.)

A number of compelling arguments have been made recently about literary fiction, genre fiction, and how the two relate—such as in Arthur Krystal's article in the *New Yorker*, and in Lev Grossman's sort-of-reply in *Time Magazine*.

And yet any attempt to describe, let alone define, genre fiction or literary fiction, or to distinguish one from the other, invites so many exceptions that the effort tends to fall apart. Supreme Court Justice Potter Stewart grappled with a similar problem in 1964, when, presiding over *Jacobellis v. Ohio*, he abandoned trying to define the genre of pornography and famously concluded, "I know it when I see it."

Any distinction between genre and literary fiction matters less than it once did. For this, I'm glad. My first book, a collection of short stories, is generally considered literary fiction. My second book, the novel *The Three-Day Affair*, is being called a thriller.

Thankfully, the tired generalizations about genre fiction being the province of stock characters and formulaic plots have eased up, as have the equally tired generalizations about literary fiction, both pro and con. (Pro: only literary fiction has graceful prose; literary fiction alone gets to the root of the "human condition." Con: literary fiction is plot-less. Literary fiction is needlessly complicated.) It takes about two seconds at my bookshelf to dispel these generalizations.

Yet as human beings, we need categories; otherwise, our lives would be impossible to navigate. We categorize and sub-categorize the food we eat, the clothes we wear, the music we listen to, and just about everything else in our lives. It would be surprising if we didn't categorize our novels, too. The trouble is finding a way to do it.

With this in mind, I offer a simple graph, meant to illustrate just *how* literary or *how* genre a work is. I call it *The Literary/Genre Continuum*, because "continuum" sounds cooler than "graph."

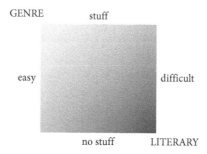

The idea is to plot a novel on the graph based on where it falls on the "stuff/ no stuff" continuum and the "easy/difficult" continuum. The closer to the top-left corner, the more genre-ness the work has; the closer to the bottom-right, the more literary-ness.

By "stuff," I mean things that are out of our ordinary experience, especially things that don't actually exist (as far as we know): interplanetary space travel, elves, vampires; and, to a lesser degree, things that do exist but that are larger-than-life: serial killers; shark infestations. "Difficult" encompasses dense paragraphs, complex sentences, ambiguity, intellectual complexity, and passages that require re-reading not because they're unclear but because they're, well, difficult.

"Stuff" and "difficult" are, of course, subjective—but not completely so. Even if you happen to speed through a Faulkner novel, you still know it's difficult. "Stuff" is a bit more objective: Vampires are stuff. A detective tracking down a murderer is more "stuff" than one investigating a robbery, but less than one hunting a serial killer—especially if the serial killer used to be CIA.

Notably, the Literary/Genre Continuum isn't prioritizing "literary" above "genre" or vice versa, nor is it quantifying how good a particular work is or isn't. Rather, it's a way to illustrate how much literary-ness and genre-ness are in a particular work.

In graphing some novels I've enjoyed recently, I've discovered that I seem to be drawn to works that sit close to the middle of the continuum.

I know I'm not alone. There's something exciting about works that try to have it all: enough "stuff" to intrigue us without dominating the story, and enough difficulty to demand something of the reader without deterring our escape into the fictional world.

I'm not exactly sure what's next on my reading list—but I'll know it when I see it.

It's Genre. Not That There's Anything Wrong With It!

Arthur Krystal

In what follows, Arthur Krystal replies to comments his essay "Easy Writers" received. Specifically referencing Grossman's essay (described in the previous section), Krystal argues that there is a dichotomy between genre fiction and literary fiction—which is not a question of how well the text is written. There are conventions that genre fiction follows that are not descriptive of literature. It is not a matter of which is better; it's a matter of noting that there is a difference.

Arthur Krystal is an author, a screenwriter, and an essayist. His works include *This Thing We Call Literature* (Oxford UP, 2016), along with several other books. (Introduction written by creative writing student Angela Compton.)

Last May, a piece I wrote about genre fiction's new-found respectability caused the digital highway to buckle ever so slightly. Despite my professed admiration for many genre writers, I was blasted for thinking that literary fiction is superior to genre fiction, and for not noticing that the zeitgeist had come and gone while I was presumably immersed in "The Golden Bowl." Apparently, the dichotomy between genre fiction and literary fiction isn't just old news—it's no news, it's finis, or so the critics on Slate's Culture Gabfest and the folks who run other literary websites informed me. The science-fiction writer Ursula K. Le Guin, for instance, announced that literature "is the extant body of written art. All novels belong to it." Is that so? A novel by definition is "written art"? You know, I wrote a novel once, and I'm pretty sure that Le Guin would change her mind if she read it.

Le Guin isn't alone in her generous estimate of literature's estate. *Time* magazine's book critic Lev Grossman also rushed to genre fiction's defense with an agile piece, "Literary Revolution in the Supermarket Aisle: Genre Fiction Is Disruptive Technology," which I heartily recommend, even if he disagrees with much of what I said. Unlike Le Guin, Grossman sees a qualitative difference between certain kinds of fiction while also insisting that good genre fiction is by any literary standard no worse than so-called straight fiction. Literature, Grossman believes, is undergoing a revolution: high-voltage plotting is replacing the more refined intellection associated with modernism. Modernism and postmodernism, in fact, are *ausgespielt*, and the next new thing in fiction isn't issuing from an élitist perch but, rather, is geysering upward from the supermarket shelves. In short, there's a new literary sheriff in town, able to bend time, jump universes, solve crime, fight zombies, perform magic, and generally save mankind from itself.

Grossman invites us to survey "a vast blurry middle ground in between genre fiction and literary fiction" inhabited by the likes of Cormac McCarthy, Kazuo Ishiguro, Kate Atkinson, and Jennifer Egan, whose books don't so much transcend genres as simply collapse them. He argues persuasively that Michael Chabon, Jonathan Lethem, Donna Tartt, and Neil Gaiman have succeeded in "grafting the sophisticated, intensely aware literary language of Modernism onto the sturdy narrative roots of genre fiction. . . . They're forging connections between literary spheres that have been hermetically sealed off from one another for a century."

There's no question that genre enthusiasts have found an eloquent spokesman in Lev Grossman, whose own novel "The Magicians" was hailed as "a postadolescent Harry Potter." Like many readers, Grossman is fed up with benighted critics who seem unaware that contemporary fiction has bloomed into "a new breed of novel" in which "plot and literary intelligence aren't mutually exclusive." He's quite rhapsodic on the subject, declaiming that "plot is an extraordinarily powerful tool for creating emotion in readers . . . capable of fine nuance and even intellectual power." Apparently, we're returning to the good old days of good old-fashioned story-telling, disdained by the modernists (who Grossman grants were "the single greatest crop of writers the novel has ever seen"), who had more high-falutin concerns. A quick side note: Graduate-school wonks may see Grossman's admiring but grudging view of modernism as a neat reversal of Dryden's poem to Mr. Congreve, in which the poet contends, "The present age of wit obscures the past. . . . Our age was cultivated thus at length; / But what we gained in skill we lost in strength."

If Grossman is correct, strength in the form of story has returned to the novel. And, in truth, a few of the writers he mentions have constructed broad canvases, crowded with colorful characters engaged on meaningful quests and journeys. But I have to disagree with Grossman: it's not plotting that distinguishes literary from genre fiction. After all, literary fiction can be plotted just as vigorously as genre fiction (though it doesn't have to be).

There's no narrative energy lacking in Richard Russo, Richard Powers, Jonathan Franzen, David Mitchell, Denis Johnson, Annie Proulx, Gish Jen, Jhumpa Lahiri, and so on. A good mystery or thriller isn't set off from an accomplished literary novel by plotting, but by the writer's sensibility, his purpose in writing, and the choices he makes to communicate that purpose. There may be a struggle to express what's difficult to convey, and perhaps we'll struggle a bit to understand what we're reading.

No such difficulty informs true genre fiction; and the fact that some genre writers write better than some of their literary counterparts doesn't automatically consecrate their books. Although a simile by Raymond Chandler and one by the legion of his imitators is the difference between a live wire and a wet noodle, Chandler's novels are not quite literature. The assessment is Chandler's own, tendered precisely because he was literary: "To accept a mediocre form and make something like literature out of it is in itself rather an accomplishment." So it is. And there are any number of such accomplishments by the likes of Patricia Highsmith, Charles McCarry, Ruth Rendell, P. D. James, Donald Westlake, Lawrence Block, and dozens of others.

Genre, served straight up, has its limitations, and there's no reason to pretend otherwise. Indeed, it's these very limitations that attract us. When we open a mystery, we expect certain themes to be addressed and we enjoy intelligent variations on these themes. But one of the things we don't expect is excellence in writing, although if you believe, as Grossman does, that the opening of Agatha Christie's "Murder on the Orient Express" is an example of "masterly" writing, then you and I are not splashing in the same shoals of language. Grossman's more powerful point derives from an article he wrote three years ago for the *Wall Street Journal*, in which he argued: "Genres are hybridizing. . . . Lyricism is on the wane, and suspense and humor and pacing are shedding their stigmas and taking their place as the core literary technologies of the 21st century." Fair enough, but how does this reify the claims of genre-loving people everywhere? It seems to me that Chabon, Egan, and Ishiguro don't so much work in genre as with genre. "All the Pretty Horses" is no more a western than "1984" is science fiction. Nor can we in good conscience call John Le Carré's "The Honorable Schoolboy" or Richard Price's "Lush Life" genre novels.

Hybridization has been around since Shakespeare, and doesn't really erase the line between genre and literary fiction. Nor should it. Ain't nothing wrong with genre, and when literary novelists take a stab at it, they relish its conventions and their ability to modulate them. Cecil Day-Lewis, the Poet Laureate of Great Britain, happened to write mystery stories as Nicholas Blake, and the Booker Prize-winner John Banville doubles as the mystery writer

Benjamin Black. Sure, their books are escapist, but their plots don't excuse or cover for bad prose. In fact, their books can actually be better than much of what passes for literary fiction, and yet still not qualify as great literature.

Quality comes in different forms: there is Cole Porter and there is Prokofiev; the Beatles and Bach; Savion Glover and Mikhail Baryshnikov—the difference between them is not one of talent or proficiency but of sensibility. When I pick up a novel with a semi-lupine protagonist, like Glen Duncan's "The Last Werewolf," I'm expecting darkness, but not "Heart of Darkness." And I'm not disappointed. Matter of fact, Duncan's foray into horror is so intelligently and exuberantly rendered that the snootiest of readers might forgive himself for letting Robert Musil and W. G. Sebald languish on the shelves.

What I'm trying to say is that "genre" is not a bad word, although perhaps the better word for novels that taxonomically register as genre is simply "commercial." Born to sell, these novels stick to the trite-and-true, relying on stock characters whose thoughts spool out in Lifetime platitudes. There will be exceptions, as there are in every field, but, for the most part, the standard genre or commercial novel isn't going to break the sea frozen inside us. If this sounds condescending, so be it. Commercial novels, in general, whether they're thrillers or romance or science fiction, employ language that is at best undistinguished and at worst characterized by a jejune mentality and a tendency to state the obvious. Which is not to say that some literary novels, as more than a few readers pointed out to me, do not contain a surfeit of decorative description, elaborate psychologizing, and gleams of self-conscious irony. To which I say: so what?

One reads Conrad and James and Joyce not simply for their way with words but for the amount of felt life in their books. Great writers hit us over the head because they present characters whose imaginary lives have real consequences (at least while we're reading about them), and because they see the world in much the way we do: complicated by surface and subterranean feelings, by ambiguity and misapprehension, and by the misalliance of consciousness and perception. Writers who want to understand why the heart has reasons that reason cannot know are not going to write horror tales or police procedurals. Why say otherwise? Elmore Leonard, Ross Thomas, and the wonderful George MacDonald Fraser craft stories that every discerning reader can enjoy to the hilt—but make no mistake: good commercial fiction is inferior to good literary fiction in the same way that Santa Claus is inferior to Wotan. One brings us fun or frightening gifts, the other requires—and repays—observance.

Against Subtlety

It sucks.

Forrest Wickman

The following piece makes a provocative argument about a literary value: subtlety. For context, it's important to gain awareness of the terms "minimalism" and "maximalism" in literature—terms that were in use by the late twentieth century to describe stylistic trends in American fiction. "Minimalism" is often associated with workshop craft principles that prioritize economy of language, concision, and subtext—or subtlety. Less often in workshop courses, perhaps, is an argument made "against subtlety." Forrest Wickman is *Slate's* Culture Editor. This piece appeared in *Slate* in November of 2015 and received many responses in multiple online venues.

Let me be blunt: Subtlety sucks. This statement might anger you. Most of us take for granted that subtlety, in the arts, is a virtue. You can see it in our critical language: It's common to say that a book or movie *lacks* subtlety—the implication being that subtlety is an essential quality. Other times, we say a song or TV show is *heavy-handed*, or *hits you over the head* with its message. Even worse is the rise of the more hair-splitting phrase *on the nose*, as in "Wouldn't you say that metaphor was a bit on the nose?" It's become an artistic sin to "hit it right on the nose," to be right on target. We have to be more oblique, less direct, more obscure.

Our obsession with subtlety, in the way we think about art, is all-pervading. You'll find it in *Mad Men* exegeses, literary criticism in the *New Yorker*, all sorts of movie reviews, theater criticism, and music reviews. Even a recap of an episode of the sitcom *Black-ish* complains, "I *get* it and it's clever enough—but . . . it's a little too on-the-nose." I confess that I've sometimes made this accusation myself. It's become such a part of the critical M.O. that I slip into it whenever I start to fly on autopilot.

For a particular case of how we police subtlety—and for evidence of just how arbitrary it can be to assess whether something possesses the proper degree of it—look no further than the reviews of Jonathan Franzen's new novel. *Purity* is like Franzen's earlier novels except "without the emotional resonance and subtlety," declares the *Economist*. The *Washington Post* and the *Independent*, by contrast, single out the book's subtlety for praise. Particular attention has been paid to the novel's parallels with *Great Expectations*. Critics generally agree that these references are "heavy-handed" (*Jezebel*) and "none-too-subtle" (the *Financial Times*), though *Kirkus Reviews* suggests that Franzen's Dickens nod "isn't heavy-handed." One of the most exasperated notices comes from *Deadspin*'s culture site, the *Concourse*, which singles out a sentence about some seals barking ("You could hear them from miles away, their *arp, arp, arp* a homing call to family members still out diving in the fog") to complain that Franzen is "a little on-the-nose with the metaphors." (The heroine is on her way to see her mother.) In *New York*, Christian Lorentzen sums up the critical response, noting that Franzen stuffs the book with "symbols and allusions that are never too difficult to catch" and "pounds the notes of guilt and shame a little too hard with his Victorian hammer."

Lorentzen is right to identify this approach as Victorian, just as Franzen, with his allusions to Dickens, is right to place the book in a stylistic lineage with the most famous (and most unsubtle) great novelist of that era. The reign of Queen Alexandrina Victoria was the last time we didn't think it so crucial—or even good—to be subtle.

The positive connotation that now accompanies *subtle* is relatively new. When most critics use the word today, they use it to mean, as the *Oxford English Dictionary* puts it, "(deftly) understated," or, as *Merriam-Webster* has it, "hard to notice or see: not obvious." (This is of course not the word's only contemporary meaning. Some still use *subtlety* to mean *nuance*, for example, which is a whole separate topic—my beef is not with nuance.) Before the 19th and 20th centuries, *subtle* was more akin to *obscure*, a word that means essentially the same thing but has a negative connotation. As the 17th-century poet Samuel Butler put it, "The subtler Words and Notions are, the nearer they are to Nonsense." But after the industrial revolutions and educational reforms of the 19th century led to an explosion in the literate population, the Modernists drove meaning deeper and deeper below the surface, with some of them explicitly hoping to wall off their work from the masses: As D.H. Lawrence wrote in one 1917 letter, "There should be again a body of esoteric doctrine, defended from the herd. The herd will destroy everything." At the same time as cultural hierarchies of *highbrow* and *lowbrow* were constructed, it became common to criticize things for being *unsubtle* or *heavy-handed*.

The critics followed the writers, and in the mid-20th century the New Criticism gave us an emphasis on close reading and locating subtext, while at the same time the rise of literary minimalism and creative writing MFA programs spread the gospel of "show, don't tell" and Hemingway's iceberg theory, which holds that the substance of a story, like the body of an iceberg, should remain below the surface.

Twenty-first-century tastemakers like to think of themselves as beyond highbrow vs. lowbrow—that monocle popped long ago—but our eye for subtlety persists. A decade ago, when TV recapping was still finding its footing, it was in vogue to look for *anvils*. By 2004, the dearly departed site *Television Without Pity*, a breeding ground for wags who were smarter than your average couch potato (the site was founded by lit majors) that helped pioneer many aspects of recap culture, made this official: They named *anvils* a part of "The TWoP Lexicon." *Anvil* or *anvilicious*, they said, meant "obvious or heavy-handed writing that has no regard for the viewer's intelligence, thus bludgeoning them over the head with parallels et al. in the manner of Wile E. Coyote and his Acme Brand anvils."

In the decade since, it's become less common to look for the clanging of *anvils* and more common to look for moments that are *on the nose*—even if it's just "a bit," "a little," or "somewhat." As recently as a decade ago, *on the nose* typically meant something positive. (Most dictionaries haven't even added the new definition yet, keeping instead only the century-old meaning of "exactly right" or "on target.") Now calling out on-the-nose—ness, like hunting for anvils before, is practically its own sport: We spot it in a callback to an 8-year-old episode of *Mad Men*, the title of an episode of *Wayward Pines*, the appearance of some portentous-seeming oranges in *Breaking Bad*, or even the lighting and staging of *Nashville*.

And so we mock obvious symbolism. We cringe at message movies and melodrama and novels that too readily reveal what they mean. And we roll our eyes at too-clear subtextual signaling even when we sit down to watch wonderfully unsubtle programs on TV. If we no longer hold the high above the low, why do we still hold the subtle above the unsubtle?

* * *

The idea that to be *on the nose* is undesirable seems to have its origins in comedy (you can see it jump from the writers' room to the screen in meta moments of *Desperate Housewives* and *Family Guy*), which brings us to one of subtlety's more defensible defenses: Being unsubtle can be a little like explaining the joke. According to this line of thought, to be unsubtle is bad because you deny the joy of realization. It's true that there's pleasure in discovering something for yourself, but we should ask ourselves whether that's more important than communicating clearly, or delivering that joy to larger audiences. Too often this defense is a form of self-flattery: This is made plain when we complain that something "talks down to us" or "insults our intelligence," as if the point of a book or TV show is to stroke your ego.

Others argue that doing interpretive work, having to search for meaning, is good not because it's pleasurable, but because it exercises your brain, like a muscle, making it strong. This is the "no pain, no gain" theory of forcing audiences to dig deeper for hidden meaning. But here's the thing: It's still just a theory. Studies have tried again and again to prove it—both for literary fiction and, more recently, for prestige television—but when it comes down to it, there's no real evidence that more subtle entertainment makes you smarter.

Even Hemingway's famous Iceberg Theory, the "Theory of Omission," only works to the extent that the reader picks up on what's omitted—i.e. to the extent that the work *isn't actually all that subtle*. Without the references Hemingway makes to an operation and, well, *white elephants*—a little on the nose, Ernest!—"Hills Like White Elephants" is just a story about a bickering couple. At worst, this kind of coy pruning makes a false virtue out of forcing readers to guess at the writer's intention rather than making that intention clear.

One last defense of subtlety I've heard is that subtle art is free of blunt, distracting gestures—the author's hand rendered visible, intruding onto the screen, stage, or page and breaking the spell. But there is nothing wrong with the hand of the author being visible as long as its presence is purposeful and of a piece with the rest of the work. Dickens can get away with names as unsubtle as Stryver (for a man who's upwardly mobile) or Mrs. Leo Hunter (for a lion hunter), because those names are no more fantastical than anything else in the story, and no less wry. He hasn't slipped and fallen onto the page; he's been sitting there all along, winking at his reader, and the novel is all the more enjoyable because of it. For heaven's sake, Hitchcock used to walk right into the frame.

* * *

The Master of Suspense happens to be a terrific example of how history shows us, again and again, that we actually don't care as much about subtlety as we might expect, given its prevalence in the critical vocabulary. Take *Psycho*, for example. At the time of its release, Bosley Crowther's dismissive *Times* review snidely remarked, "There is not an abundance of subtlety." Complained Crowther: "Hitchcock, an old hand at frightening people, comes at you with a club in this frankly intended bloodcurdler." The *New Yorker* filed a similar grievance: "It's all rather heavy-handed and not in any way comparable to the fine jobs he's done in the not so distant past." In other words, critics mistook the boldness of its style and the radicalness of its shocks—all spiraling cameras, shrieking violins, and openly leering camerawork that pulls the curtain back on viewers' desires—as obvious and regressive, rather than as precisely what would move the medium forward. The reigning greatest film of all time, Hitchcock's *Vertigo*, faced similar criticism for being too on-the-surface, but in hindsight this perceived weakness has become a strength: As James Gray puts it in the new documentary *Hitchcock/Truffaut*, "The subtext seems to be boiling up until its almost text."

Even *Citizen Kane*—the *Citizen Kane* of movies!—is not a subtle work. In Pauline Kael's epic two-part essay on the Orson Welles list-topper, she noted it isn't "a work of subtle beauty." Instead, she praised it backhandedly as "a *shallow* masterpiece" that is "overwrought" with "obvious penny-dreadful popular theatrics." Indeed, if you look at the directors who have the most movies on the American Film Institute's list of the 100 greatest American movies of all time, you come you up with a virtual Hall of Fame of Heavy-Handedness: Spielberg, who is by no coincidence also the highest-grossing director of all time, leads the pack with five entries (*Schindler's List*, which Kael also criticized for being "very heavy-handed," plus *E.T.*, *Jaws*, *Raiders of the Lost Ark*, and *Saving Private Ryan*), followed by Hitchcock, Stanley Kubrick, and Billy Wilder. The exceptionally weighty hands of Frank Capra follow not far behind. Yet these filmmakers' masterpieces stand the test of time—in part, perhaps, because their unsubtle appeal—the thrill of a man outrunning a boulder, the hilarity of a man riding an atom bomb like a bucking bronco—has encouraged generation after generation to discover and love them anew.

This phenomenon isn't limited to movies. In letters, look no further than *The Great Gatsby*, at which critics initially sniffed for being "painfully forced" and "not strikingly subtle." Some of this criticism persists, with a 2013 article in *New York* magazine disdaining the book for being "full of low-hanging symbols." Dickens, too, once was dismissed for the offense of not being subtle. The influential literary critic F.R. Leavis, in his 1948 book *The Great Tradition*, banished Dickens from his canon of "the great English novelists" for this crime, contrasting his work with Joseph Conrad (whom he found "subtler"), George Eliot (whom he praised for her "subtle . . . use of symbolism"), Jane Austen (the one author whose subtlety he did not rate), and Henry James . . . whom he praised for his "un-Dickensian subtlety." But as the years stretched on, Leavis came around on Dickens—deciding he was subtle after all.

I should note that I'm not the first to suggest a pattern here. As the novelist Michael Cunningham, author of *The Hours*, said in 2006:

> History has, it seems, a tendency not only to forgive artists their shortcomings but to value potency over subtlety. . . . Along with many other adjectives, the word "corny" can be reasonably applied to parts of *The Scarlet Letter*, *Moby Dick*, *The Great Gatsby*, and *The Sun Also Rises* (I mean, really, a guy who's had his balls shot off?), among others. Ginsberg's "Howl" is already going into history, as many more exquisitely wrought poems are not. We don't all love all those books, but there's no denying that the human race seems to have some ongoing interest in them.

To be clear, I'm not saying that *all* art must be unsubtle. (Though a lot of it would be better if it were.) Certainly there will always be people whose taste simply runs toward the subtle, and *de gustibus*, etc. Similarly, there will always be creators whose visions tend toward the understated. Even I enjoy some variety. But it's when subtlety is held up as an unquestioned virtue that it does the most damage.

Because bluntness is also a virtue. When artists don't muffle themselves in service of subtlety (or in fear of being called unsubtle), they kindle fervor and fire. When we dispense with subtlety, we're rewarded with work that resonates in every seat in the theater, not just in the orchestra section. And the more a work has something important to convey, the more it should not be subtle. Spike Lee, whose messages about race in America could hardly be more urgent, has been downgraded throughout his career for being "heavy-handed," "melodramatic," and "not exactly subtle." Even some contemporary reviews of *Do the Right Thing* and *Malcolm X* called them "hardly subtle," "shrill," and "didactic." But if Spike Lee wants to speak to the whole nation, why shouldn't he pick up a megaphone?

When we stop fussing over what's too heavy-handed, we can also start piling on the pleasure, and grabbing straight for the heartstrings. When we don't worry about taking the long way around, we gain an emotional directness that is more in tune with the way people actually feel. People's emotions, after all, are not always subtle. They are not hidden under a blanket inside their souls. People feel things, strongly, and creators that underplay that are making it harder for their audiences to connect purely and viscerally to their work. Is every enigmatic thousand-yard stare from Don Draper really better than Jesse Pinkman breaking down and saying "I killed her," or a snippet of voice-over from the Latin Love Narrator, or a "splash, punch" from Cookie Lyon?

Perhaps some of these lessons are already sinking in. However you define "the New Sincerity"—the term has described everyone from David Foster Wallace to Charlie Kaufman and Wes Anderson—we can agree that it refers at least partially to saying what you mean, to what Wallace called "single-entendre principles" and the willingness to "risk accusations of sentimentality, melodrama." As the *Atlantic*'s Megan Garber wrote in an essay on the greatness of Wallace's "A Supposedly Fun Thing I'll Never Do Again": "It is not delicate; it is not subtle. Wallace, given his remarkable talents, could easily have Shown Not Told and Onion-Peeled and Sublimated his way through the story." But instead of keeping the cruise ship seven-eighths submerged, Wallace hoists it up out of the water, examining every detail and doing all the close reading for us, better and with more insight than most of us could muster ourselves.

I see a similar trend in music criticism. Where before critics were more likely to privilege the vague, often-cryptic lyrics of singer-songwriters and alt-rockers, wincing at the direct lyrics of pop and country and hip-hop, now many are paying attention to how much more powerful these songs can be for daring to be straightforward. You can hear this in the crowds shouting along to the choruses of Arcade Fire (a band perhaps best summed up by their use of literal megaphones), or see it in the lines queuing up to cry along with Taylor Swift.

So here's to the heavy-handed ones. The bludgeoners. The Acme-brand anvilers and the ones who swing right for the nose. You can recoil from them or roll your eyes at them. About the only thing you can't do is ignore them. [. . .]

And here's to the told-not-shown ending of *The Great Gatsby*, a book that renders all criticisms of its unsubtlety ridiculous. The whole book is about the appeal of a man who favors loud colors and bold gestures, bright, monogrammed shirts and great fireworks displays of exuberance and wealth. Jay Gatsby comes out and says what he means, even when it means spelling out the themes of the book. ("Can't repeat the past? . . . Why of course you can!") There's one character in that book who hates Gatsby's parties, who thinks he can't be an Oxford man because of his pink suit. When we demand subtlety, privileging masks and minimalism over on-the-sleeve feeling and on-the-nose meaning, we turn ourselves into a bunch of Tom Buchanans.

The Politics of Literary Evaluation

Natasha Sajé

Natasha Sajé was born in Munich, Germany. She is the author of several books of poems and many essays and reviews appearing in journals such as *Kenyon Review*, *New Republic*, and *Paris Review*. Her work has been honored with the Robert Winner and Alice Fay di Castagnola Awards, a Fulbright fellowship, the Campbell Corner Poetry Prize, and the Utah Book Award. Sajé's book of literary criticism, *Windows and Doors: A Poet Reads Literary Theory* (Michigan, 2014), includes chapters on the topics of diction, syntax, rhythm, surprise, figurative language, narrative, genre, book design, and performance. The book allows writers to see their writing through poststructuralist and postmodern, as well as formalist, theories. A version of the essay below was published in the AWP *Writer's Chronicle* in 2004 under the title "Who Are We to Judge: The Politics of Literary Evaluation."

1   Many of the undergraduate staff members of our college's literary magazine have never taken a creative writing course. Once, while reviewing submissions, I suggested cuts to a particular poem and said, "With these cuts, it's not brilliant, but it's not bad." At that, one student threw up her hands: "How does anyone know what brilliant or bad is?"

2   At a Utah Arts Council literary panel meeting, one member began his evaluation of a grant for a reading by mystery novelist Mary Higgins Clark by asking, "Is this even literature?"

3   Three poets teaching in a highly ranked graduate creative writing program are so various in their aesthetics that they don't publish in the same magazines. But when the time comes to determine the top applicants to the program, these three faculty members easily agree.

Readers constantly evaluate literary texts. Picking up a book and putting it down are evaluative acts, as are buying, quoting, citing, translating, performing, alluding to, imitating, reprinting, and publishing. As for writers, they evaluate their own work when they choose what to revise, what to keep, and what to send out for publication. And yet among contemporary writers, the act of evaluation has not received much attention, partly because the criteria in place today are so well understood that there's little need to make them explicit. It is only to those new in the field, such as undergraduate students, that the criteria may seem random.

Because of their immersion in their own era, many writers do not understand that literary values change over time, and furthermore, that while criteria for evaluating literature are generally agreed upon in any given era, these criteria are weighted differently through the centuries. Meanwhile, in the critical camp, even though some literary scholars do consider evaluation and the related topic of canon formation, they tend to ignore contemporary literature. And yet *all* evaluators of literature (readers, writers, editors, and critics) have an ethical obligation to articulate their positions, however mutable. One problem with the contemporary state of affairs is that many evaluators cannot *name* their underlying values.

Rather than being timeless and universal, values are class and culture specific. M. H. Abrams discusses four theories of poetry—mimetic, pragmatic, expressive, and objective theories—in *The Mirror and the Lamp: Romantic Theory and the Critical Tradition.*[1] Both this book and the outlining of theories provided in the *Princeton Encyclopedia of Poetry and Poetics*[2] have been immensely helpful to me in understanding "where readers are coming from" when they evaluate literature. The criteria of evaluation overlap, of course, but paying attention to periods of dominance, for example the pragmatic theory's reign during the eighteenth century and its reemergence in the last thirty years of the twentieth century, clarifies the politics of literary evaluation.

Four Theories

The first theory is *mimetic.* This theory presumes that art should show us the world. The word mimesis comes from the Greek word for "mirror": Aristotle believed that art's primary aesthetic criterion was truth to nature, that art should convey reality, and Abrams points out the frequent use of the mirror as metaphor for realism, from Leonardo to Samuel Johnson, who praised Shakespeare for "hold[ing] up to his readers a faithful mirrour of manners and of life."[3] We use this theory of art when we judge a work against our experience of what is true or correct. When someone says, while critiquing a short story, "No thirteen-year-old boy would talk that way," or someone stands before a painting and says, "It doesn't look like a tomato," they invoke the mimetic theory. Abrams acknowledges that "the deviation of art from reality has always been a cardinal problem for aesthetic philosophy," solved by "claiming that art imitates not the actual, but selected matters, qualities, tendencies, or forms."[4] This is restated more elegantly in Marianne Moore's definition of poetry as "imaginary gardens with real toads in them."[5]

The second theory of art is *pragmatic*. It presumes that art has a social purpose, that art is a means to an end. Cicero and Horace applied rhetorical theory to poetry with pragmatic intent. Sir Philip Sidney said that "poesy is an art of imitation . . . a speaking picture . . . with this end: to teach and to delight."[6] Eighteenth-century satire rests on the idea that it can change the reader, as does eighteenth-century architecture. (Picture the calming effect of the Royal Crescent in Bath.) The pragmatic theory of art also operates today. In 1990, the editors of the first Heath anthology of American literature were breaking new ground (and received criticism for doing so) when they included voices of little known minority writers; now this is standard practice for anthology editors.[7] However, to be accepted and effective, the pragmatic theory needs to operate alongside the objective theory (explained below). Without ancillary attention to formal excellence, the pragmatic theory of art can lead to a misguided sense of social justice, for instance when committees choose work only because of its social content or the writer's minority status.

The third theory of art is *expressive*. It posits that artists have a special connection to emotions, and that emotions are what make us human. The expressive theory also has a long history: In "On the Sublime," Longinus praised Sappho for her ability to convey sublime emotion.[8] The expressive theory presumes that art transports us to a better or higher realm (*ekstasis* comes from the Greek root for "transport") and that art's intensity and excitement can be shared by readers and viewers. Keats' idea of negative capability has its root in the expressive theory of art, as does Harold Bloom's notion of genius. Bloom defines genius as an act of passionate intellectual engagement with the highest expressions of creativity, arguing that geniuses can express the ineffable, describing feelings that have eluded the rest of us.[9] Thus, the source of poetry is the poet himself—and that source erupts spontaneously. Two other famous articulations of the expressive theory of art are found in Wordsworth's "Preface to the Lyrical Ballads" and J.S. Mill's 1833 essay "What is Poetry?" in which he writes, "poetry is feeling, confessing itself in moments of solitude."[10]

The fourth theory of art is *objective*. It focuses on the work itself, judging its unity, probability, progression, balance, contrast, coherence, and selection.

The objective theory of art was articulated by Italian Renaissance thinkers, including Landino, Tasso, and Scaliger. Until Kant, however, the objective theory, like the mimetic, was applied only in concert with the other theories. Kant's notion of "beauty without purpose" from his *Critique of Judgment* marks the beginning of artistic judgment separated from other factors such as use or function.[11] By separating what is good from what is beautiful, Kant introduces the notion of disinterestedness, the idea that taste can be exercised "objectively." However, not until the twentieth century did the objective theory of art dominate, finding its fullest articulation in Russian formalism, explication du texte, and New Criticism. The objective theory of art is arguably still dominant today.

New Criticism and the Literature Textbook

New Criticism, the academic and critical arm of British and American modernism, was a largely American movement that grew out of the literary modernism practiced by writers such as Ezra Pound, T.S. Eliot, James Joyce, and Ford Maddox Ford. In the United States, proponents of New Criticism included Allen Tate, John Crowe Ransom, Cleanth Brooks, and Robert Penn Warren. Brooks' and Warren's 1938 textbook, *Understanding Poetry,* began a tradition in such texts of juxtaposing "good" and "bad" poems, and of identifying objective criteria by which to distinguish them. Such a focus on evaluation rests on the idea that "good" art not only rises to the top, but also that its quality is eternally lasting and easily discernable to connoisseurs.[12]

Reliance on the text itself ignores its context. For instance, Brooks', Purser's, and Warren's 1952 edition of *An Approach to Literature* includes an appreciative reading of the ballad "Frankie and Johnny" next to a reading of the ballad "Sir Patrick Spens," yet nowhere in either discussion is any mention that "Sir Patrick Spens" is from the Scottish seventeenth century or that "Frankie and Johnny" is part of the nineteenth-century African American Blues tradition and exists in dozens of variants around the country. The editors present both poems without historical context, as if their printed versions are the only versions. As an example of a "bad" poem that "will not stand up under serious contemplation," the editors use Alfred, Lord Tennyson's "The Bugle Song," a poem that reads like a song lyric and in fact was later set to music.[13]

The New Critical reader learns to discredit emotion and context, and to favor instead subtlety, paradox, irony, complexity, tension, symbols, tone, theme, and imagery. A look at the articles published during the nineteen-forties, fifties, sixties and seventies, in *PMLA* (*Publication of the Modern Language Association*), the leading journal of literary scholarship, documents the dominance of New Criticism. A New Critical "scholar" did not need to research the context of the work, era, or author to apply formalist tools to produce pages of close reading. Robert Scholes points out that literature is still taught this way in high schools, naming web bulletin boards where students desperately ask for advice on finding the symbols or irony in poems or stories assigned to them by their teachers.[14]

As a genre, poems seem particularly well suited to close reading. For example, exam questions that require the student to explicate a poem without knowing who wrote it or when. On the other hand, narrative and drama are not as well suited to New Criticism because these genres require more contextual knowledge, and they tend to contain more references to people, places, and things. The irony of all New Critical readings, of course, is that it is to some degree impossible to read anything without context: we bring our own context to everything we read, but rarely do we make that context explicit.

Two legacies of New Criticism found in literature anthologies today are the tendency to present texts without context and the attempt to teach students the difference between "popular" (or "low") and "high" art. The latter attempt is probably an effort to make students appreciate the literature they are being taught in college. For instance, *The Bedford Introduction to Literature* compares "formula fiction" by Karen van der Zee to Gail Godwin's story "A Sorrowful Woman" and greeting card verse by Helen Farries to John Frederick Nims' "Love Poem."[15] The tradition of evaluating poetry according to formalist criteria alone is also carried on by X.J. Kennedy and Dana Gioia in their textbook *Literature* (Longman, 2003). The chapter "Recognizing Excellence" begins: "Why do we call some poems 'bad'? We are not talking about their moral implications . . . [but about] some weakness in a poem's basic conception or in the poet's competence."[16] The editors juxtapose Emily Dickinson's "A Dying Tiger—Moaned for Drink" (1862) against other poems of hers that presumably do not contain the following flaws: inappropriate sound or diction, awkward word order, inaccurate metaphor, excessive overstatement, forced rime, monotonous rhythm, redundancy, simplemindedness, or excessive ingenuity.

A Dying Tiger—Moaned for Drink[17]

A Dying Tiger—moaned for Drink—
I hunted all the Sand—

I caught the Dripping of a Rock
And bore it in my Hand—

His Mighty Balls—in death were thick—
But searching—I could see
A Vision on the Retina
Of Water—and of me—

'Twas not my blame—who sped too slow—
'Twas not his blame—who died
While I was reaching him—
But 'twas—the fact that He was dead—

I imagine the editors denigrate this poem because of the abrupt ending and perhaps because Dickinson uses the phrase "His Mighty Balls" to refer to the tiger's eyes. The obscene connotations and unintentional humor of this phrase today speak to the changing context of language. But what if we restore an historical context to the poem?

Both Daneen Wardrop[18] and Shira Wolosky[19] have argued that many of Dickinson's poems express concern about Abolition and/or the Civil War. More particularly, Wardrop argues that the image of the tiger represents a slave revolt. Alfred Habegger notes that Dickinson suffered frightening eye problems.[20] Eleanor Heginbotham points out that the poem appears in Fascicle 28, where it is opposite "'Tis not that Dying hurts us so—It is Living—hurts us most—most / But Dying—is a different thing—A kind behind the door." The "Dying Tiger" ends with the clunk of death itself, and is placed in a fascicle where there are other representations of dying, yearning to die, and dying for others. Heginbotham argues that Dickinson's poems—such as this one, thought to be mere filler by the New Critics—can be read as interesting revelations of the poet's mind in dialogue with itself and with her time and its clichés, excesses, cruelties, and false pieties.[21] The problem of reading poems isolated from their context is that we use *only* the objective theory of art, and the resulting self-limitations are as destructive as reading poems only for their content or the identity of their authors.

Only recently has the literature textbook gone beyond formalism and been re-imagined using other theories of art. In addition to the aforementioned Heath anthology and others that emphasize the pragmatic theory of art by including minority voices, newer literature anthologies are additionally attempting to contextualize the works they print. For instance, *Understanding Literature* (Houghton-Mifflin, 2003), edited by Walter Kalaidjian, Judith Roof, and Stephen Watt, includes chapters titled "Beyond

Formalism: Poetry and New Historicism," "A Casebook on Poetry and Social Activism Between the Wars," and "Post-Colonial Poetics," as well as chapters on poetic form, prosody, and emotive poetics.[22] The editors emphasize context for all the genres they include. That Kalaidjian, Roof, and Watt are scholars and not creative writers is significant; their theoretical training gives them a broader base than formalism alone.

Creative writers, even those in PhD programs, tend to take only a few theory classes, and because their dissertations are collections of poems or stories or a novel, they don't practice contextual criticism. Meanwhile, formalism and the objective theory of art are practiced in every MFA workshop wherein students are taught to take apart their creations, looking at balance, coherence, and composition. They examine the thing—not who made it or what for, but *how it works*. They are taught to focus on form rather than on content. Another legacy of formalism—"blind" judging—addresses both the intentional fallacy (by discrediting the author's intentions) and the affective fallacy (by discrediting the effect on the reader).

Publishable Literature

Editors and publishers tacitly agree to use objective criteria when deciding what to print, so the term "publishable" has a recognizable meaning among the group that controls literary publication in the U.S. This category of "publishable" is of course very wide to permit variance in subject matter, personal preference, and changing fashions, and it is growing even wider as the number of books published each year increases. However, while writers are usually vociferous in making pronouncements of literary value (i.e. "What an awful book!"), they do not generally deny the publishability of the books they disdain. Thus, judges can often agree on the finalists for any literary prize but may argue over the winner. For example, while judging a neighboring state's arts council's poetry awards, the other two judges and I easily whittled down 250 submissions to the top 50. It was much harder to narrow the top 50 down to a group of ten winners.

Although some editors who are also writers use their editorial power to get their own work published (for example by trading manuscripts), and some writers offer favors to publish their work, the process of publication is by and large a meritocracy according to objective criteria—and no mystery to anyone who reads a variety of literary journals and books, as one might do while enrolled in an MFA program—which explains the general disdain for books published by vanity presses. Of course, this meritocracy is largely controlled by men, as the organization VIDA: Women in Literary Arts has documented. However, while female authors are published in smaller numbers than male authors, it's important to note they also generally submit fewer works to journals and presses. The meritocracy also explains a phenomenon that occurs when large numbers of publishable manuscripts must be whittled down to one or two winners: the regrettable phenomenon of *negative* elimination. When faced with hundreds of publishable or good manuscripts, it is often easier to find things *wrong* with some of them than to focus on what's admirable about others. The reader's evaluative machinery switches into high gear: this one isn't dense enough, that one doesn't have music, etc.

In the case of the New Critics, the practice of distinguishing between good and bad poems became a way to create an elite, academic literature composed mostly of the works of college-educated white, male writers. Robert Scholes notes that Allen Tate's 1938 review of Edna St. Vincent Millay in the *Southern Review* took her to task for writing about the Sacco and Vanzetti case, for preferring politics to [formalist] art.[23] Indeed, some New Critics separated themselves from politics in an effort to make the practice of objective art the highest value. They did not acknowledge that all writing is in some sense political: by not explicitly challenging the dominant ideology (which in the U.S. is white, male, middle or upper class, and heterosexual), a writer implicitly supports it. Writing about the beauty of trees is also *not* writing about race, gender, or class. Contemporary attempts to discredit "political" poems on the basis that they lack art often echo these New Critical attacks. Formalists hold complexity as a cardinal virtue because it gives more play to such qualities as balance, irony, and metaphor. There is a lesson to be had in seeking the virtues of complexity, namely that a text can indeed appear to be simple, because when the critic is not allowed to discuss the author, the historical period, or the implications, that leaves very little else to talk about.

Structuralism, Poststructuralism, and Deconstruction

Structuralism is a kind of criticism that takes its practice from formalism, but differs from it in awareness of itself as a critical practice. Swiss philologist Ferdinand de Saussure believed that language is above all a system (*langue*) within which individual utterances (*parole*) must be understood. The study of codes, signs, and rules helps us understand the cultures that produce them. The linguistic structuralism of Ferdinand de Saussure and the anthropological structuralism of Claude Levi Strauss both look at the formal and repeated features of a language or a culture, but recognize the political aspects of their practice and try to make their own assumptions explicit. Jonathon Culler notes that structuralism's attempt to make its processes explicit results in a greater awareness of literature as an institution.[24] Conversely, the New Critics assumed their hierarchies and practices were "natural" and thus did not question them. A New Critical study of a short story might focus on the contrast between light and dark to demonstrate the story's art, while a structuralist study of that contrast might focus on *why* light and dark are oppositional—in other words, on the values of the culture.

Literary scholars working in gender studies, new historicism, and psychoanalysis emphasize context alongside text. While relying on close reading techniques and/or formalist criteria, they also venture into issues that for much of twentieth-century criticism were deemed inappropriate: how and why texts get produced, who writes them and out of what need, how the texts shed light on social and economic issues. To understand culture, such critics chip away at the division between "high" and "low" art, for instance, between a Jorie Graham poem and a Hallmark card verse (which might be written by Maya Angelou). They presume that "low" art might tell us something interesting about a culture and, moreover, that the very distinction is political.

Deconstruction, associated with French philosopher Jacques Derrida, is a philosophy of language that grew out of postmodern concerns with the instability of language. Deconstructive readings of texts, not unlike New Critical readings, focus on the text itself. However, deconstructive readings look for slippage, gray areas, and inconsistency, while New Critical readings make the text into a coherent whole. Among other ways of bringing culture into criticism, deconstruction questions the "not said"— the gaps—to expose and interrogate the binary oppositions that rule our lives, oppositions between black and white, male and female, gay and straight, body and mind, reason and emotion, etc. Ideology inevitably constructs hierarchies for oppositions, and the default is dominant: *white, male, straight, mind, reason*. Deconstructive readings are difficult (we're not trained to notice what's not there, for instance) and rarely practiced in isolation from other poststructuralist criticism. And deconstruction, like other poststructuralist criticisms, is highly conscious of itself as a critical and political practice.

Class Preferences

Since the Renaissance, recognized artists and writers have been mostly middle-class, and since the beginning of the twentieth century, mostly university educated. French sociologist Pierre Bourdieu has researched issues of class and taste in his groundbreaking study, *Distinction: A Social Critique of the Judgement of Taste*.[25] Bourdieu points out that cultural capital equals academic capital, and that universities educate students in taste. Thus, social classes share certain tastes—for example a preference for abstract art or realist art. While social class in the United States is more fluid than in France, a university education in both countries maintains one's class status or causes it to rise. Once we receive an advanced degree in creative writing, we join a club, and our membership in that club depends on guarding the entrance gates. Joining the club gives us certain privileges, for instance the authority with which to critique the work of other members. There's a different club for scholars, however, and accompanying differences in their attitudes toward art can produce tension in English departments. Creative writers tend to rely on the objective theory of art, while poststructuralist scholars have been trained also to consider context. Formalism, however, is the default that unites everyone with an advanced degree in writing or literature or equivalent years of reading. Moreover, this education makes its recipients eager to judge, to evaluate, and to discriminate.

Avant garde and postmodern art tend to be bourgeois, Bourdieu points out, bourgeois meaning middle-class and college-educated. The French working class of the 1970s preferred mimetic art and insisted that every image must perform a function. When asked to rank the artfulness of various images (what would make a better subject for a work of art) working class respondents chose things like flowers and sunsets, while bourgeois respondents preferred car wrecks. The separation of form and content is linked to a higher level of class and education in Bourdieu's studies; thus, intellectuals, taught to believe in representation more than the thing represented, take bourgeois attitudes toward art one step further. The notion of a pure aesthetic (the objective theory of art) is rooted in a chosen distance from the necessities of the natural and social world. In other words, a pure aesthetic is founded on a belief that artists, writers and their products can be separated from issues of class, race, gender, etc. The contradiction between postmodern theory (that strives to be political) and an aesthetic that privileges form over content has made twenty-first century poetry a particularly interesting evaluative time. Poets who make an issue of their race, class, and gender, etc. offer challenges to American poetry that strike at the very heart of "objective" assumptions. Their increasingly numerous voices have made U.S. poetry more vital, and criticism of their work tends to practice the pragmatic theory of art in tandem with the objective.

The Academic and the "Average" Reader

Literary professionals achieve a boost in class status through an education that also separates them from general readers. Janice Radway argues that there's a gulf of purpose between academics and general readers, and that one longstanding artifact of "middlebrow" art is the Book-of-the-Month Club. Book-of-the-Month Club editors and readers choose books to know, to connect, to communicate, to share, (and to sell), while academics read to evaluate, to explicate, to explain, to discriminate, and to judge.[26]

Academics are trained to dissect and judge literature in formal ways and this training unites them, something made clear to me in Fall 2002 when I was asked to participate in a model book group at the Salt Lake Public Library. The leaders put together as diverse a group as possible: a disabled Chicano lawyer, an amateur Mormon poet in her seventies, a Mormon writer of adolescent fiction, a Latina professor of communication, a humor writer, a judge, a recent college graduate and poetry-slam winner originally from Tonga, the associate director of the Utah Humanities Council, and two university poets. Not surprisingly, despite our age, racial, religious, gender, or ethnic differences, those of us with graduate degrees in literature had more in common with each other than with anyone else because we had been trained to look at literature as formalists, and were eager, above all, *to evaluate it*. Everyone else in the group discussed the general content of Barbara Kingsolver's *The Bean Trees,* but the four academics with PhDs focused on form—and on how it wasn't a very good book because the message was too simple and the characters were not complex enough. Perhaps the academics would have preferred a book that gave us more to do.

Although some books taught by university professors are also Book-of-the-Month Club selections, the overlap is not large, partly because contemporary literature is marginalized in the academy. As poet and professor Alicia Ostriker says, in the academy "a living author is an embarrassment."[27] A living author usually has a lot to say about her writing, which refutes the intentional fallacy, and a living author cannot be unmeshed from the culture that produced her. The popularity of book readings and signings testifies to the current interest in living authors among the general reading public and other writers, but not necessarily the interest among literary scholars. The audience composition of a university reading series will generally consist of undergraduate students who are required to attend, graduate creative writing students, and a sprinkling of English faculty members. Very often the latter sprinkling consists of people who have devoted their working lives to literature—to texts written by dead authors—and so they are inclined to find literature written by living authors to be insufficiently weighty. Hindsight, of course, is an aid to evaluating the worth of any text, and the more that's been written about a text, the more value it seems to have.

The struggle between the academy and the general reading public is a struggle to control reading practices, and the division of "high" art from "low" and "middlebrow" art is part of this struggle. Academic writers routinely look down their noses at The League of Writers and The State Poetry Society, grassroots organizations that sponsor workshops and contests, and organize readings by writers of mystery, fantasy, and romance. Proclaiming themselves the gatekeepers of "high art," academic writers in advisory positions on arts councils attempt to keep the distinctions clear and sometimes prohibit access to public funds. They do so because they have been trained to see themselves as superior, and because the limited funds for art in this country seem to necessitate a battleground mentality.

The struggle between "high" and "middlebrow" art was made clear in Jonathan Franzen's 2001 encounter with Oprah's Book Club. According to Franzen, the typical Oprah novel (note that she never chose a book of poems) is a "schmaltzy, one-dimensional book" that made him "cringe."[28] Franzen neither outwardly rejected being an Oprah pick, nor took the distinction with good grace, as James Wolcott points out in The New Republic, but when Oprah caught wind of his ambivalence, she withdrew her first offer to have him appear on her show. Of course, the resulting flak gave him even more publicity. Interestingly, upon publication of his 2010 novel Freedom, Franzen seemed happy to appear on Winfrey's show and be featured on her website.

Celebrity and Popularity

Publicity is allied to popularity and thus reeks of "low" art. In her essay, "I Know Why the Caged Bird Cannot Read," Francine Prose goes so far as to hold the popular poet Maya Angelou partly responsible for the decline in literacy among high school students, citing Angelou's sloppy metaphors and infelicitous syntax.[29] Perhaps Prose was prompted to this measure by Angelou's simple writing and her popularity. Angelou's poem written for Bill Clinton's inauguration, "On the Pulse of Morning," was sold in drugstores as a chapbook. Angelou received $35,000 per appearance, and her memoirs were bestsellers. It seems that Angelou needed to be brought down a notch, as anyone does who rises to stature—whether real or imagined. But I can "remember when": In 1974, I took a course in women's literature at the University of Virginia (one of the first offered there), taught by James Joyce scholar Suzette Henke, and the course included a serious study of *I Know Why the Caged Bird Sings*. In the intervening quarter of a century, Angelou's unforeseen rise in popularity resulted in her being stricken from the ranks of "high" art. When she appeared in Salt Lake City in 1999, the audience was composed of the general reading public and high school students. The academic poets stayed away.

Some celebrities write literary books (e.g., Carrie Fisher, Steve Martin, Jewel, Jimmy Carter, Paul Reiser), and their books sell simply because of who they are, usually not cause for outcry from writers whose work is formally better but financially less remunerative. But when writers become celebrities—as is the case with Maya Angelou or, in the previous generation, Anne Morrow Lindbergh—"high" art writers discipline their celebrity peers. In 1957 in *The Saturday Review* John Ciardi reviewed Anne Morrow Lindbergh's vastly popular seventh volume of poems, *The Unicorn and Other Poems*, and called it "an offensively bad book—inept, jingling, slovenly, illiterate even, and puffed up with the foolish afflatus of stereotyped high-seriousness, that species of aesthetic and human failure that will accept any shriek as a true high-C."[30]

While negative reviews are an essential part of the critical dialogue, it is their tone and timing that I call attention to here. The reviewer often attempts to distinguish himself or herself from the "low" art subject. In "If Only We Couldn't Understand Them: How Contemporary American Poets Are Denaturing the Poem," Joan Houlihan denigrates popular poets: "the Billy Collins poem . . . is also a Mary Oliver poem, a Rita Dove poem, a David

Lehman poem, a Maya Angelou poem, among other contemporary poets, because it is a poem we can understand. Immediately. We feel no drive to delve. It is not a poem we need to analyze. There are no pesky layers of meaning. What you see is what you get."[31] Jeredith Merrin similarly takes Collins to task in an article entitled "Art Over Easy" in the *Southern Review*.[32] These critics make excellent points. But it is useful for our discussion here to ask whether the criticism is motivated by the writer's popular ascent. Formalist criteria are often used to discipline writers who transgress the bounds of decorum (and poverty?) by becoming too popular.

But what of a writer like Toni Morrison, a writer who is popular *and* critically acclaimed? Her books are Oprah picks, and made into movies, *and* she won the Nobel and Pulitzer prizes and is widely taught and studied. It seems that Morrison's novels give the objective theorists enough symbols, paradox, and ironies, while also pleasing poststructuralist and pragmatic critics because of their social content. Toni Morrison, like William Shakespeare, writes texts that appeal to a broad range of readers for a variety of reasons. Yet there may come a time when her novels, like the plays of Shakespeare, fall out of fashion. We have no way of knowing when that will be. A look at the anthologies and prizewinners over the past hundred years proves that some acclaimed writers later disappear from prominence.

Critic Jane Tompkins explains what poststructuralist critics understand—that "literary classics do not withstand change, rather they are always registering, promoting, or retarding alterations in historical conditions as these affect their readers, and especially, members of the literary establishment."[33] That Shakespeare's tragedies were rarely performed for over a hundred years during the eighteenth century suggests they do not have universal and timeless appeal. His sonnets, as Barbara Herrnstein Smith notes, were despised by many nineteenth-century critics. Herrnstein Smith posits that the academy has remained "beguiled by the humanist's fantasy of transcendence, endurance, and universality," and thus is unable to acknowledge the mutability and diversity of literary values. All value is radically contingent because it is produced within a particular economy. Thus texts that endure often "appear to reflect and reinforce establishment ideologies" and never radically "undercut establishment interests."[34]

When Herrnstein Smith refers to the "academy" of forty years ago, she is pointing to those scholars trained in the New Criticism, not to poststructuralists like herself. Her idea that enduring texts are *conservative* texts is chilling, and a wake-up call for those of us who teach. It also casts a shadow on Oprah's reinvented book club, which focused on "classic" novels by writers such as Austen, Dickens, and Faulkner. The previous version of Oprah's Book Club emphasized character and plot, and revered the author's ability to provide ancillary information—a mix of biographical criticism and formalism. Her website notes that "[The newer] show originate[d] from a site connected with the selection—the author's birthplace, the book's setting or some other relevant locale. Oprah.com feature[d] comprehensive support, including companion study guides, for readers' keener appreciation." A quote from Oprah herself (since withdrawn from the website) suggests a Harold Bloomian emphasis on greatness, tinged with pragmatism: "I cannot imagine a world where the great works of literature are not read. My hope is *The Oprah Winfrey Show* will make classic works of literature accessible to every woman and man who reads . . . I hope to invite readers throughout the world to visit or revisit a universe of books of enduring usefulness, because I believe that the sublimity of this experience, this gift to ourselves, is something that we owe to ourselves."

Texts by Shakespeare, Morrison, and Hawthorne might "endure" because they contain elements that appeal to a variety of audiences for a variety of reasons. Tompkins argues that the claim to "classic" status rests on different texts read within a different frame of assumptions. For example, nineteenth-century readers of Hawthorne favored domestic sketches like "A Rill from the Town Pump" and "Little Annie's Ramble," not the stories we prize today like "The Minister's Black Veil." Moreover, Hawthorne was praised in the 1830s in the same terms as writers like Harriet Beecher Stowe and Susan Warner—primarily for their ability to evoke sentiment (i.e. the expressive theory of art). Hawthorne as a writer interested in psychology is a post-Freudian creation. Tompkins' own aim is revealed in the subtitle to her groundbreaking book, "The Cultural Work of American Fiction." We can see then that restoring (or attempting to restore) original context to a literary work enables it to be read for reasons other than formalist "complexity" and "irony." Tompkins succeeded in reviving interest in sentimental authors like Stowe who were vastly popular during the nineteenth century but rarely read in the twentieth: rather than holding their books up to modernist standards, Tompkins reads them in an historical context and values them for what they are.

It is no accident that many of the authors of the eighteenth and nineteenth centuries who are no longer widely read are female. The novel's earliest practitioners in England were women who wrote potboilers to support themselves—women like Eliza Haywood, Mary Davys, and Charlotte Lennox—and there are even some instances of men writing under female pseudonyms for the same purpose. As the novel gained legitimacy and status during the eighteenth and nineteenth centuries, more men started writing novels, which helped turn the genre into "high" art. Gay Tuchman's *Edging Women Out: Victorian Novelists, Publishers, and Social Change* offers evidence for this gender and status shift from the records of Macmillan publishers in London.[35] The rise of the female poet in the United States since the 1970s is a phenomenon that also deserves study. As greater numbers of women started writing and publishing poetry, the genre declined in status, even in academia.

Poetry and Academia

Each generation of poets in the twentieth century has its academics and its populists— Ezra Pound and Vachel Lindsay, for instance, in the 1920s. The "difficult" poet's work is taught in universities and studied by scholars, something that poets in academia can't help but notice. So, which do we want—to be popular or to be critically acclaimed? Shortly after Billy Collins was named Poet Laureate, my conversation with several other women poets turned to his poems. "They're nice enough, but they're too simple," said one. "They don't hold up to re-reading," said another. "People will say to me, why can't *you* write like Billy Collins?" said the third. "Easy-listening," we chorused. I didn't realize it then but our session marked our effort to distinguish ourselves from Collins' popular, accessible, non-academic poetics as well as our attempt to secure our own membership in elitist poetry circles, ones until recently closed to women. The fact that Collins' work is read and loved by many readers immediately makes it suspect. An additional irony in the debate over Collins' accessibility is the fact that he earned a PhD in Romantic literature. He has *chosen* to be accessible and accordingly is criticized for it by fellow academics.

Critic Helen Vendler blames a waning student interest in poetry on the shift back toward the pragmatic theory of art and away from objective "perfection,"[36] but I would argue that it is New Critical readings of difficult poems practiced by experts like Vendler with their emphasis on "excellence" that are responsible for any decline in student interest in poetry. As a Poet-in-the-Schools, I found that students like poetry until that liking is regimented, restricted, and *judged*; in other words, until they are expected to evaluate the products they are being taught to produce. One might cite the increase of creative writing degrees, the number of poetry magazines and books published, and the poetry slam phenomenon as evidence of a healthy interest in poetry. Vendler, of course, along with many others, would draw a distinction between popular forms of the art, like the poetry slam, and the "high" art that she herself authorizes through her criticism. While fiction has always been complicated by money—fiction writers can sometimes make a living from their writing—poor poets must rely on academic positions. What better way to show you hang with the right crowd than to distance yourself from those who make their poems accessible to the masses? Interestingly, no one would claim that The Beatles and Jay Z are not sophisticated artists. What is it about poetry that creates a bifurcated lens?

The irony of this trend toward academic poets—who write high art for a small audience—is that scholars in their own departments simultaneously may be studying the phenomenon of the poetry slam or nineteenth-century greeting cards or "vanity" publications by working class writers, topics that are interesting for the light they shed on cultures, rather than for formalist values of complexity and paradox. Of course, while "difficulty" and "obscurity" are relative terms, another irony of "difficult" poetry is that the political aims of the l=a=n=g=u=a=g=e poets—to reveal the constructedness of language and identity—are heard only by their peers. The average print run of Potes and Poets Press, for instance, is less than one thousand copies; the average print run of a university press poetry series is two thousand; Louise Glück's books sell more than 10,000 copies; a book by Billy Collins might sell 100,000 copies. Compare this to the million copies sold of every novel featured on Oprah's book club. Historically, of course, poetry has always had a smaller audience than fiction because reading poetry—even that of Billy Collins—takes more effort than reading prose, and a lot more effort than listening to music. Poetry offers, in Emily Dickinson's words, "more windows and doors" than prose.[37] In other words, to various degrees, poetry can challenge the dominant ideology because of its form—the white space that makes us read differently and changes the rhythms of our breath and speech. Readers of poetry can change themselves—and subsequently their worlds—because they can breathe outside convention.

I have found myself on every side of each of the debates presented here: academic poet, high art gatekeeper, defender of popular literature, instructor of context, formalist standard-bearer. In my role as faculty advisor to our literary magazine and teacher of creative writing, I teach student editors formalist criteria; as a teacher of literature, I teach formalism alongside poststructuralism through a combination of "enduring" and "unproven" literature; as a judge for poetry book contests, I allow my own prejudices about pleasure and experimentation to guide my choices; as an arts council board member, I defend the right of "low" art organizations to receive public funds. I don't always realize the contradictions inherent in these roles, and I believe that other writers and readers find themselves in similarly vexed positions. Yet we *must* try to see our own blind spots; we have an ethical obligation to be clear about "where we are coming from" when we evaluate literature. And the literary world will become larger and more interesting when we open ourselves to as many ways and kinds of reading as possible, when we realize that evaluation is contingent on our values, and when we question those values.

Notes

1. M. H. Abrams, *The Mirror and the Lamp: Romantic Theory and the Critical Tradition* (New York: Oxford University Press, 1953).
2. M. H. Abrams, "Theories of Poetry," in *Princeton Encyclopedia of Poetry and Poetics*, ed. Alex Preminger (Princeton: Princeton University Press, 1965), 639–49.
3. Abrams, "The Mirror and the Lamp: Romantic Theory and the Critical Tradition," 32.
4. Ibid., 35.
5. Marianne Moore, "Poetry," *Poets.org*, June 22, 2012, http://www.poets.org/viewmedia.php/prmMID/15654
6. Sir Philip Sidney, "The Defence of Poesy," *Poetry Foundation*, June 22, 2012, http://www.poetryfoundation.org/learning/essay/237818?page=3
7. Paul Lauter et al., *The Heath Anthology of American Literature* (Lexington, MA: Heath, 1990).
8. W. Roberts, *Longinus, on the Sublime* (Cambridge: Cambridge University Press, 1899) Peithô's Web. April 15, 2003, http://classicpersuasion.org/pw/longinus/desub003.htm
9. Harold Bloom, *Genius: A Mosaic of One Hundred Exemplary Minds* (New York: Warner Books, 2002).
10. John Stuart Mill, "What is Poetry," The University of Texas at Austin, June 22, 2012 http://www.laits.utexas.edu/poltheory/jsmill/diss-disc/poetry/poetry.s01.html
11. Immanuel Kant, *Critique of Judgment*, trans. Werner Pluhar (Indianapolis: Hackett Publishing, 1987).
12. Cleanth Brooks and Jr. Robert Penn Warren, *Understanding Poetry* (New York: Henry and Holt Company 1938).

13. Cleanth Brooks et al., *An Approach to Literature* (New York, 1952), 282–86.

14. Robert Scholes, *The Crafty Reader* (New Haven: Yale University Press, 2001).

15. Michael Meyer, *The Compact Bedford Introduction to Literature*, 6th ed. (New York: St. Martin's, 2003).

16. X. J. Kennedy and Dana Gioia, *Literature: An Introduction to Fiction, Poetry, and Drama*, 3rd Compact ed. (New York: Longman: 2003), 718.

17. Kennedy and Gioia, *Literature: An Introduction to Fiction, Poetry, and Drama*, 721.

18. Daneen Wardrop, "'The Ethiop Within': Emily Dickinson and Slavery," in Gurdrun Grabhers' *Emily Dickinson at Home: Proceedings of the Third International Conference of the Emily Dickinson International Society in South Hadley, MA* (WVT: Wissenschaftlicher Verlag Trier, 2001), and "'That Minute Domingo': Dickinson's Cooptation of Abolitionist Diction, and Franklin's Variorum Edition" in *The Emily Dickinson Journal* 8, no. 2 (1999).

19. Shira Wolosky, *Emily Dickinson: A Voice of War* (New Haven: Yale University Press, 1984).

20. Alfred Habegger, *My wars are laid away in books: The Life of Emily Dickinson* (New York: Random House, 2001).

21. Eleanor Heginbotham, *Reading the Fascicles of Emily Dickinson: Dwelling in Possibilities* (Columbus: Ohio State University Press, 2003).

22. Walter Kalaidjian, Judith Roof, and Stephen Watt, *Understanding Literature: An Introduction to Reading and Writing* (Boston: Houghton-Mifflin, 2003).

23. Robert Scholes, *The Crafty Reader*, 17–20.

24. Jonathan Culler, *Structuralist Poetics: Structuralism, Linguistics and the Study of Literature* (Ithaca: Cornell University Press, 1975).

25. Pierre Bourdieu, *Distinction: A Social Critique of the Judgement of Taste*, trans. Richard Nice (Cambridge, MA: Harvard University Press, 1984).

26. Janice Radway, *A Feeling for Books: The Book-of-the-Month Club, Literary Taste, and Middle Class Desire* (Chapel Hill: UNC Press, 1997).

27. Alicia Ostriker, Email correspondence, February 18, 2003.

28. James Walcott, "Advertisements for Himself," *The New Republic* Online, June 22, 2003. http://www.tnr.com/article/advertisements-himself

29. Francine Prose, "I Know Why the Caged Bird Cannot Read," *Harpers* (September 1999): 76–84.

30. John Ciardi, "The Reviewer's Duty to Damn," *The Saturday Review* 40 (February 16, 1957): 24–25.

31. Joan Houlihan, "The Sound of One Wing Flapping: The Art of the Poetry Blurb. How Contemporary American Poets are Denaturing the Poem,

Part VI." *The Boston Comment*, April 15, 2003. http://www.webdelsol.com/LITARTS/Boston_Comment.

32. Jeredith Merrin, "Art Over Easy," *Southern Review* 38, no. 1: 202–14.

33. Jane Tompkins, *Sensational Designs: The Cultural Work of American Fiction* (New York: Oxford University Press, 1985).

34. Barbara Herrnstein Smith, *Contingencies of Value: Alternative Perspectives for Critical Theory* (Cambridge, MA: Harvard University Press, 1988).

35. Gaye Tuchman, with Nina Fortin, *Edging Women Out: Victorian Novelists, Publishers, and Social Change* (New Haven: Yale University Press, 1989).

36. Helen Vendler, Radcliffe Quarterly Interview, April 20, 2003, http://www.radcliffe.edu/quarterly/200001/shape-1.html

37. Emily Dickinson, "I dwell in Possibility (466)," Poetry Foundation, June 22, 2012. http://www.poetryfoundation.org/poem/182904

Chapter Reflection

Questions for Discussion

(Some of the following questions were generated by creative writing student Angela Compton.)

1   Where have you encountered the distinction that is sometimes made between "high" versus "low" art? Or the "sacred" versus the "profane"? Or "literature" versus "entertainment", and so on? Do you see these constructs in your classes, or in how people talk about books, films, TV, and other media? What do you think about these distinctions? And, thinking of Sajé's essay, how is this issue "political" and about the *politics* of literary evaluation?

2   How would you describe the difference between "genre fiction" and "literature"? Is there a difference? Do the university, the marketplace, or other institutions have a role in establishing a difference between "genre fiction" and "literature"? How would you respond if someone called your work "genre fiction"?

3   If you were to make your own continuum, graph, or illustration to chart differences in literature, like Michael Kardos has done, how would you do it? Think of a work of "literature" that you've read for class; then think of a work of fiction you've read for pleasure—compare the two: Where would you chart each on your continuum, graph, or illustration?

4   How is the word "genre" used when it is not referring to "genre fiction"? What is "genre"? Is genre a set of constraints or conventions? Is genre a tradition? Is it a formula or a patterned response? Is genre a form that content is poured into? Is genre a classificatory device or interpretive tool? Does genre identify a text's relationship to a social context?

Writing Prompt

Write a story, poem, essay, script, or song that is meant for one audience. Then translate that same piece for a different audience. Reflect on the choices you made in creating this "translation": what was your rationale? How did you go about tailoring a piece of writing for one audience and another? What does this process of translation uncover about the values, desires, and expectations of different readerships? How would your writing be evaluated differently by different audiences?

Suggestions for Further Reading

1   Collins, Jim. *Bring on the Books for Everybody: How Literary Culture Became Popular Culture*. Duke University Press, 2010.
2   Davis, Ben. *9.5 Theses on Art and Class*. Haymarket, 2013.
3   Mukherjee, Bharati. "Immigrant Writing: Give Us Your Maximalists!" *New York Times Book Review* (August 1988): 28–29.
4   Mullen, Harryette. *The Cracks Between What We Are and What We Are Supposed to Be: Essays and Interviews*. University of Alabama Press, 2012.
5   Poddar, Namrata. "Is 'Show Don't Tell' a Universal Truth or a Colonial Relic?," *Literary Hub* (2016).

Acknowledgments

The editor would like to thank those who granted permission to use their work. Thanks also to Jan Calderon, Angela Compton, Bri Lucero, Zachary Harris, Kelley Ellion, and Mirabai Collins for editorial contributions and to David Avital, Clara Herberg, and Mark Richardson at Bloomsbury for their support and vision. Deep gratitude to Lisa Adsit, Eric Adsit, and John Johnson for showing so much care and encouragement along the way.

Credits

"Inappropriate Appropriation." Published in *PEN America: A Journal for Writers and Readers,* Issue 7, M Mark, ed. New York: PEN American Center, 2006.

Adsit, Janelle. "Unpacking Privilege in Creative Writing." Originally published as "Exclusionary Constructions of the Writer's Life" in *Toward an Inclusive Creative Writing: Threshold Concepts to Guide the Literary Writing Curriculum,* published by Bloomsbury, 2017.

Borich, Barrie Jean. "The Craft of Writing Queer." Originally published in *Brevity,* September 2012. Reprinted by permission of the author.

Cruz, Conchitina. "The Filipino Author as Producer." Originally published on Curious Couch (curiouscouch.wordpress.com), March 10, 2017. Limited copies of the full essay in pamphlet form were given away at traveling small press expo Better Living Through Xeroxography (BLTX), Quezon City in May 2017. Reprinted by permission of the author.

Das, Kavita. "On Parsing." Originally published on the VIDA Women in Literary Arts website, February 6, 2016. Reprinted by permission of the author.

DiFrancesco, Alex. "Writing Trans Characters." Originally published in *Brevity,* issue 49, May 2015. Reprinted by permission of the author.

Edmond, Jacob. "On Not Repeating 'Gone with the Wind': Iteration and Copyright." Originally published in *Jacket2,* December 2012. Reprinted by permission of the author.

Green, Chris. "Materializing the Sublime Reader: Cultural Studies, Reader Response, and Community Service in the Creative Writing Workshop." Originally published in *College English,* volume 64, number 2, November 2001. Reprinted by permission of the author.

Harmon, Kristen. "Writing Deaf: Textualizing Deaf Literature." Originally published in *Sign Language Studies,* volume 7, number 2, Winter 2007. Reprinted by permission of Gallaudet University Press.

Kardos, Michael. "The Literary/Genre Fiction Continuum." Originally published in the *Huffington Post,* September 5, 2012. Updated November 5, 2012. Reprinted with permission of Brandt & Hochman Literary Agents, Inc.

Khakpour, Porochista. "The Others." Originally published in *Guernica,* November 2011. Reprinted by permission of *Guernica* Magazine.

Krystal, Arthur. "It's Genre. Not That There's Anything Wrong With It!" Originally published in the *New Yorker,* Page Turner Section, October 24, 2012. Reprinted by permission of the *New Yorker;* permission conveyed by Condé Nast Licensing.

Mathis, Ayana. "Which Subjects Are Underrepresented in Contemporary Fiction?" Originally published in *The New York Times,* Book Review Section, April 12, 2016. Reprinted by permission of *New York Times;* permission conveyed by PARS International Corp.

Miller, Isaac Ginsberg. "The Racial Politics of *The Best American Poetry 2014.*" Originally published in the *American Poetry Review,* volume 44, number 22, March/April 2015. Reprinted by permission of the author.

Mura, David. "On the Response to Junot Díaz's 'MFA vs. POC,'" from *Revolver.* Originally published on the author's personal blog (https://blog.davidmura.com), May 5, 2014. Reprinted by permission of the author.

Nardone, Michael. "On Settler Conceptualism." Originally published in *Jacket2,* February 5, 2016. Reprinted by permission of the author.

Paloff, Benjamin. "Poetry and Catastrophe." Originally published in *The Nation,* September 30, 2014. Reprinted by permission of the author.

Perez, Craig Santos. "Poetry, Politics, and Letters to Empire." Originally published on the Poetry Foundation's Harriet blog, April 2012. Reprinted by permission of the author.

Row, Jess. "American Fiction's Racial Landscape." Originally published in *Boston Review, August 2013.* Reprinted by permission of the author.

Sajé, Natasha. "The Politics of Literary Evaluation," from *Windows and Doors: A Poet Reads Literary Theory,* published by University of Michigan Press, 2014. Originally published in *Writer's Chronicle,* May 2004, as "Who Are We to Judge: The Politics of Literary Evaluation." Reprinted by permission of the author.

Salesses, Matthew. "'Pure Craft' Is A Lie." Originally published on *Pleiades* online, 2015. Reprinted with permission of Ayesha Pande Literary.

Selasi, Taiye. "Stop Pigeonholing African Writers." Originally published in *The Guardian,* Books section, July 4, 2015. Reprinted by permission of *The Guardian;* permissions conveyed by Guardian News & Media Limited.

Silko, Leslie Marmon. "Language and Literature from a Pueblo Indian Perspective," from *English Literature: Opening Up the Canon, Papers from the 1979 English Institute,* edited by Leslie A. Fielder and Houston A. Baker, Jr., published by John Hopkins University Press, 1981. Reprinted by permission of The English Institute, Yale University, Whitney Humanities Center, 53 Wall Street, New Haven, CT 06511.

Wang, Dorothy J. "Aesthetics Contra 'Identity' in Contemporary Poetry Studies," from *Thinking Its Presence: Form, Race, and Subjectivity in Contemporary Asian American Poetry,* published by Stanford University Press, 2013. Reprinted by permission of Stanford University Press.

Wickman, Forrest. "Against Subtlety." Originally published in *Slate,* November 1, 2015. Reprinted by permission of *Slate*; permissions conveyed by PARS Internationals.

Index